DEFENSE XXIII

America Faces a Very Different World

Edited by

ROBBIN LAIRD

SLDinfo.com

This book is dedicated to my friend and colleague Erik P. Hoffmann. Erik believed in me and my career and helped me get my initial professional footing. Without his friendship, help and professional support, I certainly would not be creating this book.

In addition, he talked with the woman I hoped to marry and conveyed to her that whatever my faults, she would never be bored with me. That seemed to help and she did marry me.

Unfortunately after a long period of illness, he died last year at the age of 82.

CONTENTS

INTRODUCTION

This is the fourth annual publication we have published at *Second Line of Defense* and *Defense Information*. Each of the four publications highlight themes from essays we have published during that year.

We are living in a time of compressed history, and our essays in each volume captures the history emerging in that year. We focus on defense issues, so we have highlighted some of the key developments affecting the evolution of defense and security challenges facing the United States and its key allies in that year, as well as innovations and developments in selected military technologies and concepts of operations.

The first volume was entitled *2020: A Pivotal Year? Navigating Strategic Change at a Time of COVID-19 Disruption*. The book focused on the impact of COVID-19 and the strategic change evidenced in 2020. The 2020 book focused on the pandemic, notably as it played out in France and Britain. The book provided an overview of the challenge of navigating strategic change at a time of COVID-19 disruption.

The second volume was entitled *Defense XXI: Shaping a Way Ahead for the United States and its key Allies*. The book focused on the key drivers of change in defense, which reshape force capabilities, and the strategic context within which those capabilities are being shaped. It is about technology, concepts of operations, and strategic purposes for defense. One theme we explored in 2021 was the increased challenge to the liberal democratic order from authoritarian powers.

This was a major theme in the third volume entitled *Defense XII: A World in Transition*. We focused on how major allies are changing their focus on how to defend themselves in the context of their broader alliances. This is especially notable in Australia and the Nordic region, and we highlighted our work on these regions, which is based on travel to those regions and discussions with policymakers and analysts in these regions.

The four volumes read together provide a succinct overview of contemporary history over the past four years, a period in which a new historical era is emerging. My dissertation at Columbia University was entitled "On Historical Change." It served as useful preparation for the historical upheaval we are living through.

An additional book which is highly interactive with the annual publications but highlights the work of one our major contributors was published in 2023. The book is entitled: *Kenneth Maxwell on Global Trends: An Historian of the 18th Century Looks at the Contemporary World.*

This book brings together Professor Ken Maxwell's essays published since 2011 on global trends. This book is most likely to be read initially by the many followers of the work of Dr. Kenneth Maxwell, the historian. He is a well-respected and well-known historian of the history of Brazil and the Iberian Peninsula. Even though much of his work focuses on the 18th century, he is not an expert as understood in today's society. He is more like the philosophes of the 18th century, focusing on a subject but with a wide view.

Together, these essays provide a comprehensive perspective on the modern world as seen through the eyes of a professional historian who has worked extensively on the 18th Century. These essays reflect an understanding of the world through an unusual lens. The book provides an essayist view on the changing global order seen through the perspective of specific events, countries, and leaders. It provides an important contribution to our thinking about the new global disorder and what comes next.

This year's volume highlights a number of key developments and dynamics in 2023. This year has been characterized by growing conflict worldwide and further devolution of the global order. We are clearly in a period of history which challenges our fundamental values and challenges us to navigate through a very difficult period of history.

Rather than a world of multi-polarity or great national power competition, a key aspect of the new historical epoch we have entered is multi-polar authoritarianism. Authoritarianism is clearly globally ascendant, but these regimes or groups do not share a common ideology or action program.

They are not in alliance, although they cooperate when convenient for their particular interests. They support splintered globalization which is when global rules exist to some extent to handle globally important exchanges but the authoritarians are not contributing political capital to maintaining the "rules-based order."

Many of these authoritarian states or groups have roots deeply inside Western democracies and through various means operate within Western societies, rather than simply being an external threat.

These means are diverse: cyber, economic investments, economic partners who advocate their economic interest, or in the case of a number of Middle Eastern states, the impact of a migration which has not been characterized by new arrivals in the West shedding their cultural or political identities from where they came.

At the same time, the liberal democracies or the West as it used to be called, is in the throes of significant self-questioning, internal debates, rejection of capitalism as practiced the last 50 years, and the emergence of disaggregated societies in each of the Western states.

These states work together on common issues, but cooperation is challenged by internal national or regional debates (in the case of Europe.)

This new era is a major challenge to the United States and its governing elites. It no longer commands a Western shaped global order. There is no great crusade as Eisenhower wrote about.

It is about national interests and winnowing commitments to the availability of resources, whether military or financial. The governing elite has not practiced or thought in terms of such discipline and the gap between the evolution of the new era and American leadership is clearly out of phase.

The war in Ukraine is not about democracy: it is about a NATO war with Russia to constrain Russian ambitions. What is the end game and how can America define and protect its interests?

We are not in with Ukraine to the end because Ukrainian and American interests are not the same. I remember the same team in Washington now promised the same to the Afghans. How did that turn out?

The war in the Middle East is one which the United States needs to be careful not to get sucked into a negative relationship with the Arab world and avoid being the paymaster for the rebuilding of Gaza by an Israeli run process.

And neither of these actions has much to do one another.

It is a case-by-case world in which national interests need to be carefully defined and resources calibrated to those interests.

The size and weight of the American debt and the limitations on American military power are real.

We need a re-calibration of polices for the new historical era in line with our interests and a realistic understanding of our resources and capabilities, and their strengths and limits.

Finally, a procedural item.

As with the other volumes in this series, when I wrote the essay there is no name attached to that essay. If one of the contributors wrote the essay, their name is indicated. And the dates listed for every essay are the date they were published on one of our websites. The cut-off date for articles included in this volume was of 15 December 2023.

❧ I ☙

GLOBAL DEVELOPMENTS

THE NEXT PHASE OF THE XI ERA: CHINA'S STRATEGIC
SHIFT IN A WORLD IN FLUX

March 23, 2023

The recently concluded Party Congress in Communist China has both consolidated Xi's control of the Chinese system and turned the country further from its earlier legacy of global engagement built on its powerful export engine. According to my colleague, Dr. Harald Malmgren, Chinese policy under Xi has taken a significant strategic turn in its economy and with it in terms of how he seeks to shape the China of the next decade.

This shift is significant and has significant implications for a world which is in flux in terms of the Western countries who have been the focus of exports, the authoritarian partners of China and the global system which my colleague Ken Maxwell has referred to in an essay published in 2022 as the arrival of the new world order.

In this new world order relationships by multiple power centers which would not described either as Western or as great power authoritarians have emerged and are shaping new global linkages. And China under Xi is focused on enhancing these relationships at the expense of its recent decades of reliance for high growth on its export relationships with the West.

Dr. Malmgren and his colleague Nicholas Glinsman have highlighted and summarized the Chinese shift in their seminal paper written earlier this year entitled, "China and its Lost Decades Ahead."

In this paper, the authors assess that China is moving on from its neo-mercantilist economic model which relied heavily on exports for growth. At the Party Congress, the importance of global exports was replaced by placing highest national priority on domestic consumption within China itself. The dramatic shift in priority from its external relations in economic growth and the drawdown of their ability to rely on foreign capital to domestic growth drivers poses huge challenges for China in shaping a new way ahead.

Malmgren has also noted in a recent discussion I had with him that up to now President Xi had kept reporting of his military exclusively to himself. All other matters, including state security, were under the direction of the Chinese Communist Party. In March, Xi declared that state security was removed from CCP jurisdiction and would henceforth report exclusively to Xi personally.

All matters that he deemed to be essential in managing internal security would be subject to his personal decisions. Thus, from now on the entire CCP was subordinated to the supreme leader, and the Party would function under decisions made by state security and the Central Military Commission, which Xi chairs.

To better control the domestic economy, Xi has decided to intensify centralized direction of all segments of the economy. Since Deng, state owned enterprises had been subject to Party direction, but large segments of the economy functioned with considerable autonomy. Xi made it clear that he wanted greater public and private coordination, and that Party political officials would be placed into the management of all private businesses.

Moreover, the Party would assign its officials to participate in all scientific research projects and the development of technological innovations. This would, of course, complicate relations between Chinese scientific innovators who were participating with American scientists and investors, calling into question whether either the Party or the U.S.

Government would permit continuation of such ongoing businesses and R&D projects.

Innovations which had been spurred by foreign investments and engagements of various foreign academics and scientists would likely be re-crafted to become more Soviet like with commissars within the key companies and domestic economic sectors.

The Covid pandemic lockdowns paralyzed the Chinese economy during the period from the start of 2020 to the very end of 2022. Throughout the world markets, there has been an expectation that 2023 pandemic end would result in a strong Chinese economy rebound, bringing back to life the powerful Chinese engine of growth that had long provided momentum to the rest of the world.

As it turned out, 2023 showed little sign of a Chinese rebound. New orders for exports did not appear. Demand for ocean going cargo carriers remained depressed.

What the world had forgotten was that world trade in manufactures had already slowed down in the years since the Great Financial Crisis of 2008-09. During 2019, just before the pandemic struck, the IMF warned that a synchronized industrial downturn was evident throughout the world. The pandemic then took over, slowing and even halting all economic activity virtually everywhere. Now, in post-pandemic 2023 much of the world is back where the economy of 2019 left off, in an economic downturn.

None of the world's great trading nations, Japan, China, South Korea, Germany, or the U.S. showed any signs of increased demand for manufactures, whether automobiles or consumer appliances. World-wide inflation was being attacked by central banks everywhere, raising interest rates to subdue spending and rising wage demands.

In February 2023, the Government Investment Corporations of Singapore, one of the world's biggest Sovereign Wealth Funds, announced it was pulling back from exposure to investments in China. This agency is known throughout the world as the most knowledge-able entity able to make objective assessments of the inner workings of the Chinese economy.

The U.S. Government was also showing concern about U.S. private investment into China that might be supporting technologies of national security concern. This was casting a negative blanket over previous years of optimism among high tech American and European technology investors.

Malmgren noted that China has reached an economic plateau similar to that reached by Japan in the late 1980s, where Japan shifted its economic growth to direct engagement in the United States and other Western states. China will not be able to do that because of the Western concern with regard to how China has distorted "globalization" to its advantage.

According to Malmgren, with the United States cutting the umbilical cord to its technology and technological investment's, there is growing Chinese recognition that their own pace of innovation could slow significantly.

With the economic slowdown by China, the role which China played in the 2008 global economic crisis will not be repeated. The authors concluded in their paper that "China will not come to the world's rescue, as it did in 2008-09 under Hu Jintao."

Malmgren also underscored that the focus on enhanced domestic consumption will prove difficult as well with the economic drawdown and internal protests. Most of the major protests have been highly disciplined in forms that the government felt unable to contain.

These protests have taken two forms: the so-called white paper protest whereby significant numbers of Chinese have simply hoisted blank paper in protest without actually indicating what they are protesting.

The second is Chinese parents of childbearing age are refusing to have children and, wives asserting their rights to continue active professional lives and simply avoiding raising any children. The birth rate per thousand Chinese continues to fall dramatically, alongside a growing number of the elderly. The total number of Chinese counted in 2022 showed year on year decline, and world population experts are now forecasting steep decline in Chinese population over the next 50 or 100 years.

I will include here the first part of their paper, a paper which brings together a wide range of data supporting their arguments in the paper.

"In late October, when Xi Jinping consolidated his hold on China's communist party at its five-yearly congress, the world cringed. Xi seemed determined to push China back to the age of Mao Zedong, his role model. Hardline ideology would tighten its grip on the world's second-largest economy, with dire implications for the rest.

"The last thing anyone expected from a strongman president entering his 11th year in power was a sudden about face. Yet within weeks, Xi's government reversed its efforts to control Covid-19, Big Tech companies, the Chinese property market and more.

"It has shown signs of reduced support for Russia's war in Ukraine while trying to ease diplomatic tensions with the U.S. and in its territorial disputes regarding the South China Sea. This softening seemed so uncharacteristic of Xi that rumors began circulating that his political power was weakening, as other high officials were intervening to alter policy.

"That's unlikely, given that at the congress, Xi had purged enemies and installed allies throughout the party. Yet the 180-degree turn on multiple policy fronts was unmistakable and raises doubts about everything the world thought it knew about Xi, the unbending hardliner. Was he now bending to pressure from worried officials, the public, the deteriorating economy?

"The answer may be all of the above. Xi's Covid policy, the tech crackdown and the property bust had brought the economy to a standstill in 2022. The economy contracted in the fourth quarter, which is likely to bring growth for the year down to 3 per cent.

"That is according to official Chinese data; the reality was probably worse, as the reliability of such has declined under Xi. Nevertheless, and back on point, China has not grown this slowly since the late 1970s and is growing no faster than the rest of the world, also a first since the 1970s.

"A performance that weak was a serious threat to an authoritarian state that rests its legitimacy on promises to restore China's prosperity and its global stature. As the slowdown fueled street rallies against the pursuit of "zero-Covid lockdowns", some protesters dared to call for Xi to step down. Officials in his own government were reportedly urging him to act to save the economy. Still, few if any China watchers thought the paramount leader would change course.

"Aiming to revive the economy after the congress, Xi's government started sounding less Maoist. It has dropped the "three red lines" on borrowing by developers and announced that the "rectification" campaign against fintech firms is nearly complete. After tightening state control for years, it is sending out messages of support to the private sector, even offering details of its new global data market that suggest respect for private data ownership.

"The irony: Xi may be trying impractically hard to revive growth. His plans to build "a modern socialist economy" imply an annual gross domestic product growth target of 5 per cent, which is no longer possible. China's population growth has slowed sharply, as has productivity growth.

"With fewer workers and slumping output per worker, the country's potential growth rate is 2.5 per cent. Beyond this year, when spending by Chinese consumers released from lockdown may temporarily boost growth, 5 per cent is an unrealistic target. And more debt-financed spending will only increase China's already massive debt load.

"Global investors, who often blow hot and cold on China, have again flipped, this time to embrace the new Xi. Before November, the country's stock market was tanking with the economy. Foreign fund managers were launching emerging market mandates excluding China.

"Now, they are bullish on hopes of a post-pandemic "reopening" bounce and have been pouring money into Chinese stocks. The benchmark MSCI China index is up a staggering 50 per cent since the late October lows.

"Yet questions about China's policy direction remain. Xi's pivot is a pragmatic course correction, but it raises doubts about his steadiness. His impulse to control may reassert itself when the economy starts to recover.

"However, we just do not see it lasting, and hence there will be no repeat of the Chinese reaction to the Great Financial Crisis of 2008/09, wherein the enormous stimulus introduced by the Hu Jintao administration was accredited with helping the world economy avoid a broad and deep global recession.

"Back to the present and despite the dangers, there are nevertheless signs that the economy is stirring. Subway ridership in major cities is rapidly returning to normal. Consumers who accumulated savings while shut in their homes for much of the past year have money to spend.

"And the government is rolling out policies to support a rebound, or more accurately, reversing policies that had previously constrained growth. China's ability to recover from nearly three years of self-imposed isolation "is very likely the single most important factor for global growth in 2023," according to Kristalina Georgieva, the managing director of the IMF.

"Indeed, the global economy's other main engines are far from firing on all cylinders. The U.S. economy, despite a strong end to 2022, will struggle this year as higher interest rates bite, according to the World Bank's latest forecast. Europe is in recession, and Japan is projected to eke out just a 1 percent growth rate.

"As for China, the World Bank forecasts growth of 4.4 percent this year, and of course, some private estimates are even higher. Goldman predicts a 5.2 percent gain. 'Evidence of a rapid China reopening is accumulating,' the investment bank said in a note to clients last week.

"Still, it will take time for the Chinese to re-establish their pre-pandemic routines, including links to the outside world that the government severed in hopes of keeping the virus at bay. The next few months may bring a stop-and-go recovery before a more widespread resumption of activity in the spring.

"Even with a smooth Chinese reopening, the global economy faces a year of anaemic growth, according to World Bank and IMF projections. As mentioned above, China could theoretically provide a big world economic impetus, but we do not expect China to have growth surge and ride to the rest of the world's rescue.

"One area that commentators are expecting a growth impetus is Chinese exports, but we would argue against that too..."

In other words, we are seeing a sharp break from the economic orientation of China and from how China has engaged with the West economically. How then does this affect the Chinese place in the world, and affect the evolution of the evolving global situation and order?

CHINA'S STRATEGIC SHIFT: WHAT ARE THE IMPLICATIONS FOR THE EVOLVING GLOBAL ORDER?

March 25, 2023

Dr. Harald Malmgren has described what he and his colleague see as a strategic shift in China associated with the next phase of President Xi's leadership.

The shift from an export-oriented growth economy which is deeply intertwined with the developments in the Western world to one more focused on domestic consolidation and a global shift to the rest of the non-Western world carries with it significant implications for the global competition with the West.

How can we characterize this shift?

What is the nature of the changed competition?

What are the implications for the West?

Although it is early days in providing answers to these questions, we can identify some possible key developments and questions going forward.

My objective here is to raise such questions rather than providing answers, which will be determined interactively between China, its allies, its friends, and its competitors.

But that is really the central point: the nature of the new global order will be determined by competition among key states and how they cooperate or don't in shaping what has been called frequently a "rules-based order."

There might be several "rules-based orders" rather than one as the outcome.

The kind of authoritarian regime being crafted by President Xi and his allies puts a priority on how to shape working relationships with other authoritarian powers.

The relationship with Russia is the most visible for China, but there is a global effort to come to terms with other authoritarian powers built around working relationship's shaped by the enemy of my enemy is my friend dynamic.

We are simply not very good at analyzing how authoritarian leaders work with one another, how they think, how they act and how they are deterred from actions we fear or do not like. We need to recognize that this is a key field of study which has little to do with how liberal democracies compete and cooperate with one another.

This raises a key question when we address conflict and notably military conflict in the years ahead.

We have coined a series of concepts such as hybrid warfare and gray zone conflict which simply reflect that we don't know how to deter let along compete in an area which is neither hard nor soft power nor in which force is used to gain objectives short of a general war. The American-led wars in Iraq in Afghanistan have demonstrated that the art of statecraft in dealing with this level of conflict is in short supply.

Authoritarian leaders clearly do not all think alike and have their own version of their national interest.

How do and will they work together?

How do and will they influence each other?

For example, when President Xi restored the former Chinese name to Vladivostok, what did Putin discern its meaning?[1]

How in fact can Western states most effectively influence authoritarian behavior?

The track record with regard to Putin certainly is not a showcase for European or American statecraft.

What would have deterred him from the Ukraine invasion?

This is a subject worthy of analysis, not simply from the minds of Westerners but conceptualizing how Putin and his allies think. This is hardly just historical analysis because it is tied up with how we would end such a war and deal with the evolving global order.

Another key area to explore are the changes in the global economy associated with the projected shift led by President Xi.

This can be seen on many levels but here I will focus on two.

The first is the need for foreign capital to fuel Chinese domestic development. The recent peace overture led by China with Saudi Arabia and Iran was largely interpreted as dealing with oil and the future energy needs of China. But it is much broader than that.

The American political process led by Biden attacked the legitimacy of the ruler of Saudi Arabia, and Biden turned his back on the Abraham Accords. President Xi could care less about the internal ethics of the Saudi leader, but the global future of Saudi is important. They are building new technologies and new defense systems which China could support, China has personnel to replace the current heavy reliance on Pakistanis and the Saudis have capital to invest.

The second is the shift associated the West and China.

There is a clear shift towards innovation in terms of energy, of better use of resources which are loosely associated with dealing with the global climate change.

In dealing with this new phase or age of innovation, there is a shift towards critical minerals and other commodities of enhanced importance, somewhat reminiscent of the shift from coal to oil at the beginning of the 20th century.

Countries which have these critical minerals and commodities are in a pole position for enhanced global influence and the reshaping of the "rules-based order" to their advantage.

The visit of President Lula to China can be seen in this light. Brazil is not simply part of the South or the developing world. Brazil should be described differently with the Western world increasingly preoccupied with the "climate emergency."

But such a shift in terms of global economic focus raises the question of how Xi will balance his calculation in terms of the use of force and for what purpose with his shift away from the Western economies.

Does an invasion of Taiwan make any sense from his point of view in terms of the global fallout from his shift away from the West?

Or does it become more desirable as a show of force which can enhance his ability to demonstrate the weakness and "moral bankruptcy" of the West?

Then I would like to raise an issue very relevant to the future direction of military conflict. Dr. Pippa Malmgren, Hal's daughter and a noted global analyst in her own right, has raised for some time the secular change in operational capabilities for military forces associated with the growth of AI-enabled machines.

Recently, she argued that following: "The next war for China is a digital operation run by highly responsive and obedient self-replicating robotics, informed by the best data sets and AI that exists anywhere in the world today. Humans won't even be needed for decision-making. In conjunction with super-computing, AI is replacing Generals, especially as the warzone expands beyond a battlefield and across the entire supply chain."[2]

If we look at the question of what one is prepared to do in terms of machine-led destruction to support your version of statecraft, how will China led by President Xi use his machines to support gray zone operations or his global reach?

I would like to close with a sobering thought.

Will the West really rebuild their ability to defend their interests?

Will we really find ways to work supply chains in common?

Will we be able to recover the art of statecraft along with military force innovations to provide deterrence of the authoritarian powers with China being a key leader?

And will the West do so while being able to find ways to cooperate with China in those areas that are critical for global survival?

Accompanying the economic shift described by Harald Malmgren might well be a broader global shift.

China would shift from being the economic export growth engine of globalization as understand by the West.

The focus would be upon managing the economic drawdown internally but working globally with key authoritarian allies and non-Western countries in the South to create an alternative to the legacy rules-based order.

China does not have to be formally allied to other authoritarian powers but just play off what the challenges these powers pose to the West.

And with the Brazil's of the world new resource and trade relationships can be built as alternatives to the capital-intensive belt and road approach.

The growth of China's informal empire becomes a key priority for the Chinese leadership as opposed to the export engine to the West. As Kenneth Maxwell has noted: "China has focused under the regime of President Xi on building out its global informal empire.

"By trade and investment, China has become a key player in Africa and Latin America. Its practices in doing so have a number of questionable dimensions, but instead of highlighting the reality of Chinese informal empire practices, Western states have largely ignored the opportunity to do so. They have focused on issues like Taiwan and the South China Sea, both very important but not part of the informal empire geopolitical strategy.

"But the reality is that China poses a global threat to the Western order underwritten by its economic, cultural, and third world narrative efforts along with an expanding fleet of both military and commercial shipping and ports as well."[3]

The concept of informal empire was developed by John Gallagher and Ronald Robinson in a 1953 article published in *The Economic History Review*, as Kenneth Maxwell has underscored in his discussions about Latin America and China. Ronald Robinson was Maxwell's tutor at St. John's College at Cambridge University.[4]

"It ought to be a commonplace that Great Britain during the nineteenth century expanded overseas by means of 'informal empire' as much as by acquiring dominion in the strict constitutional sense. For purposes of economic analysis, it would clearly be unreal to define imperial history exclusively as the history of those colonies coloured red on the map.

"Nevertheless, almost all imperial history has been written on the assumption that the empire of formal dominium is historically comprehensive in itself and can be cut out of its context in British expansion and world politics. The conventional interpretation of the nineteenth-century empire continues to rest upon the study of the formal empire alone, which is rather like judging the size and character of icebergs solely from the parts above the waterline."

As far as military issues go, China has internal problems – significant and growing.

But in terms of defense. their nuclear arms buildup makes them a territory one would not wish to strike, and with the growing domination of Russia, the internal resource trade routes are secure.

This means that their outreach with regard especially to naval power becomes more significant less in terms of directly confronting the United States and the West, then building a force that can operate globally around them.

At the same time, building a global navy of course enhances their ability directly to deter or fight the West if it comes to that. The recent exercises off of South Africa_with the Russians illustrate this approach.[5]

China shifts along with the global order.

DETERRENCE IN SHAPING AUSTRALIA'S PATH IN THE GLOBAL TRANSITION

April 18, 2023

As global conflict continues apace, and Australia navigates its way ahead, there is a clear desire to defend Australia's interests and to deter actions by China which significantly undercut those interests. But what does Australia wish to deter?

How does it do so?

And how does it work its allied and partner relationships in conjunction with defining its new relationship with China?

During my current trip to Australia, I had a chance to discuss these questions with Dr. Andrew Carr of Australian National University. We started by focusing on the salience of deterrence and its discussion and debate in Australia to shaping Australia's way ahead in dealing with China.

Carr: "What are we deterring China from doing? This is not just a military task. We need to address it publicly, both to gain ongoing support from the public but also to clarify what we expect from government coordination across the whole of government to deter China.

"Deterrence is very new in the Australian experience. We have been part of a Western coalition for a very long time, but we have never had to do the kind of messaging and communication which is a crucial part of deterrence. There is not a lot of muscle memory in Australia for deterrent discourse."

China has become a different kind of competitor and adversary and partner as it changed from the reform years and building its economy to that of the China under President Xi who is combining elements of power to shape the global system more in the Chinese image.

What will Australia accept in working with its main trade partners? And what will it not?

What role will foreign students from China play in Australian universities?

What actions by China are clearly to be countered? Which tolerated? Which ignored?

All of this is part of shaping deterrent language and narrative. What tools does Australia need to deter against which types of actions? Where does the military fit into a broader deterrent effort involving broader Australia economic, social, cultural, information and security interests?

Carr's key point s that such questions need to be central to Australian debate and consideration, and regularly so. There are ongoing considerations of what is to be deterred and what means need to be developed to do so.

Carr concluded our conversation by highlighting a central problem facing Western policy makers. Simply put, with the end of the Cold War and the seeming end of history and the victory of liberal democracy underwritten by the United States, policy makers saw the rules-based order as global with little clarity with regard to what are core versus peripheral interests.

The term global commons came into vogue and suggested a global interdependent order in which interests were dictated by the need to deal with the gaps in the seams wherever and whenever they occurred.

Deterrence is national in character and to be effective requires clarity with regard to core interests versus peripheral interests. It also requires a realistic sense of limits. What can the nation actually do that will be seen as credible by the adversary? And will the nation have the will to do so?

As Carr put it: "The gray zone challenge comes from this global lack of clarity. With our "rules-based order" language, we tend to suggest that everything in the status quo is of interest for the West. Chinese actions in the South China Sea and Russia's actions in Crimea in 2014, called our bluff.

"Deterrence is then a policy of limits as well as focus. But it cannot remain a policy only pursued by the military, while absent from the discussions of the political class and the public."

The China relationship shaped in the past two decades cannot continue; but what kind of relationship can it be? What are its limits and what are the paths of cooperation and the focus of deterrence?

A FRENCH DEFENSE UPDATE: FEBRUARY 2023

February 16, 2023

By Pierre Tran

France took a financial hit of €409 million ($440 million) as a result of its 2015 cancellation of the sale of two helicopter carriers to Russia, the national audit office said in its report on French arms exports.

"In total, taking into account the result of negotiations with Russia, cancellation of payments, payments to Naval Group, modifications and the sale of the ships to Egypt, this transaction cost France €409 million," the independent office said in its report, Support for Export of Military Matériel. The report was cleared 24 January 2023 for publication.

The then French president, François Hollande, cancelled in August 2015 a controversial sale of the Mistral class warships, under pressure from the U.S., central European and Baltic nations, after Russia seized in 2014 the Crimean Peninsula from Ukraine.

The then U.S. president, Barak Obama, said Paris should "press the pause button," while the U.K. also called for Hollande to ax the arms deal.

How the audit office arrived at that €409 million was unclear, but one view is that amount includes an estimated €340 million-€350 million paid out by Coface, the export credit agency, to the prime contractor, Naval Group, then known as DCNS, and other contractors including STX and CNIM.

STX built the two Mistrals at Saint-Nazaire shipyard, while CNIM supplied two L-CAT landing catamarans for the warship deal with Moscow.

That overall €409 million might also include €56.8 million spent on training Russian crews and adapting the ships to Russian specifications. The hangers had been built large for a naval version of the Kamov Ka-52 Alligator attack helicopter, and the helicopter deck could be heated, to sail in Arctic waters.

STX, the shipbuilder, received €661 million from Coface, Thales €80 million for supply of electronics, and CNIM €40 million, September 2015 parliamentary reports from the lower house National Assembly and Senate said.

France paid Russia total reimbursement of €949.75 million for cancelling the order for the Mistrals, comprising a core payment of €892.9 million, and a further €56.8 million, the Sept. 15 2015 National Assembly report said.

It is understood the core repayment was based on Russian advance payment for the first ship – Vladivostok – which had been built and was ready for delivery, and partial advance payment on the second vessel – Sevastapol – which had yet to be completed when Hollande called the deal off.

There is a view the costs were covered by insurance claims through Coface, rather than French taxpayers, with export insurance for building the warships, buying them back from Russia, and selling them on to Egypt in 2015.

There is also a view the Mistral sale to Egypt was worth €960 million, although press reports at the time said the Cairo deal was worth €950 million.

Egypt's purchase of the two Mistrals followed Cairo's 2015 order for French weapons worth €5.2 billion for 24 Rafale fighter jets, a FREMM multi-mission frigate, and air-to-air and naval missiles.

The audit office was not available for comment.

Coface consistently made money between 2010-2021, with premiums exceeding claims, the report said, with only 2015 showing a net loss of €82 million due to the claims made on cancellation of the Mistral deal with Russia. The sale to Egypt limited the amount of claim, the report said.

Naval Group, the French shipbuilder, received payment that covered the cost of production, but it had to forego an estimated profit of €100 million on the Russian deal due to the cancellation.

There was much debate in France at the time, with some calling for delivery to Russia, to bolster a perception of France as a reliable trading partner.

The previous French president, Nicolas Sarkozy, had approved the Mistral sale to Russia in 2011, for around €1.2 billion, with options for two more. That deal with Russian president Vladimir Putin drew criticism, with critics pointing to Russia's 2008 invasion of Georgia, and concern rising when Russian troops seized Crimea and Moscow-backed separatists took control of the Donbas region, Eastern Ukraine, in 2014.

The incursion into Georgia would have taken 40 minutes rather than 26 hours if Russian forces had sailed the Mistral carrier, a Russian general had said.

The then executive chairman of Naval Group, Hervé Guillou, told parliamentarians in September 2015 that lawyers had said the company faced penalty payments of some €1 billion if the Mistral deal went into a lengthy legal dispute with Russia, on top of repaying almost €1 billion of advance payments.

The then French secretary general for defense and national security, Louis Gautier, negotiated with the then Russian deputy prime minister, Dmitry Rogozin, and they agreed on repayment, avoiding a legal wrangle. Hollande and Putin had agreed there should be a negotiated settlement and gave those senior officials mandate to strike a deal.

Those high-level, confidential talks appeared to spark a Russian free and frank expression of views.

Rogozin had not been "very favourable" to the Mistral deal, Gautier told Sept. 8, 2015, parliamentarians, the Sept. 15 parliamentary report said.

The Russian official, in a brusque manner, stated his opposition to cooperation, that Russian yards could have built the helicopter carriers, and that they had not exercised the option for two more Mistrals, which would have been built in Russian yards, the senior French official told the parliamentary committee.

"His point of view was opposition to execution of the contract," Gautier told parliamentarians. "Nonetheless, there were representatives of other ministries sitting round the table."

The big French companies which use U.S. components in foreign arms deals are each thought to apply every year for an estimated 800-1,000 export licenses from the U.S. Directorate of Defense Trade Controls (DDTC), as required by the International Traffic in Arms Regulations (ITAR), the report said.

The directorate is part of the State Department.

That reliance on ITAR approval leads to a process which is "long, heavy, constraining, and risky to business confidentiality," the report said, pointing out that American inspectors go on site to verify companies' commitments. Once an export license has been issued, restrictions on use must be observed and the State Department can make further checks.

The application of ITAR leads to slowness of procedure, higher costs, and can result in withdrawal of technology – leading to lower weapon performance. There may be delays as an alternative solution is sought, in an approach dubbed "ITAR free," the report said. Or the project is cancelled.

"In every case, the supplier's reputation is sullied," the report said.

ITAR, which applies to export of equipment for dual military and civilian use, is very broad, the report said. The authorization applies not just to products, but also technical data, and services such as assistance, training, design, development, production, operational use, maintenance, and repairs.

A component which has been "ITAR-ized" may lead to approval needed for the whole weapon system, the report said. Export of civil equipment may need authorization if they use components which have been ITAR-ized.

The defense trade directorate has power to conduct criminal inquiries, the report said, and can change rules, apply them retroactively, and revoke license.

"The U.S. could decide on its restrictions as much for strategic reasons as for commercial," the report said.

Companies found guilty of breaking ITAR can be denied the right to apply for future licenses and be hit with sanctions, the report said. Penalties include being banned from operating and selling on U.S. soil, hefty fines, and prison sentences of up to 10 years for company directors.

In addition to ITAR, there are checks on dual-use equipment covered by export administration regulations, boosted by the 2018 Export Control Reform Act, the report said. Licenses for foreign use of U.S. semiconductors and avionics are under close scrutiny. The Commerce Department oversees those export rules.

France seeks to pursue arms programs which are "ITAR free," as can be seen in government instruction 1618, drafted by the Direction Générale de l'Armement (DGA) procurement office, the report said.

That Feb. 15 2019 instruction from the ministerial cabinet outlines the protocol for weapons programs.

The European Union should pursue this approach, the report said, urging the EU's European Defense Fund to avoid supporting European projects for products and components which might fall under the control of ITAR.

Fresh Ties with Berlin

The report considers an updated agreement with Germany on arms exports following "serious difficulties," which saw French deals stalled in 2014 and 2018.

The fresh accord revised the Debré-Schmidt agreements signed Dec. 7, 1971, and Feb. 7 1972, which allowed the export of weapons built in cooperation, without the partner nation blocking the deal.

The projects for a future combat air system, based on a new generation fighter jet, and a main ground combat system, based on a new tank and unmanned vehicles, underscored the need for a new Franco-German pact, the report said.

France and Germany signed Oct. 23, 2019, agreement on export controls on weapons, the report said, with both countries were free to sell abroad without authorization from the partner nation when the latter had less than 20 percent of content in the weapon.

That 20 percent – based on the principle of de minimus, when something is so small there is no breach of agreement – excluded service, spares, training, and repairs, the report said. Tucked into the annex of the agreement was a list of weapons excluded from that 20 percent rule.

Apart from the 20 percent ruling, a partner nation could not block exports of weapons designed and developed in cooperation, unless the sale went against the partner nation's interest or national security, the report said.

It is not clear whether national interest and security were clearly set out.

Some French executives saw that 20 percent threshold as giving Berlin vast sway over French arms exports.

A permanent committee was set up to oversee the smooth running of the agreement, the report said, and it was too early to tell if that was working well. Much will depend on the German parliament, which has oversight over contracts worth more than €25 million.

All nations reserve the right to authorize foreign deals when components come from their country, the report said.

The authors led with the U.S. and Germany. The report also refers to cooperation on missiles between Britain and France.

It's About Politics

Export arms sales depend on relations between nations, their appreciation of the international situation, balance of power and how they change, the report said.

The foreign arms trade is subject to changes in the political tide, the report said, with deals made more fragile, or suspended, or talks broken off in recent years.

Such vagaries stem from various factors, such as strategic change, shifts in diplomacy, change in the political majority, a determination to show respect to contracts, or the search for independence and alternative suppliers, the report said.

An arms embargo on Russia and the curtailed Mistral deal was the leading example of five recent "emblematic" cases involving breach of a French contract or the foreign pursuit of other suppliers, the report said.

- Those cases included Poland's pick of American kit due to its close ties to Washington and stationing of U.S. troops in the East European nation, the report said, citing the following cases:

- Warsaw picked Sikorsky Black Hawk helicopters over the Airbus Caracal in 2016, Patriot missiles over MBDA weapons in 2018, and Lockheed Martin missile launchers in 2019.
- Brazil's selection in 2019 of four corvettes from German shipbuilder ThyssenKrupp Marine Systems over an offer from Naval Group. That reflected weaker ties between Brasilia and Paris after the election of Jair Bolsonaro in 2018.
- Egypt's opting in 2020 for two FREMM multi-mission frigates from Italian shipbuilder Fincantieri over an offer from Naval Group, mainly due to French criticism of Cairo's lack of respect for human rights.
- A fresh analysis by the Australian and U.S. authorities of the "strategic situation" in the Indo-Pacific region led to Canberra's 2021 cancellation of Naval Group's work to build 12 Shortfin Barracuda attack submarines for the Australian navy.

Alternatively, rising tension has led some nations to speed up arms deals, such as Greece ordering Rafale fighter jets and FDI defense and intervention frigates, the report said.

Strategic partnership agreements can also help arms deals if they are watched over with care. A strategic agreement signed with India in 1998 helped lead to Naval Group's 2005 sale of six Scorpene attack submarines, and New Delhi's 2016 order for 36 Rafale fighters.

Companies Owe Money

The DGA – which the audit office says plays a pivotal role in exports – can in theory claim payment of two percent when companies win overseas deals, stemming from paying for studies, research and development, and machine tools for production, the report said. But the reality is quite otherwise, with some companies opting out of payment.

"In fact, problems in calculation, the determination of some companies to exonerate themselves from these payments and the complexity of relations between the DGA and companies" lie behind corporate reluctance to show the money, the report said.

The report pointed up companies failing to inform the DGA when an export deal had been pitched, delaying communication of the estimated payment, and lateness in fixing the final amount due.

There may be a ministerial decision to exonerate payment partially or fully, if the DGA accepts the company's request, usually based on the corporate effort in the export sale campaign, the report said. That capacity for partial or full exoneration of company payment was not available until written into administrative guidelines revised last year.

The report pointed up lengthy legal disputes and loss of income for the DGA. Some €16 million was due on a contract signed back to 2015, the report said, with the company disputing that as an excessive claim in January 2020. The lawsuit was still pending when the audit office report was being written, the authors said.

The DGA was owed some €154 million in company payments at the end of 2021, the report said, of which €148 million was tied to contracts signed in 2015 and 2016, and these will undoubtedly be contested in the courts. The total amount owed by companies at the end of 2022 was €170 million.

Payments to the procurement office were late, with the payment of one year sometimes including back payments of several years, the report said. The amounts received by the DGA appeared to be "particularly low," even after including the contested payments.

The DGA has not made the effort it should have to be fully paid, the report said.

The procurement office said exports were worth more than "the few dozens of millions of payments," the report said, and greater importance lay in exports supporting the defense industrial and technological base, companies' economic performance, which cuts costs, helps the defense budget and its effect on jobs and tax revenue.

The audit office called for a tougher approach.

"Even if these factors are beyond dispute, they do not justify the lack of tight management of returns the government has the right to expect," the report said.

The DGA received €26.4 million in payment from companies in

2021, up from €15.3 million in the previous year, a table in the report shows.

"The armed forces ministry should pursue a more aggressive policy on the subject of payments, as it is inadmissible that, after several years of signing a contract, some companies continue to contest the amounts," the report said.

DGA and the Services

The procurement office assigned respectively an estimated 231 and 270 staff on support of exports in 2019 and 2020, although that was not a complete tally, as there were some 40 full time equivalent personnel who could be accounted for, the report said.

The DGA technical and operations departments consider they make big contributions to supporting exports, with the appointment of "architects of export programs," the report said. These officers work closely with teams working on programs and operations, with three program architects assigned to Rafale contracts.

DGA technical centers are working on flight tests to assess readiness of Rafales for India, Caracal helicopters for Kuwait, and NH90 helicopters for Qatar. There is certification work to ensure standards matches those for use of French forces.

The procurement office recruited 182 staff between 2016 and 2021 to help support exports, assigning around a third to work on the Rafale, 17.5 percent on submarines, 12.6 percent on the CaMo (mobilized capability) program with Belgium on armored vehicles, 11.6 percent on satellites, and 7.7 percent on helicopters, the report said.

In 2016, the then procurement head, Laurent Collet-Billon, said the DGA planned to recruit more than 500 staff to support exports by 2019-2020.

The DGA invoices for payment for supporting exports, with its international development department negotiating directly with client nations on technical services.

A senior DGA official, Thierry Carlier, won promotion last year to five star general and deputy director of the procurement office after heading the international development department for five years. That department leads the French export drive, and foreign arms sales were expected to exceed €30 billion over 2021 and 2022, mostly due to winning pitches of the Rafale abroad.

The joint chief of staff invoices for the services' support of exports, drawing on the SISTEX computer program for an overall view, the report said. The air force particularly helped in sale of the Rafale overseas. The invoices are sent to the companies or to the forces of the client nation.

The French forces, much like the DGA, prefer billing companies, rather than having to directly invoice the client nation, the report said. The billing of client nations for training pilots proved to be particularly trying.

The armed forces invoice after "tough talks" with companies, the report said, as much on the basic principle of what can be invoiced – such as service support, as the details of each export project. The companies put on pressure in a bid to cut costs "to maintain competitiveness."

"The aeronautics sector has benefited on several occasions from favorable ministerial decisions in this area," the report said. "Such was the case in 2017, with aircraft being made available for air shows, without being invoiced."

China, France, Germany, Russia and the U.S. ranked as the top five arms exporters from 2017 to 2021, the report said, holding between them 78.5 percent of the world market for weapons.

France rose to third from fifth ranking in the world, the report said, doubling its market share to 11 percent, helped by selling €11.7 billion of weapons abroad in 2021.

LULA AND XI IN THE EVOLVING NEW WORLD ORDER

April 18, 2023

By Kenneth Maxwell

"Brazil is Back" is the slogan of President Luis Inácio Lula da Silva after returning with a very narrow majority to the Planalto Palace in Brasilia for his third presidential term.

The presidential palace was badly damaged by the mob of pro-Bolsonaro rioters on January 8, 2023. Jair Bolsonaro the former right-wing populist president had left for Florida two days before Lula's inauguration. He claimed, like his friend Donald J. Trump, that the election had been rigged.

President Lula visited Joe Biden at the White House on February 10, 2023. The two presidents discussed "democracy and environmental commitments."

Many international observers welcomed Lula's return to office as a beacon of hope for the rainforests of the Amazon and for the global environment. In addition to his meeting with President Biden, Lula met with Senator Bernie Sanders, and Democratic Party law makers. Lula then went to the environmental summit in Egypt where he was received as a hero.

Last week Lula was in China on a official state visit where he attended the formal installation of former (and impeached) Brazilian president, Dilma Rousseff, as the president of the BRICS development bank in Shanghai. Lula also visited the factory of the Chinese telecom giant Huawei.

In Beijing Lula met with president Xi. On his way on back to Brazil he visited the United Arab Emirates (UAE) where he was received by the president, Sheikh Mohamed bin Zayed al-Nahyan.

After arriving back in Brasilia, he received Sergei Lavrov, the Russian foreign minister, who is on an official visit to Latin American visiting in addition to Brazil, Venezuela, Nicaragua, and Cuba. Latin America is according to the Russians "one of the centres of the forma-tion of the multipolar world."

The question is what precisely does "Brazil is Back" mean for Brazil's position in the emerging international system, and what role does Lula see for himself now in his third incarnation as Brazilian pres-ident on the international stage?

Last week Thomas A. Shannon Jr. said in an interview with the Rio de Janeiro based newspaper, *O Globo*, when asked about Lula's proposal in Beijing that the Chinese currency, the renminbi, replace the dollar in international trading: "Good Luck! with that! "

When asked about Lula's peace plans for the Ukraine, and Lula's suggestion that Ukrainian president Volodymyr Zelenskyy give up Ukrainian claims to the Crimea, Shannon responded that perhaps Lula might suggest that Brazil give up the southern Brazilian state of Rio Grande do Sul to Argentina!

Shannon was the United States ambassador to Brazil between 2010 and 2013, which coincided with the last year of Lula's second administration and the first of Lula's chosen successor, Dilma Rousseff, is no mean observer of things Brazilian. Shannon was the special assistant and senior director for western hemisphere affairs on the national security council between 2003 and 2005 under President George W. Bush.

Andrew Hill Card, better known as Andy Card, was Bush's White House chief of staff between 2001 and 2006. On September 11, 2001, it was Andy Card who whispered in George Bush's ear as he was visiting the Emma E. Booker elementary school in Sarasota, Florida, that a second plane had struck the World Trade Center in Manhattan.

Thomas Shannon, together with Andy Card, had coordinated a week-long series of private briefings for Brazilian officials at the request of José Dirceu after Lula's inauguration in January 2003. José Dirceu was Lula's principal political adviser.

Shannon also served for twelve days as Secretary of State until President Donald J. Trump's nominee, the former ExxonMobil CEO, Rex Wayne Tillerson, was approved by the U.S. Senate.

Lula has refused the request from the German chancellor, Olaf Schulz, to supply arms to Ukrainian forces. Like much of the "global south" Lula is neutral on the war in the Ukraine. He seeks the role of a peace maker. It is a large part of his post-Bolsonaro foreign policy agenda to assert that "Brazil is back,"

During his state visit to China last week Lula attended in Shanghai the inauguration of Dilma Rousseff as the head of the BRICS development bank. Dilma Rousseff was his chosen successor as the President of Brazil. She was impeached and removed from office in 2016.

Lula himself had spent 580 days in prison at the Brazilian Federal Police headquarters in the city of Curitiba. He had been sentenced to 12 years for corruption and money laundering in April 2018 as part of the "car-wash" investigation by Federal Judge Sérgio Moro.

Lula was released by the Supreme Court after the website "intercept" revealed that Judge Moro had collaborated with the prosecutors.

However, "Operation car-wash" had revealed widespread corruption and kickbacks involving the state petroleum company Petrobras, business leaders, middle man, and leading politicians. José Dirceu, Lula's chief of staff, had also been imprisoned. The scandals also had major international consequences.

Dilma Rousseff's appointment to the BRICS bank was Lula's response to her impeachment which he claims was politically motivated (it was). He also claims that his own imprisonment on corruption charges was politically motivated which is also in part true. The Chinese press quoted the statement of General George S. Patten, that success for you only begins when you hit the bottom. Dilma Rousseff appeared to have hit the bottom after her impeachment and removal from office.

Lula also appeared to have hit the bottom when he was imprisoned.

Dilma Rousseff had been a long-term member of Lula's Workers Party (PT) and was a former left-wing militant who had been imprisoned by the Brazilian military regime. The New Development Bank (NDB) is headquartered in Shanghai. The idea for the bank was first proposed by India at the BRICS summit in Delhi in 2012.

Dilma Rousseff hosted the BRICS summit in Fortaleza, Brazil, while she was the Brazilian President in 2014. The BRICS bank was established in 2015. The BRICS are Brazil, Russia, Indian, China, and South Africa.

The next BRICS summit, the fifteenth, will be held in Durban, South Africa, in late August of this year. According to Russian Foreign Minister, Sergei Lavrov, the next BRICS summit will be a "manifestation of global multi-polarity."

Dilma Rousseff in her inauguration speech in Shanghai with Lula present, thanked Lula for "introducing her candidacy" for the bank's presidency, and said that the BRICS bank was "committed to multilateralism and south-south cooperation" as well as to "a world undergoing profound transformation."

Lula also visited the factories of Huawei while in Shanghai and said that "no one will prohibit Brazil from prioritizing its link with China." Huawei is a multinational technology leader, headquartered in Shenzhen, Guangdong, China, and is the maker of telecommunications equipment, consumer electronics, smart phones and small electronic devises, and roof top solar panels.

Huawei has been heavily invested in Brazil. It is seen, however, by many western governments as a security risk because of its intimate links to the Chinese government and the Chinese security services a connection which the U.S. government has warned Brazil about.

The BRICS bank is part of an alternative to the World Bank, the IMF, and the Breton Woods institutions which made the US dollar the global settlement currency. Dilma Rousseff in her inaugural speech as the new BRICS bank president specifically mentioned "the renminbi, the dollar, and the euro" and in that order.

Lula was very "multi-polarity" in Beijing. After a stellar reception at the palace of the people in Beijing, and inspecting the serried ranks of a resplendent Chinese people's liberation army guard-of-honor, and a meeting with Chinese president Xi Jinping,

Lula reiterated his attack on the dollar, said that the U.S. should stop "encouraging war in the Ukraine and start talking about peace." Above all it was "necessary to convince the countries that supply weapons, encouraging war to stop." Brazil's relations with China was "non-negotiable," and that the Ukraine should formally cede the Crimea to Russia as part of any peace deal.

On the way back to Brazil, Lula made a one-day official visit to Abu Dhabi in the United Arab Emirates (UAE) where he was received by the president Sheikh Mohamed bin Zayed al-Nahuan. Lula said he had signed deals worth US$10 billion in China.

Lula said he had discussed with the UAE and China joint mediation for Russia's war in the Ukraine. He again accused the U.S. and Europe of prolonging the war. And he said he has proposed "a political G-20 to try to end the war." He also lashed out at the dollar's domination of global trade calling for a new currency for transactions between the BRICS.

On the Middle East, China had just brokered in Beijing a rapprochement between Iran and Saudi Arabia, which has already produced a positive outcome in negotiations between the Saudi backed and Iranian backed forces in the civil war in Yemen. Saudi Arabia and

Russia have recently agreed to rise the price of petroleum, despite entreaties from Washington not to do so.

On his arrival back in Brasilia Lula will meet with the Russian foreign minister, Sérgio Lavrov, who is on Latin American tour, visiting Brazil, Venezuela and Cuba. Latin America is considered by the Kremlin to be "one of the centers of the multipolar world."

Brazil's repositioning is not surprising. But Lula 3 seems much more aggressively anti-American than Lula 1 or Lula 2. He was it seems profoundly marked by his imprisonment. Before he was an eminently pragmatic leader, a tough labor union negotiator, with strong links to the U.S. Labor movement, especially United Auto Workers, and he was never an ideological Marxist.

José Dirceu was also in practice a pragmatic politician and he was very willing to reach out to the U.S. before and after Lula's first presidency. The U.S. ambassador in Brazil at the time, Donne J. Hrinak, was also extremely skillful in her dealings with the new Lula government.

Dirceu had been a communist student activist in 1965-1968, but he broke with the Brazilian communist party and joined more radical groups. He had been imprisoned and in 1969 was among the 14 leftist prisoners exchanged in return for the release of the kidnapped American ambassador, Charles Burke Elbrick. José Dirceu was flown into exile in Mexico and later spent time in Cuba. He returned clandestinely with a new identity and a changed appearance with plastic surgery living in São Paulo and the northeast of Brazil.

Dirceu was later caught up in the scandals of Lula's first term and was imprisoned by Judge Moro"s car-wash operation. During the early Lula administration as Lula's chief-of-staff, however, he was extremely sensitive to the U.S. and acted to mitigate possible tensions and misunderstandings and in this he was aided by Andy Card and Thomas Shannon in Bush's White House

Lula's (and Dilma Rousseff's) long term long term foreign policy adviser in the Planalto, however, was the late professor Marco Aurelio Garcia (1941-2017), as well as less directly, Luiz Alberto Moniz Bandeira (1935-2017). Bandeira who was a descendent of one of the oldest families in Bahia was a prolific author who had been a socialist militant as a young man in Rio de Janeiro. Exiled after the military coup of 1964 he had lived in Uruguay before returning to Brazil clandestinely.

Bandeira was arrested by the Brazilian navy and spent two years in jail. His books included a history of "U.S. hegemony" and a book on "a perilous relationship: a history of U.S. wars from the war against Spain to war against Iraque." And a book on the "American Empire." Bandeira died on 2017 at the age of 81 in Heidelberg, Germany.

Marco Aurélio Garcia from Rio Grande do Sul was a professor of Latin American History at UNICAMP in São Paulo. He had also been an exile in Chile and Paris where he taught at the university of Chile and in France at Paris-VIII and Paris-X. A long time PT militant on his return to Brazil he was the convener of the forum of the São Paulo which was a meeting (first suggested to Lula by Fidel Castro) of the leftist parties of Latin America.

Celso Amorim who was Lula's Foreign and his defense minister in his previous presidential incarnations came late to the Lula fold, originally via José Dirceu at the time of Lula's first election as president. Celso Amorim is now the dominant force in Brazil's foreign policy as Lula's special foreign policy advisor in the Planalto. He is extremely anti-American, and his wife is even more so. He visited Putin in Moscow prior to Lula's visit to China.

Brazil's closeness to China makes sense both economically and politically for Lula. Economically China is Brazil's major trading partner. And it makes political sense because the powerful agro-business interests in the south and west of Brazil export most of their soya production to China. And China takes much of Brazil's iron ore.

The strongest support for Bolsonaro is also concentrated in the west and the south. So it was very smart of Lula to include major figures from Brazilian agro-business as part of his delegation to China, and the deals which were stuck during Lula's visit to China also involved Brazilian made aircraft and opened up Chinese collaboration with the Brazilian space agency's base at Alcântara.

Not everyone in Brazil is enamored by Lula's foreign excursions and love-in with president Xi. Duda Teixeira on the Brazilian website "Crusoe" quoted from Lula's speech on Beijing where he urged "groups of countries disposed to find a jeito to make peace". The "jeito" is an untranslatable Brazilian term for a "fix."

But as Duda Teixeira point out to have any impact it will be necessary to convince the president of Russia, and that "the best thing that could happen for the war in Ukraine is to keep Lula as far a possible from any path to end the conflict."

Other Brazilian commentators are equally skeptical. And in any case most Brazilians who have the money much prefer Florida to Shanghai. Larry Summers, the former U.S. treasury secretary and Harvard president, said in an interview on the sidelines of the IMF and World Bank meetings in Washington .D.C., that the U.S. was getting "lonely" and that we are facing the "fragmentation of the global economy" and that the Bretton Woods settlement is under challenge. He said that he was told that "what we get from China is an airport, what we get for the U.S is words."

Lavrov's visit to Lula in Brasilia seems to have eventually got Washington's attention. John Kirby, the White House's national security spokesman said on Monday that Lula's comment were "simply misguided" and that Lula was "parroting Russian and Chinese propaganda."

Lavrov told journalists in Brasilia on Monday that "he was grateful to our Brazilian friends for their clear understanding of the situation." The only European leader who has welcomed Lula's initiative has been Emanuel Macron of France. But then Macron too has just returned from a state visit to China

One hopes the new U.S. ambassador to Brazil, who only arrived on February 3, 2023, Elizabeth Frawley Bagley, who was previously the successful U.S. Ambassador in Portugal, will have the skills displayed by her predecessor, Donna Hrinak, at the beginning of Lula's first term. She will need them.

But the challenges for the U.S. are considerable. While Lula was in Beijing, the "leader of the free world", the increasingly geriatric Joe Biden, who barely seems to know what direction he is facing, was busy wallowing in faux-Irish nostalgia (with his son, Hunter Biden no less) in Dublin, and at his "ancestral town" of Ballina in County Mayo.

It is a great pity that there is not a French type of retirement age for the retirement of aging politicians in the U.S., which would also remove the New York County district attorney Alvin Bragg's revitalized Donald J. Trump's from his presidential contemplation.

The truth is that while the U.S. is consumed with domestic contention, Brazil is indeed "back."

But much more significantly is the fact that "China is Back" and that Xi is busy orchestrating the "new world order" in China's national interest, and that Brazil and Lula are willingly going along for the ride.

WHO WILL COMPETE WITH CHINA IN CENTRAL ASIA?

May 31, 2023

By James Durso

Instead of being "Being Fustest with the Mostest" in Central Asia, an area of intense interest to China and Russia, the U.S. and Europe may be "too little, too late."

The dwindling relevance of Washington and Brussels to Central Asia was on display when Chinese leader Xi Jinping hosted the leaders of the five Central Asia republics at the China-Central Asia Summit in Xi'an, the terminus of the ancient Silk Road. (In the future, the meetings will alternate between China and a Central Asian capital; the next meeting will be in Astana, Kazakhstan in 2025.)[6]

Xi unveiled his vision for Central Asia that was, like most top-level political documents, laden with vague declarations like "helping each other," "common development," "universal security," "shared future," and that old Beijing favorite, "win-win."

China's strategy for Central Asia is to secure economic gains and help alleviate the high youth unemployment rate, create prosperity in the Xinjiang region to calm separatist tensions, and to build an alternate trade corridor in the event of a U.S.-led naval blockade of China's maritime trade routes.[7]

Kazakhstan's president, Kassym-Jomart Tokayev, responded "We consistently assert that Central Asia is a creation place.[8] We oppose turning the region into a place of geopolitical confrontation" and Turkmenistan's president, Serdar Berdimuhamedov, added, "As emphasized, the peoples of our countries have centuries-old friendly relations, a vast experience of interaction and good neighborliness."[9]

But despite all the official bonhomie – and group pictures – the leaders put pen to paper and, according to Silk Road Briefing, "... approved US$3.72 billion in regional grants, signed 54 major multilateral agreements, created 19 new regional platforms and signed a further 9 multilateral cooperation documents."[10]

Among the agreed points were to coordinate China's Belt and Road Initiative with the republics' national development strategies, upgrade border checkpoints, expand agricultural exports to China, award scholarships to Central Asian students to study in China, and develop cooperation in the fields of irrigation and green energy.

Kazakhstan and China signed 47 agreements worth $22 billion which should increase trade, a record $31 billion in 2022, and investment.[11] China is one of the five biggest investors in Kazakhstan with a total investment exceeding $23 billion.

Kazakhstan's exports to Russia increased 15% in 2022, and trade turnover by September 2022 was $18.4 billion, but Astana would be more comfortable if Moscow adopted the philosophy "When you're only No. 2, you try harder" in its dealings with its now-wary Central Asian neighbor.[12]

Uzbekistan and China adopted a "comprehensive strategic partnership" and inked 41 official documents, and Chinese and Uzbek businesses concluded $25 billion in deals.[13] The official agreements addressed joint efforts in higher education, alternative energy, agricultural innovation, hydroelectric power, and logistics.

A "comprehensive strategic partnership" is just below a "comprehensive strategic co-operative partnership," which is generally regarded as the highest level of bilateral relations for China.

Uzbekistan now joins Kazakhstan and Turkmenistan as the third Central Asian republic at this level of engagement with China, giving China privileged access to the two biggest economies in Central Asia, and the country with 10% of the world's natural gas reserves, that all sit astride Eurasia's East-West transport links.[14]

So where were America and Europe when all this was going on?

Their leaders were at the G-7 meeting in Tokyo where they castigated China for "economic coercion" which probably caused some confusion in Beijing as Washington is the source of economic sanctions "that currently cover 29 percent of the global economy and 40 percent of global oil reserves," according to the Quincy Institute.[15]

But even if it was momentary bemused by the G-7 outburst, Beijing probably welcomed the opportunity to contrast threats from the G-7 with what it could highlight as practical steps to grow mutually beneficial partnerships.

The U.S. announced its strategy for Central Asia in 2019 with an emphasis on the republics' "sovereignty, independence, and territorial integrity," but it was in reference to the U.S. occupation of Afghanistan.[16]

After the hasty U.S./NATO retreat from Afghanistan in 2021, the republics know their utility to the Americans in limited and they must find partners that will help them increase economic opportunity for their mostly under-30 populations.

The U.S. hasn't helped with relatively small projects like the Economic Resilience in Central Asia Initiative that trumpeted a $50 million effort to "diversify trade routes, expand investment in the region, and increase employment opportunities" – which is what China intends to do at industrial scale.[17] (The U.S. did, however, provide significant economic assistance to the republics in the immediate post-Soviet period.)[18]

The American actor Woody Allen said, "80 percent of success is showing up" and that is something an American president has never done in Central Asia. The presidents of Russia, Vladimir Putin, and China, Xi Jinping, leave nothing to chance: Xi has visited every one of the republics and has been to Kazakhstan four times and Uzbekistan three times; Putin has visited Kazakhstan twenty-seven times (the countries share a 7,644-kilometre border), and has been to Kyrgyzstan and Tajikistan at least a dozen times each.[19]

China's Belt and Road Initiative has pumped about $40 billion into the region, but recent surveys by the Central Asia Barometer showed a decrease in public sentiment towards China, even as China increases local investment.[20]

Positive sentiment was down in Kazakhstan and Uzbekistan since 2017, but held steady in Kyrgyzstan.

If Russia has a weak presence in future years this is an opportunity for the U.S., Europe, and India, Japan, Turkey, South Korea, Singapore, and the Persian Gulf petrostates to build grass roots support.

The Persian Gulf states have increased their investment in Central Asia and no longer regard the area just as a place to exercise their falcons.[21] The government-led development of the Gulf states appeals to the leaders of the republics and can offer a counter-weight to China's projects.

The Gulf states have invested_in traditional projects, such as coal and chemicals, power generation and distribution, cargo handling, and oil pipelines, and ACWA Power of Saudi Arabia recently committed over $2 billion for a wind farm in Uzbekistan's Karakalpakstan region, part of a $12 billion commitment to the country.[22]

Aside from all that cash, the Gulf states can create good will by helping the republics rediscover and preserve their history and heritage by assisting the restoration of local Islamic heritage sites, such as the Bibi Khanum Mosque in Samarkand, Uzbekistan.[23] And it gives the local leaders the opportunity to not be beholden to one primary creditor – China.

Investing in Central Asia also gives Saudi Arabia and the United Arab Emirates the opportunity to establish a foothold to the North of their competitor Iran. Relations between the Arabs and the Islamic Republic are improving lately, but it is prudent for the petro-states to diversity their political portfolio at the same time they are diversifying their foreign direct investment. And allying with the republics gives the Gulf Arabs allies in multilateral organizations such as the United Nations and the Organization of Islamic Cooperation.

The U.S. can also make gains even though it can't match China's investments in the region. It can deploy the expertise of organizations like the U.S. International Development Finance Corporation to address areas of concern to Central Asia, such as the impact on the cotton crop caused by reduction in the flow of the Amu Darya river due to the Afghan Taliban's irrigation canal project.[24]

Washington can also help the region though mechanisms such as the C5+1 Regional Border Security Program, and by helping local participants in the Global Methane Pledge (Uzbekistan, Kyrgyzstan) achieve their goals, and lobbying Turkmenistan, whose methane leaks exceed the carbon emissions of the United Kingdom, to join the pledge.[25]

One element of China's progress has been its readiness to transfer technology, which it has done in Kazakhstan, Uzbekistan, Kyrgyzstan, and Tajikistan.[26] Local leaders may argue that China can advance regional connectivity if it transfers the technology to help the region develop a high-speed rail network, as it recently did in Thailand.

The good news for Central Asia is that it has China's undivided attention; the bad news is that it has China's undivided attention. But the region can pursue its development objectives and not be in thrall to creditor China or the social engineers in the U.S. and Europe.

The region used China to balance the U.S., Europe, and Russia, and can now deepen its relations with the Gulf states, Turkey, India, Japan, South Korea, and Singapore to offset the China influence.

One result of the China focus may be more local coordination by the republics. Uzbekistan's president Shavkat Mirziyoyev started this trend by resolving outstanding border demarcation issues after he assumed office in 2016.

The worsening water crisis caused by Afghanistan's diversion of the water of the Amu Darya will force close collaboration on this most sensitive issue for the water-starved region between countries with water but little energy (Kyrgyzstan and Tajikistan) and countries with energy but less water (Kazakhstan, Turkmenistan, and Uzbekistan.)

Success in this task will reinforce cooperative habits that will ensure the future benefits of China's investments in the republics don't all go one way.

In 2017, the Asia Development Bank estimated Asia would have to invest $1.7 trillion dollars annually until 2030 to maintain growth momentum, tackle poverty, respond to climate change, and, now, recover from the COVID-19 pandemic.[27]

The funding would be shared by the public and private sectors. Central Asian leaders are acutely aware their plans for economic and liberalization are limited by infrastructure shortfalls and will be receptive to partners who will share funding and know-how to help the region be not just a low-cost workshop or provider of natural resources, but a full partner in 21st century Asia.

NATO SUMMIT IN VILNIUS: EXPECTATIONS IN CENTRAL EASTERN EUROPE

June 12, 2023

By Robert Czulda

Between July 11-12, 2023, Lithuania will host the NATO Summit in the capital city of Vilnius. This event is extremely significant for several reasons.

Firstly, this summit will have symbolic value, as it will be the first summit in a former Soviet republic and the second ever in Central Eastern Europe (the first being the NATO Summit in Poland in 2016).

Secondly, Central Eastern Europe is particularly vulnerable to Russia's aggressive and unpredictable policies, and is counting on concrete resolutions, including the implementation of decisions from the NATO summit in Madrid, which was held in June last year.

The topic of NATO and the upcoming summit in Vilnius was one of the dominant issues at Defence24 DAY – one of the largest international symposiums on security and defense in Poland. This two-day event was organized for the fifth time in Warsaw, this time at the National Stadium.

The conference was attended by a strong representation from Lithuania. Greta Monika Tučkutė, Deputy Minister of National Defense of Lithuania, and Rima Malakauskienė, Security Advisor to the President of Lithuania, expressed Vilnius' expectations. In addition, the discussions involved, among others, Gen. Ian Oprisor, Security Advisor to the President of Romania, Janis Kazonics, Security Advisor to the President of Latvia, Jacek Siewiera, Head of the National Security Bureau of Poland, and Tomasz Szatkowski, Permanent Representative of the Republic of Poland to the North Atlantic Council.

Nine countries of the region form an informal group known as the B9 (Bucharest Nine). The Bucharest Nine consists of NATO members from Central and Eastern Europe: Bulgaria, the Czech Republic, Estonia, Lithuania, Latvia, Poland, Romania, Slovakia, and Hungary. The official inauguration of the group took place on November 4, 2015, during a mini-summit of NATO's Eastern Flank countries in Bucharest (hence the name of the alliance).

"I am convinced that the B9 identifies common threats and interests. A formation of a new identity of this group is now taking place," said Minister Siewiera. The same attitude was expressed by Romanian General Oprisor, who confirmed that Bucharest would increase defense spending from 2% of GDP to 2.7%.

Malakauskienė compared the B9 to a puzzle: each country is a piece of a larger picture, and its fate depends on the security of the other "bricks".

Tučkutė presented Lithuania's expectations for the Vilnius Summit. As she stated, Lithuania hopes that concrete, clear, and binding decisions will be made on key aspects, particularly regarding the Russian threat in Central Eastern Europe.

She also simultaneously mentioned three key points from the perspective of the Lithuanians.

Firstly, Lithuania expects the adoption of defense plans and the full implementation of decisions which we made earlier at the Madrid Summit.

Secondly, there are expectations regarding the establishment of a rotational model for NATO's air defense and missile defense component.

Thirdly, the development of defense industries in Europe needs to accelerate, which are necessary to meet current and future requirements.

In this context, Tučkutė raised an issue of transitioning from peacetime to wartime mode and a challenge of increasing production while maintaining high standards. It is also important to ensure interoperability among allies.

In her opening statement, Tučkutė briefly touched upon a significant topic of Ukraine's perspective of NATO membership.

"We expect clear and achievable mechanisms to be established that would allow Ukraine to achieve this goal. Ukraine has already proved that it is capable of defending itself and could become a very strong, well-organized member state capable of using the latest weaponry available to NATO".

Ambassador Szatkowski confirmed that Poland's position regarding key issues, including the vision of Ukraine's NATO membership, is similar to Lithuania's position. "In our discussions, we must focus not so much on ideal visions but on what is actually achievable."

He added, "NATO summits essentially have two goals. Firstly, communication, and the ability to send a message. Secondly, they provide an opportunity to manage concepts and ideas. Gathering decision-makers in one place creates an opportunity to make concrete decisions."

Participants of Defence24 DAY agreed that without Ukraine's victory over Russia, it will not be possible to ensure security and stability in the region. Without the security of Central Eastern Europe, a safe Western Europe cannot be created.

As for the summit in Vilnius, Ambassador Szatkowski agreed that it is expected that it will fully implement NATO's new concept of deterrence and defense strategy.

"This action has not yet been completed, as it is important to incorporate a new concept into operational plans and force structure documents. Communicating this information to the public will be very challenging, as a significant portion of the details are classified."

In the context of Ukraine, Szatkowski stated that "NATO must demonstrate its credibility. This includes a vision of Ukraine in the Euro-Atlantic family. Such declarations were made back in 2008.

It is difficult not to notice that the lack of implementation of our own words from 2008-2014 and later from 2014-2023 did not help Ukraine. Leaving this country in the realm of ambiguity has caused significant harm to European security."

Additionally, Poland maintains the position that discussions should be initiated in Vilnius regarding the future relationship with Russia.

Tučkutė added that, given all difficulties in quickly inviting Ukraine to NATO, the Alliance should develop other mechanisms that would bring Kiyv closer to NATO.

The representative of Lithuania stated that in the absence of consensus, any other option for integration should be considered, but these mechanisms should not replace the ultimate goal, which is full NATO membership. Tučkutė expressed support for the idea of developing and adopting a timeline that would facilitate the implementation of further steps.

BASTILLE DAY 2023: MODI BRINGS AN INDIAN ACCENT

July 14, 2023

By Pierre Tran

Paris - President Emmanuel Macron welcomed on July 14 the Indian prime minister, Narendra Modi, as guest of honor to a prestige-laden military parade marking the 1789 French revolution, a day after New Delhi green lighted high-level talks to order 26 Rafale fighter jets and three attack submarines for the Indian navy.

Modi attended the televised event to mark the sun-soaked national holiday which celebrates a storming of the Bastille prison, sparking a revolution which led to the execution of King Louis XVI by the guillotine.

Three Indian air force Rafales flew with a Rafale from the French service in the highly orchestrated fly past, and 240 personnel from the Indian air force, army, and navy marched in the parade down the Champs Elysées.

Foreign tourists attended the parade, and French nationals were heard questioning why public spectators were barred from entering the famous avenue to watch the parade close up, rather than catch glimpses of the military showcase from neighboring streets.

It has been on, off, then on again for the Indian arms announcement to coincide with Modi's two day official visit, with the Bastille day parade serving as the media high point.

Finally, Indian defense minister Rajnath Singh said July 13 the high-level Defence Acquisition Council had that day approved plans to order 26 Dassault Aviation Rafale, and three more diesel-electric Scorpene boats from Naval Group, a French warship builder.

It remains for the Indian and French authorities to negotiate financial details, in what looks like a government-to-government deal, with

Reuters reporting the total deal for fighters and submarines could carry a price tag of $9.75 billion.

"The price and other terms of purchase will be negotiated with the French government after taking into account all relevant aspects, including comparative procurement price of similar aircraft by other countries," the Indian Defence Ministry said in a July 13 statement.

The prospective order consists of 26 Rafale M, a naval model with strengthened undercarriage for flying from an aircraft carrier. That planned order includes four Rafale for training navy pilots, Reuters reported.

France winning that fighter deal suggests India could order more French missiles and powered smart bombs, opening up sales prospects for MBDA and Safran.

This year marks 25 years of a French strategic partnership agreement with India, which includes defense cooperation, a senior officer of the Direction Générale des Relations Internationales et de la Stratégie (DGRIS), told journalists July 6. DGRIS serves as a think tank for international relations for the armed forces ministry.

Paris is keen to promote close ties with New Delhi to help strengthen the French presence in the Indo-Pacific region.

French Fighter for Indian Aircraft Carrier

The Indian navy will fly the Rafale from its new Vikrant carrier, built with a ski lift deck for short take-off and landing. The navy also sails the Vikramaditya, a modernized version of a Russian carrier, which dates back to the Soviet era.

For France to win an export deal for its carrier-based Rafale has been reported as an extraordinary feat, beating out the Boeing F/A-18 E/F Super Harrier.

The contracts with France could be signed next year, media reports said, but it remains to be seen when the deals will be sealed as it has been previously noted New Delhi is inclined to stretch out negotiations.

Three Indian air force Rafale flew with a Rafale from the French service in the Bastille day fly past, just after the Patrouille de France display team opened the public event, flying the Big Nine formation.

A British RAF Typhoon and two Polish F-16, elements of the Nato enhanced air policing team, took part in the fly past, flying with a Rafale and Mirage 2000-5.

The French Rafale fighter had competed in the Indian navy competition against the Super Hornet, and Russia had reportedly offered its MiG-29K and MiG 29KUB carrier fighters for the Vikrant and Vikramaditya.

If New Delhi had picked the MiG fighter, even upgraded with a more powerful engine and active electronically scanned array radar, that would likely have drawn severe criticism from western allies, which have rallied around Ukraine's struggle against Russian forces.

There were reported Indian concerns over the Super Hornet, which is nearing the end of manufacture in 2025 - unless Boeing won an export order.

There was a strong U.S. presence at the Bangalore air show in February, Reuters reported, with Boeing pitching its Super Hornet to the Indian navy, and Lockheed Martin presenting its F-21, an F-16 modified for the Indian air force.

There was close interest on social media of the Indian navy's ski-jump tests of the Super Hornet and Rafale at the shore-based test facility at Goa, western India.

More Scorpene Boats

The planned order for three more Scorpene boats would be in addition to the six Scorpene subs ordered for the Indian navy in 2005. Mazagon Dock Shipbuilders will build the three new boats if the deal goes ahead.

The navy has commissioned five of the Scorpene diesel-electric boats, with the sixth sub undergoing sea trials and due to enter service next year.

India awarded that Project 75 deal, worth $3.75 billion, to Naval Group in 2005. The submarine project ran some four years behind schedule, and was part of Modi's Make in India policy drive, seeking to boost jobs and secure transfer of technology.

The India navy is looking to add a further six, more advanced attack submarines with its competition for Project 75 (India). German shipbuilder ThyssenKrupp Marine Systems is seen as a serious contender in that tender, which seeks extensive technology transfer, an advanced air independent propulsion system, and advanced missiles and torpedoes.

Dassault last year completed delivery of 36 Rafale fighters to the Indian air force, meeting the timetable despite the lock down stemming from the Covid pandemic.

The French family-controlled company won the 2016 fighter order, worth €7.8 billion ($8.7 billion), and the Indian air force is looking to add more fighters to the three Rafale squadrons.

India has previously had effectively two air forces, namely French Mirage, and Russian MiG and Sukhoi fighter fleets, pursuing its policy of non-alignment in the Cold War.

That reliance on Russia has waned, as could be seen with Modi going to Washington D.C. last month to meet president Joe Biden, part of India's plan to boost its place in the world, counter the power of China, and strengthen its border with Pakistan.

THE IRISH OPPORTUNITY: IRELAND RETHINKS ITS ROLE IN SECURITY AND DEFENSE IN EUROPE

March 2, 2023

Ireland in my lifetime has been more likely a defense problem than part of a defense solution for Europe. But joining the European Union and the Good Friday Agreement in 1998 set Ireland onto a new path, one in which peace in Ireland plus significant economic growth became the reality.

Then Brexit posed the possibility of division in Ireland once again, this time fostered by the uncertain relationship of Northern Island and the UK with the EU. And then the war in Ukraine has made neutrality in Europe an historical discussion, rather than a realistic policy for a number of states within Europe itself.

Last year, the Irish government began a process of rethinking and reworking their role in European security and defense. This can be clearly seen in the February 2022 report issued by the government entitled the Report of the Commission of the Defence Forces which was accompanied by a more detailed plan "Building for the Future—Change From Within."

The government announced plans to reverse declines in defense spending with a new commitment to security and defense. A simple question is: What book should I read to provide an understanding of the context of Irish defense and security policy and the opportunity which the rethink can provide?

Not easy to answer for there really is not a good answer. Well, at least until now.

My friend and colleague, Dr. Dale Herspring has written such a book and plans to publish it in the near future. Dale and I wrote a book published in 1984 shortly after the greatest threat of nuclear war we faced (perhaps until now) about the strategic arms control process between the United States and the Soviet Union. After a distinguished career at the State Department, Dr. Herspring taught at Kansas State University for many years.

The book describes and analyses Irish civil-military relations from 1922 until the current day. When I discussed with Dale this week, what he thought was a central message from his work it was really simply put: there is an opportunity for Ireland to play a role in North Atlantic security and defense but that the EU and NATO leadership needed to pay attention to the opportunity and nurture progress in shaping and working with Ireland in terms of a relevant role and contribution.

He underscored that the current government is tackling the problem but Ireland like other smaller countries in Europe seeks to contribute and the challenge for the larger countries is to craft a realistic context in which such a contribution can be made.

One area of importance for example facing both Denmark and Ireland is the security of the underwater cables entering Europe. Perhaps this mission can be a major one in which Ireland participates.

This is how Eoin Micheál McNamara put it in a 21 December 2022 article: "Ireland is a global data hub and a base for many multinational technology giants. 75% of the Northern Hemisphere's telecommunications cables pass through or near its maritime Exclusive Economic Zone (EEZ). Hybrid threats to global connectivity mean that Ireland is no longer an island 'safely tucked away behind Britain."[28]

There is virtually no literature of Ireland and defense. Herspring's book not only fills a gap but raises key questions of the role of Ireland in the evolving European order.

Is the historical stance of Ireland on neutrality acceptable to its European partners, who increasingly are focused on the absolute necessity of a stronger European defense allied with North America? If not, what is Ireland prepared to do about it?

As Herspring concludes: "While it may come as a shock to some, Ireland is becoming increasingly important militarily to the defence of Europe." Herspring explains why and identifies the challenges facing Ireland to live in the new world.

EUROPEAN DEFENSE ARMAMENTS COOPERATION: AN AUGUST 2023 UPDATE

August 6, 2023

By Pierre Tran

There is a view that politics is really about personalities. That notion comes to mind after Airbus chief executive Guillaume Faury pointed up the frustration of Europe failing to cooperate on arms programs in the light of war in Ukraine – apart from the future combat air system (FCAS).

The Airbus top executive told July 26 CNBC that Europe was not "showing unity in addressing the new threats and solutions."

"That's very challenging, and it's quite frustrating to see that the responses that have been provided so far are mostly of a national nature and not much of a European nature," he said.

That national drive can be seen as a damper on building a strong European industry – including Airbus – to design and manufacture advanced weapons, and from which to place a steady flow of high-margin orders.

Instead, there is a view there are lucrative orders for U.S. systems, such as the iconic F-35 fighter jet, or deals sealed with dynamic allied nations such as Israel, South Korea, and Turkey as well as domestic manufacturers, which employ vote wielding workers whose wages boost the local economy.

There has been some cooperation, notably in the naval sector, and on a bilateral basis. There was a July 28 contract for upgrade of the Aster 30 new technology (NT) missile for the four Horizon air defense frigates of the French and Italian navies – two for each of the allied services. That anti-missile weapon arms British, French, and Italian navies, the French armed forces said in a statement, pointing up the cooperative aspect of the Aster program.

In another cooperative naval deal, the Direction Générale de l'Armement procurement office took delivery July 18 at Toulon base the Jacques Chevalier, the first of four fleet auxiliary ships, based on the Italian Vulcano logistic support ship. The DGA will hand over the supply vessel to the French navy.

The Jacques Chevalier represented "a strategic European industrial partnership," French shipbuilders Naval Group and Chantiers de l'Atlantique said in a July 19 joint statement.

On the wider European front, a study led by Italy for a European Patrol Corvette is among studies funded by the European Union permanent structured cooperation. There are 25 EU states backing PESCO, Brussel's expansion into support for the arms industry in the EU.

Another cooperative PESCO study, led by France, considers an airlifter, dubbed Future Mid-Size Tactical Cargo, which would fly alongside the A400M and replace the lighter Lockheed Martin C-130, Airbus C-295, and Leonardo C-27J.

Airbus is leading that industrial study for a future cargo aircraft, backed by €30 million from the European Defense Fund, which supports research and technology studies.

The EU has scrambled to respond to the Russian invasion of Ukraine, with the quaintly named European Peace Fund acting as financial conduit for €1 billion of EU funds to reimburse in part member states which have sent ammunition and missiles to Kyiv, and a further €1 billion for EU states jointly to buy ammunition to refresh depleted national stocks.

The third part of the EU-backed program is Act in Support of Ammunition Production (ASAP), with €500 million to help companies in the European Union boost production of ammunition and missiles.

Show Me the Program

While there are EU funds for R&T weapons studies, and to pay for shipment of munitions and missiles to war torn Kyiv, Faury's point remains – where are the new programs?

There may be renewed interest in a Franco-German project for a new heavy tank and un-crewed vehicles in the main ground combat system (MGCS), but apart from that there appears little else on the horizon.

Just now, it looks like something of a personal and political dispute over what constitutes European, with French president Emmanuel Macron at loggerheads with German chancellor Olaf Scholz, who leads a plan to build a missile defense system against Moscow.

That Berlin-led project, dubbed European Sky Shield Initiative, draws on German, Israeli, and U.S. missiles to hit any incoming Russian weapons.

But the absence of Franco-Italian SAMP/T Mamba missiles in that planned system has sparked Macron's ire, as he sees the German approach as undermining European strategic autonomy, a concept the French commander in chief has promoted as an alternative to European dependence on Washington and the Beltway.

Now Berlin has unrolled the red carpet for Israel, with its Israel Aerospace Industries Arrow-3 missile, in a deal reported to be worth almost €4 billion.

The French pursuit of autonomy is underpinned at a strategic level by an independent French airborne and seaborne nuclear weapon.

Jupiter is the code name for the duty officer carrying a black briefcase with nuclear launch codes for the French president, as noted in a book, *The President and The Bomb* (Odile Jacob), by authors Jean Guisnel and Bruno Tertrais.

Jupiter leads the Greek gods from Mount Olympus, keeps a watchful eye over mortals down below, and wields deadly lightning.

Limits of Autonomy

The Russian invasion of Ukraine points up the limits of European pursuit of autonomy, with Finland and Sweden applying for membership of NATO, a military alliance led by the U.S. Some in France see that transatlantic partnership as favoring orders for U.S. over European equipment, perhaps the price to pay for the American protective umbrella.

Finland has joined the alliance, and Sweden awaits formal approval from Hungary and Turkey, both expected soon.

The U.S. has reportedly given approval for Finland's order for the Israeli David's Sling missile, a procurement approved by the Finnish government in April, just after it joined Nato.

Underlying the pursuit of European missile defense against Moscow might be the question, who leads Europe – Macron or Scholz?

Underpinning that is – where are the orders for European kit?

The German chancellor invoked a Zeitenwende, a turning point in history, after Russian president Vladimir Putin ordered the bloody incursion into Ukraine. In response, Scholz pledged an extraordinary €100 billion military budget for Germany and to hit the two percent target of gross domestic product, as requested by Nato.

Skepticism has crept in since Scholz grabbed headlines with his drive for martial modernization, as Berlin bureaucracy slowed the arms procurement process.

Across the Rhine, Macron's invoking a "war economy" in response to Putin's belligerence, has left some in the French arms industry disappointed as expectations of bumper orders were largely left unmet. Here, an exception might be missile maker MBDA, which has received hefty orders from Macron's administration.

A 2024-2030 military budget law was published Aug. 2 in the Journal Officiel statute book, with a 40-percent increase in spending to €413 billion from the previous multi-year program.

For some analysts, much of that went to a scheduled modernization of nuclear weapons, and inflation is expected to wipe out €30 billion or maybe more.

Cool Relations

On the political front, France and Germany last month marked the 60th anniversary of the Elysée treaty, a bilateral agreement signed by the then president Charles de Gaulle and then chancellor Konrad Adenauer, marking a determination to forge close cooperation to rebuild Europe after the second world war.

But on the personal front, there appears to be little warmth between Macron and Scholz, making it harder to advance cooperation between the two nations, seen as key partners in forging European defense – and launching those programs.

Despite that coolness between the two political leaders, Germany has seen the need to pursue European cooperation to hedge the transatlantic bets, after Berlin saw how Trump won the 2016 election and forged an America First policy, with consequences for foreign allies. Even with the latest set of indictments, Trump is ahead in the polls for leading the Republican party in the forthcoming election.

A reflection of the importance of close personal ties can be seen with the then chancellor Angela Merkel and Macron agreeing at the 2017 bilateral summit, held here, the FCAS project, seen as a signature project for European autonomy.

Berlin's backing for that key project has not prevented an order for the F-35, to extend the German air force's capability to carry Nato B61 nuclear bomb after the fleet of Tornado fighters is retired.

On the industrial front, it can be argued that for Dassault Aviation, European cooperation on a fighter project is fine as long as it is led by the French family-controlled company.

That privileged approach can be seen in Dassault's insistence on being the sole prime contractor on the new generation fighter in FCAS, despite Airbus Defence and Space seeking a joint prime contractor status.

France backed Dassault's position, so in that respect, there was a national approach on a project held as key for European cooperation. Such is the perceived importance, Belgium has joined as observer on FCAS, joining the partner nations France, Germany and Spain.

Less Tension with the UK

On broad cooperation, Macron has long sought to keep the U.K. in the European defense fold in response to the Brexit departure from the European Union.

Britain and France are the two leading military powers in Europe, both equipped with nuclear weapons and holding a sought after permanent seat in the U.N. security council.

Rishi Sunak as prime minister is seen on the French side as welcome change from the previous tenant of Downing Street, Boris

Johnson, seen as happily exploiting difficulties with France as welcome distraction from unsettling events at home.

Putin's drive into Ukraine brought the cross-Channel allies together, but the question remains – where are the arms programs?

Britain and France are signatories of the 2010 Lancaster House treaty for bilateral defense cooperation, but there has been a lack of newly launched programs.

Italy has applied to join the Anglo-French future cruise/anti-ship weapon program, which will extend European cooperation in missiles, a key area of the Lancaster House pact. On the A400M, Britain and France share spare parts for the airlifter, underlining cooperation.

Meanwhile France and Germany each went its own way for service support, with the former signing with Air France Industries, and the latter with Lufthansa Technik.

The U.K. has attended both meetings of the European Political Community, a broad group of nations promoted by Macron and part of his attempt to keep Britain close to Europe after leaving the E.U.

The most recent EPC meeting, attended by 48 European leaders, was held June 1 in Bulboaca, Moldova, just a short distance from the border with Ukraine, signaling support for Kyiv. Security and defense were high on the agenda, with the president of Ukraine, Volodymyr Zelenskiy, attending the high-level meeting.

Political conferences are undoubtedly crucial policy tools, but for contractors it is a government order and down payment that count.

Maybe nationalism as a political movement sweeping across western Europe hampers a government's willingness to sign up for a large, ambitious, cross-border arms programs. Far-right parties have gained populist ground in Austria, France, Germany, Italy, Finland, The Netherlands, and Sweden, making it harder to forge common projects with partners abroad.

It seems patience is indeed a virtue.

BRICS-PLUS SIX: FROM COHESION TO CONGRUENCE: NEW PATTERNS OF GLOBAL (DIS)ORDER

September 4, 2023

By Kenneth Maxwell

Lord Jim O'Neill (Baron O'Neill of Gatley) invented the acronym BRIC in 2001 to describe the rising economic powers of Brazil, Russia, India and China. Jim O'Neill originally developed the idea in the context of Goldman Sachs foreign investment strategies when he was the chairman of Goldman Sachs Asset Management.

But the original protagonists of his asset management strategy took up his acronym and made it a reality. South Africa joined in late 2010 at the invitation of China making it the BRICS.

The initial meeting of the foreign ministers of the four countries met in September 2006 in New York City on the fringes of the UN General Assembly. A full-scale diplomatic meeting was held in Yekaterinburg, Russia, on June 16, 2009.

At this first formal summit Luiz Inácio Lula da Silva represented Brazil, Dmitry Medvedev Russia, Manmohan Singh India, and Hun Jintao China. When South Africa joined the BRICS became a formal intergovernmental organization with the heads of state meeting annually in formal summits.

The expansion of the BRICS to incorporate six new members (Argentina, Ethiopia, Saudi Arabia, Iran, Egypt and the United Arab Emirates) was agreed at the BRICS summit in Johannesburg on August 24th, 2023, and will take place on January 1st next year.

Lord O'Neill, however, does not see much traction from this expanded BRICS, nor does he see it as much of a challenge to the dominance of the US dollar in global international exchange. He dismissed the notion of BRICS developing their own currency as "ridiculous."

But this is a very economist-centric view. The geopolitics of the enlargement are much more challenging in the emerging poly-centric world. The Manchester born Jim O'Neill served briefly in the British conservative-liberal democrat coalition government under David Cameron when he was charged by the Chancellor of the Exchequer,

George Osborne, with the developing the "Northern Powerhouse" aimed at "leveling up" northern Britain.

This is when he was made Lord O'Neill. But he resigned under prime minister Theresa May and he now sits in the House of Lords as a cross-bencher.

The eleven members of the expanded BRICS will collectively represent 37% of the World's GDP and 46% of the World's population, contesting the Western-led G-7. Six of the ten oil producing states will be members. Chinese President, Xi Jinping, who pushed for the admission of the new members of the group, described the expansion as "historic."

Vladimir Putin did not attend the BRICS Summit in Johannesburg as there is an outstanding arrest warrant for him for war crimes committed by the Russian forces in Ukraine issued by the international criminal court (ICC). He attended "virtually" from Moscow and he was represented in Johannesburg by Sergio Lavrov, the long-time Russian foreign minister. Chinese president Xi Jinping described the expansion of BRICS as "historic."

Next year Russia will host the expanded BRICS summit and the gathering of the BRICS+ heads of state. The meeting in 2024 will be chaired by Vladimir Putin.

A BRICS Development Bank headquartered in Shanghai already exists. It is now led by the former (but impeached and removed from office) Brazilian president, Dilma Rousseff, who was nominated to the position by the current (and formerly imprisoned) Brazilian President, Luiz Inácio Lula da Silva. Dilma Rousseff and Lula are strong promoters of an 'independent" foreign policy for Brazil that favors the "global south."

This stance has as its principal critical proponent within the Planalto, the presidential palace in Brasilia, Celso Amorim, Lula's former foreign and defense chief, who is profoundly anti-American.

This is in striking contrast to the role of José Dirceu in Lula's first term. Ze Dirceu was then Lula's de-facto chief of staff. Dirceu was exiled during the military regime when he and several other imprisoned leftist activistas were exchanged for the kidnapped American Ambassador.

But Dirceu was a highly pragmatic guide to Lula and he personally greatly soothed Lula's relationship with a skeptical (and at the time in large part hostile) Washington. Lula since his long and contentious imprisonment seems much less willing to compromise and much more committed to a policy hostile to the west.

Dirceu meanwhile fell victim to the corruption scandals (essentially the buying of votes and political support in Congress) during Lula's first terms in office (the "mensalão" affair). President Cyril Ramaaphosa of South Africa said on the eve of the Johannesburg summit, that South Africa "would not be bullied" into taking sides with global powers. President Luis Inácio Lula da Silva has been promoting a "peace plan" for the war in Ukraine.

These views are far from being isolated. They reflect the widespread skepticism revealed at the UN general assembly last year in the vote on the the U.S. motion to suspend Russia for human rights violations in Ukraine. 58 countries voted to abstain. These included in the Middle East, Bahrain, Saudi Arabia, Egypt, Qatar, Oman, Iraq, Kuwait, and Jordan.

They were joined in the abstentions by India and South Africa. Brazil under former Jair Bolsonaro voted with the U.S., though he criticized his vice-president, Hamilton Mourão, for condemning the Russian invasion of Ukraine, saying that it "was not Mourão's job to speak about Eastern Europe." China, which promoted the expansion of the BRICS, has recently brokered the opening of diplomatic conversations between Saudi Arabia and Iran.

The new configuration of the expanded BRICS should not be underestimated. In fact, the results have been quick. India has just done a deal with the UAE which ditched the U.S. dollar and purchased one million barrels of oil paid for in rupees, the first sale in a currency other than the US dollar. 90% of oil deals are settled since 1973 in petrodollars.

Saudi Arabia will be the next to watch. Saudi Arabia's de-facto ruler, Crown Prince Mohammed bin Salman, is reported to be prepared to commit US$ 16 billion from Saudi Arabia's foreign reserves to BRICS initiatives: South Africa and Egypt and potentially Argentina could be beneficiaries. Saudi Arabia and the UAE supply most of China's energy imports. Saudi Arabia and UAE could make local currencies the only way to procure oil and gas.

China has also just completed a deal with Petrobras, the Brazilian oil and gas giant. In late August Petrobras signed a memorandum of understanding (MOU) with China's Development Bank (CCHDB.UL) and the Bank of China (601988.SS) to partner in a series of projects covering low carbon initiatives, green finance, supply chain investments, and trade exchanges.

The chief executive of Petrobras, Paul Prates, said that Petrobras plans to create a Chinese subsidiary in an effort to triple oil exports to China over the next decades, and that Chinese partnerships were foreseen in oil refineries, fertilizer projects, and in efforts to renew the Brazilian naval industry.

President Lula recently visited China where he attended the installment of Dilma Rousseff at the BRICS Bank in Shanghai, criticized the IMF, visited the Huawei research center, and was received with full honors in Beijing by President Xi. China has since 2009 been Brazil largest trading partner, receiving soya beans, beef, iron ore, poultry, pulp, cotton and oil.

Lula dropped in on the UAE on the way home from China were he was received by the UAE prime minister, Sheikh Mohamed bin Zayad Al Nohyan. He signed a series of deals including an investment of $2.5 billion for a biodiesel project by UAE controlled Matasipa refinery in Brazil. The two leaders also discussed the Ukraine and Lula promoted the idea of a BRICS based currency.

Lord O'Neill is right that the BRICS+ currency is an illusion, and there is no serious indication that the BRICS are currently contemplating this. Much more likely are deals in currencies other than the dollar.

The notion of the "global south" is also a shibboleth. Most of the countries involved in BRICS+ are north of the equator, including China and India and the Middle East. Argentina which was invited to join the BRICS at the insistence of Brazil, and most of Brazil, and South Africa, are south of the equator. But so too are Chile and Australia, and there is little indication of any Australian desire to join the BRICS+.

China and India are at loggerheads over a border dispute in the Galwan region of Ladakh and Indian and Chinese armed forces clashed in the high Himalayas in mid-2020. Xi Jinping will not apparently attend the G-20 meeting in New Delhi hosted by Indian prime minister Narendra Modi.

India is basking in its recent (and very cost effective) successes in Space, where unlike the Russians, it landed a vehicle on the moon and has just successfully launched a rocked towards the sun. President Xi will send his prime minister, Li Qiang. It will be the first time he has not attended a G-20 summit since he became president of China in 2013.

Lula believes the G-20 needs revision to better reflect the changing global distribution of power.

The geo-politics of Middle East are certainly in flux. The Persian Gulf states and Saudi Arabia have very successfully deployed their "soft power" (backed by the hard cash of their vast and gas wealth) into the heart of Western Europe. Middle East money is irresistible to golf and soccer stars who care little about human rights when vast payouts are involved. Qatar found this by hosting the soccer World Cup last year.

Moreover, the Trump Administration initiated Abraham accords have brought Israel and the Gulf States together in a mutually reinforcing agreement, and Saudi Arabia cannot be far behind. This is smart. Soccer engages many millions, many more than the antics and bluster of Western politicians.

But the clandestine and open links are not inconsiderable. The pipelines bringing Russians oil to China. The clandestine at sea transfers of Russian oil to India. The consequences of catastrophic withdrawal of U.S. (and NATO) from Afghanistan by Joe Biden.

The consequences of the endless and non-UN sanctioned Bush-Blair invasion of Iraq on the false pretense of searching of Saddam Hussain's supposed weapons of mass destruction. The rise and fall of Isis in Iraq and Syria and the Islamist international terrorist cells it inspired in Western Europe. The consequences of the British and French intervention in Libya to overthrow Gaddafi.

Is it any surprise that the Sheikhs in the Gulf and the potentates in Beijing and Moscow (let along the rulers in Brasilia and New Delhi) draw their own conclusion. The issue is not whether the BRICS+ will form a coherent block. What matters is that are a congruent bloc where they may agree on some questions but not on all.

And that does not matter. What matters is they are a forum of nations which are not automatically in favor of the West, and many are hostile to the institutions which have defined the international order since WW2, and they going about consciously to create alternatives.

Is is not as Lord O'Neill would have only a question of the continuing dominance of the U.S. dollar, and of the World Bank, and the IMF.

The challenges are real and ongoing for Europe and North America. The migrant crisis was first weaponized on the border of Belarus and Poland. The Sahel in Africa is consumed by military coups and proxy Russian military interventions. The Sahel is the route for many migrants from West Africa who are crossing the Sahara and entering Europe across the Mediterranean from North Africa.

This migration is aggravating the cross-channel surge of small boats crossings from the coast of Belgium and France into England, reviving and reversing the route of the heroic escape on small boats of British and French soldiers evacuated from Dunkirk during WW2. For years Turkey has been the route for refugees fleeing from Syria and into Greece and the Balkans and on to Germany.

Like the migrant crisis on the southern border of the U.S., with hundreds of thousands fleeing from Central and South America, this large-scale illegal migration fuels populist anger and opposition in the U.S., Britain, France, Germany and Italy.

And underlying these very visible challenges is the vast clandestine commerce in cocaine from South America to Europe, undermining regimes like that in Ecuador, and corrupting police and custom officials, and young "county line" drug runners from Amsterdam and Rotterdam to small towns in rural England.

Meanwhile the war in Ukraine continues with its innovation in the use of killer drones matched on the ground with the return of the grinding, bloody, and man consuming, old fashioned WWI style trench warfare in the killing fields of the battles on the eastern Ukrainian front.

Meanwhile the U.S. faces endless internal disarray and deep political, social, and cultural divisions, with an utterly sclerotic leadership. Biden is deeply unpopular even among Democrats, and barely seems to know at times which way he is facing and is lost without his cue cards.

The Senate Republican leader, Mitch McConnell, freezes mentally at news conferences. Senator Feinstein does not seem to know what is going on half the time or where she is. Not to mention the phenomenon of the "mug shot" resurgent and indestructible Trump.

The UK has just appointed as defense Secretary, Grant Shapps, who has had five jobs in the past year, and was revealed to be a fantasist "multimillion dollar web marketeer' when first elected as an MP.

In Germany the creaky coalition under Olaf Scholz has not begun to meet its promised 3% defense commitment. In France President Macron is once again promoting the idea of a compromise settlement between Russia and Ukraine.

The one thing that can be said with any certainty is that it is not a pretty picture. The outdoing UK Defense Secretary Ben Wallace, was quite right to say in his resignation letter to the Prime Minister: "I genuinely believe that over the next decade the world will get more insecure and more unstable". He is quite right. The world is becoming a very much more dangerous place.

WHO BENEFITS FROM THE TRADE WAR BETWEEN UKRAINE AND POLAND?

September 19, 2023

By Robert Czulda

On September 19th, 2023 Ukraine filed a complaint with the World Trade Organization against Hungary, Poland, and Slovakia. This is Kiev's response to the decision by these countries to extend the embargo on grain. Furthermore, Ukraine is threatening retaliation – a ban on the import of Polish fruits and vegetables is being considered.Polish commentators share a common view – Ukraine is starting a senseless war with its most vocal advocate and friend.

What is the root of this problem?

Due to the blockade of Ukrainian ports by the Russian warships,

Ukrainian grain reaches its recipients through the territory of Poland. It is sent in transit, but in practice, some of the Ukrainian grain remains in Poland, which is a blow to Polish agriculture. The grain from Ukraine − often of lower quality and not meeting the strict European Union standards (unlike Polish grain) − is simply cheaper.

In mid-September, the European Commission lifted its embargo on Ukrainian grain for five countries — Poland, Hungary, Slovakia, Bulgaria, and Romania. Following this decision, Warsaw, Budapest, and Bratislava extended the ban on the import of agricultural products from Ukraine.

This is undoubtedly a significant blow to some Polish politicians and commentators − those who had hoped that the current rapprochement between Poland and Ukraine would continue even after the war. In fact, just a few months ago, the concept of a common, federative state was actively discussed in Poland. Now, voices of disappointment and even outrage can be heard in Poland.

Ukraine's actions are perceived in Poland as self-destructive, as Kiev is suing one of its closest allies. Poland is one of the leaders in providing military assistance to Ukraine, an active advocate on the international stage, and a critical transport hub − any military and humanitarian support to Ukraine is directed through Poland, using the port of Gdańsk for maritime transport and the Rzeszów airport for air traffic. Since the outbreak of the open war in February 2022, Rzeszów airport has become one of the most important airports within NATO.

Now, in the face of Ukraine's actions, there have been voices − though not from decision-makers − suggesting that, as a retaliatory measure, Rzeszów airport should be temporarily closed (which, of course, will not happen).

So why is Kiev taking such action?

After all, it leads to a deterioration of relations between Poland and Ukraine (which have also experienced other problems in recent months). This action weakens Ukraine's capital of support and sympathy among the Polish population, some of whom have begun to see Ukrainians as ungrateful.

It is also a self-destructive action in the sense that if Ukraine actually started negotiations with the European Union. Ukraine and the

European Union would have to contend with the reluctance of some Central and Eastern European countries, which – mindful of the current crisis – could slow down negotiations in the agricultural sector.

When analyzing Ukraine's actions, the first thing to note is a specific nature of Ukrainian agriculture. There are very few individual farmers in Ukraine. The sector is dominated by companies – it is estimated that there are around 70,000 of them, and they control about ¾ of all land.

Among them are particularly powerful companies that use their position and corruption to pursue their interests. Top firms controlling agricultural land in Ukraine are registered outside Ukraine – they are international conglomerates.

In other words, this dispute is perceived in Poland as an illustration of corruption in Ukraine, and above all, enduring power of oligarchs. A quarrel with Poland is a result of financial interests of a small group. It is noteworthy that Leonid Kozachenko – a Ukrainian politician and President of the Ukrainian Agrarian Confederation – has spoken out against the trade war with the countries of Central and Eastern Europe.

Secondly, attention is drawn to the beneficiaries of the Polish-Ukrainian dispute. Primarily, it is Russia for whom breaking a deep cooperation between Warsaw and Kiev is a crucial matter. However, in Poland, it is noted that a true architect of the current dispute is Germany, which has recently increased its presence in Ukraine.

Germany is not interested in close cooperation between Poland and Ukraine because it undermines Berlin's ambitions to be an architect and executor of the European Union's eastern policy. A stronger and more active Central and Eastern Europe is seen as a threat to Germany – especially after the current war, when Berlin will seek to rebuild its relations with Moscow.

The current agricultural dispute is increasing Germany's position. It is not coincidental that almost immediately, German Minister of Agriculture Cem Oezdemir criticized the grain embargo without addressing any problems faced by Polish, Hungarian, and Slovak farmers.

Financial connections are not known, but some commentators in

Poland argue that German money is also behind Ukrainian agro-firms, and behind that, there may also be Russian money (some of mentioned agricultural firms in Ukraine are registered in tax havens such as Cyprus, which has also been favorable for Russia).

Thirdly, it is believed that a timing of the dispute's onset is not coincidental. Parliamentary elections will take place in Poland in mid-October. The right-wing party that has been in power for eight years (which, by the way, is economically and socially left-leaning) is not certain of victory.

The still influential agricultural communities in Poland may turn away from the government in the current situation and vote for the opposition. The Confederation, a coalition of far-right groups, could also benefit. Its main stream is characterized by an anti-Ukrainian approach and generally pro-Russian stance.

If Ukraine truly believes that Germany — which now portrays itself as a great ally of Kiev and an advocate for the Ukrainian cause in the European Union — will become its partner, they are very naive. Since the beginning of the war, it has been clear that Germany primarily aims to strengthen itself, while any increase of power of Central and Eastern Europe, including Ukraine, is not their goal.

COUNTERING CHINESE ESPIONAGE REQUIRES MORE THAN A GOVERNMENT RESPONSE

September 21, 2023

By Richard Weitz

Recent incidents make clear that Chinese hacking and espionage remain a core U.S. national security concern. The scope and scale of these activities are breathtaking. Defeating this threat requires an optimized public-private partnership since the magnitude of the challenge far exceeds what the federal government can combat on its own.

The Federal Bureau of Investigation has been sounding the toxin about Chinese cyber-espionage for years. On September 18, FBI Director Chris Wray reiterated that Beijing's cyber-espionage program has grown so vast that it transcends the size and scope of all its major competitors combined.[29]

The People's Republic of China (PRC) employs tens and perhaps hundreds of thousands of skilled hackers, whether as government employees or semi-private contractors, in a full-court campaign to steal foreign secrets.

There have been many reports over the years of major PRC espionage operations targeted against the United States that have severely compromised U.S. secrets; many more cases are likely unreported.[30]

Though Chinese human agents and spy balloons often gain the most popular attention, the most pervasive threat to Americans' secrets comes from the PRC's massive cyber espionage. Even in recent months, senior cyber officials fear Chinese hackers so deeply penetrated some sensitive U.S. computer networks that they still may have access to them.[31]

In a major foreign policy speech earlier this week at Hudson Institute, former Vice President Mike Pence acutely observed that, "China is the greatest strategic and economic threat facing the United States in the 21st century."[32]

It is imperative that the United States prevent the Chinese Communist Party from accessing our sensitive information, especially classified U.S. defense and intelligence data.

Though government bodies like the Office of Personnel Management (OPM) seem inclined to assume more responsibilities in this area, the United States would do better by having the private sector hold, manage, and store more of this data.

OPM has not been a reliable guardian of Americans' secrets. Its vulnerabilities permitted one of the most egregious data breaches in history.[33] In 2015, a PRC entity, likely the Jiangsu State Security Department, which is a subsidiary of China's Ministry of State Security spy agency, stole the records of more than 22 million Americans.

Despite years of congressional hearings and generous appropriations designed to strengthen its cyber defenses, the OPM still received a cyber score of F on the July 2022 Federal Information Technology Acquisition Reform Act (FITARA) scorecard.[34]

Since OPM is the Human Resources authority for much of the federal government, cyber security issues often receive insufficient attention as the Office strives to provide and implement human resources policy and guidance for myriad other issues across many federal government agencies.

Unfortunately, many other U.S. government bodies are also not well positioned to secure U.S. cyber security efforts. In May of this year, the Government Accountability Office (GAO) found that an array of government agencies have not implemented critical cloud security practices, including defined security metrics. GAO listed almost three dozen recommendations that these government bodies had to follow to fully implement these practices.[35]

In contrast, private sector companies have a more consistent and effective track record with preserving the integrity of the U.S. sensitive information. They must receive FedRAMP authorization, which means they must use sophisticated cloud technologies that have modern security and protection protocols to keep federal information safe and secure. Furthermore, private sector companies focus more closely on human capital needs and data security.

As the Chinese cyber espionage threat continues unabated, it is critical that the government lean more heavily on these entities in the years to come.

MEETING THE CHALLENGES FACING THE WAY AHEAD FOR AUSTRALIAN DEFENCE

October 10, 2023

During my current trip to Australia in support of the Williams Foundation 27 September 2023, I had a chance to talk with my colleague Dr. Andrew Carr of Australian National University. He is a regular interlocutor for me on strategic issues affecting Australia and the broader alliance.

With the main issue in Australia being the impact of the DSR on shaping a way ahead, Dr. Carr argued that underlying the DSR and the shift to deal with the China threat, there was a process change underlying thinking about the way ahead for Australian defence.

He argued that the basic approach of higher-level defence thinking in Australia since the 1970s has been very pragmatic and assessing change and adjusting Australian engagement in response to the particular crisis or event.

Government's commissioned Defence White Papers if and when needed, and the link between strategy and force structure has not always been well-maintained. Instead, the focus has been on correlating what Australian capabilities are available with crafting a response package to today's events.

This has allowed Australia to be flexible and to think about if not through events and how to protect Australian interests. But now with a clear focus on the region and a direct threat to Australia in the form of the Chinese along with the broader association of 21st century authoritarian powers, this is no longer adequate.

What now does Australia do to defend itself and protect itself in its own region?

How does it work with and manage allies?

How does Australia manage threats and work through how the broader society deals with the comprehensive Chinese challenge?

Dr. Carr argued that the defence processes are having to become more scenario focused and threat focused.

How does Australia built relevant forces in light of core scenarios of the threats and crises to be anticipated?

Australia cannot do everything. What will the government pare down and focus upon within the defence force?

And how will this thinking correlate with broader considerations for security and economic development of Australia?

In other words, because Australia is facing enduring challenges, Dr. Carr asks: "Does the past practices of pragmatism and ad hoc strategic planning, such as irregular Defence White papers' still make sense?"

Such a shift poses three major challenges.

The first is within the defence establishment. Carr underscored that today's ADF has been built around a balanced force structure approach and sharing of resources. A threat based or scenario-based approach will prioritize some forces compared to others.

How will defence adjust to a culture of a threat-based force?

The second challenge faces the political class. A threat-based focus will require a discipline in the political class to manage defence in a way it really did not need to do in the age of pragmatic responses. We show up to a crisis and convince ourselves, our allies and, hopefully, our adversaries that we are contributing meaningfully to the crisis. And then we go home.

But now home is precisely the center of the defence challenge.

How to avoid the infamous 'tyranny of dissonance' as Michael Evans put it, where defence plans said one thing, but our political class often asked the ADF to do something else?

And the third challenge is to strategic thinking.

How do we build an effective strategy for a world in profound change and in many ways chaos? Strategy has been shaped since the 1990s around the end of the Soviet era, global terrorism and wars of choice and the hidden hand of supporting a "rules-based order."

But in the context of profound change within the allied world, the growing impact of authoritarian powers and the end of the globalization of the past thirty years, what is our strategy?

As Carr warned: "We're locking in now to a process that is making bets about what the future will look like, so that we can shape policy in an orderly way. Will such an approach deliver real benefits in coherence and focus tomorrow, and will these offset the inevitable costs to our ability to adapt and innovate in response to what's happening today?"

My own sense is that we are in era of profound change, different from the three historical eras I have already lived through. We need to consider the nature of that era rather than simply go on auto-pilot from the past twenty hears, or think that our war games really capture in any way the nature of the new historical era.

PRESIDENT XI IN SAN FRANCISCO: KISS AND MAKE UP WITH THE BIDEN ADMINISTRATION?

November 15, 2023

By Harald Malmgren and Pippa Malmgren

The world has suffered deeply from the breakdown of relations between the U.S. and China. Since the heady days when Bill Clinton welcomed China into the World Trade Organization, things have run so far downhill that the two superpowers have consolidated into opposing geopolitical blocs that are increasingly engaged in ever more aggressive shows of force.

China aligned with Russia, Iran, and many emerging market nations. This meant the U.S. had to consider the real possibility of multi-front wars. The U.S. found itself aligned with the Five-Eyes nations, NATO and hardened regional alliances worldwide with selected nations like the Philippines in the Pacific and Morocco in the Atlantic. Ukraine had already become tricky, especially given Russia's persistent threat to revert of nuclear weapons. The prospect of a breakout of regional war in the Middle East is making all the parties reassess.

Now a new critical challenge to these geopolitical realignments has become painfully evident: Wars are brutally expensive. And costs of preparing for possible wars are threatening to overwhelm national economic policies. Increased defense and national security require-ments are boosting borrowing needs of nations at the very time when national economies are hovering on the edge of economic downturn. Bond markets on which nations depend are threatening to reject over-reaching global aspirations of their leaders.

The leaders of China and the United States are becoming aware they simply cannot afford to proceed on this present path leading towards greater confrontation.

Biden and Xi Jinping meeting in San Francisco. The two are very likely to strike a deal that will diminish the scale of geopolitical confrontation under a theme of "stabilization", agreeing to halt the seemingly relentless slide into decoupling large segments of the world economy.

Given the significant present possibility of a hard landing for their stumbling economies, both leaders need to demonstrate an historic "win" to strengthen their precarious positions of leadership. "win". They both need it right now.

China staked out a role as a peace broker by opposing Putin's threats to deploy nuclear weapons. As soon as Putin said "nukes" China said "truce".

But that is not enough for President Xi. He now faces the existential risk that China falls apart. The economy has collapsed. The massive failure of Evergrand exposed a simple truth. It wasn't just one huge property company that had gone bust. It was the realization that the whole idea that Chinese people could be safe by buying property to get rich was over.

The losses have dented every citizen's hopes for the future. Meanwhile, Foreign Direct Investment into China has gone negative for the first time in modern history as foreign investors rush to escape the tightening grip of the Communist Party on private business. The hardworking youth in China are protesting the fact that there's nothing at the end of the rainbow – no jobs, no income, no reward. Nobody believes they'll get rich before they get old anymore.

America cancelled China under both Trump and Biden. This killed any hope of rising export sales pulling China into the return of domestic growth. The Belt and Road Initiative should have become a revenue generator for China, but it has turned into a system that bleeds cash. The poor emerging market nations used to pay China or borrow money from China to cover the cost of China's seemingly kind offer to build physical infrastructure.

But now those emerging markets cannot pay back those loans, thanks to rising inflation and the global slowdown. When the Chinese Communist Party last month convened a multi-year national review pf the Chinese economy, they concluded the economy was sinking with inadequate demand to keep its production engine running.

The conclusion was reached that a new source of demand was needed, but Xi Jinping personally opposed free handouts to the working classes. Instead, the participants in the review agreed to return to the "tried and true" promotion of manufacturing to produce goods for export to the U.S. and Europe. But it has become evident that demand for more manufactures from China was not likely as both the U.S. and Europe were entering a period of slowdown in their own demand.

Frustrated that the U.S. and Europe seemed to be entering economic slump, days ago President Xi visited China's Central Bank (PBOC) and China's national economic regulatory agencies to express unhappiness with their technocratic policies' failures. No doubt he demanded that they make the numbers prettier even though the world lost faith in the veracity of their numbers a long time ago. Xi insisted the CCP must impose greater oversight to ensure policies brought about stronger economic growth.

But greater command and control at the center of the economy likely will make China's. economy more brittle and fragile and impede innovation. His internal opponents are murmuring. They all want to get back to making money. They don't want to waste the already declining youth demographics on a senseless war with the world's most formidable military power. For the Chinese people, Taiwan can wait.

Meanwhile, President Biden's popularity is collapsing. Both President Trump and total long-shot Robert F Kennedy Jr are way ahead of him in the polls and in fundraising with all the key swing votes. Democratic Senator Manchin looks likely to launch a campaign for the Presidency under a "no labels" candidacy. Only 14% of Americans think that Biden has improved their standard of living.

Unexpectedly confronted with a shock Hamas terrorist attack on Gaza and growing Iranian threats to ignite a wider Middle East war, Biden has engaged in a serious show of force.

The U.S. economy for now still seems to be doing ok but few give Biden any credit for that. Meanwhile the war in Ukraine seems to have reached an impasse. Russia is not losing, and Ukraine is not winning.

The appetite for spending money on foreign wars dropped further once the problem in Israel stole the headlines from Ukraine. It became almost impossible for Biden to justify further funds for Ukraine once President Zelensky announced that he is refusing to hold elections. This killed any idea that the U.S. and Ukraine were fighting for democracy.

Also, the unlimited defence of Israel has now become hotly controversial. It is splitting the all-important Jewish vote and splitting the young voters, both of which are critical for Biden's re-election chances. So, the President needs a win. He needs a historic win. Short of having a war, he needs a peace deal. He needs an historic peace deal.

Now could be the moment that both the U.S. and China agree to play nice for the sake of the world. This means China must burn tight links with both Russia and Tehran which had served their purpose but are now obstacles to stabilizing China-U.S. relations. Their bullying forced changed the U.S. perception of risk and brought The President to the negotiating table with China.

The U.S. wants to support Ukraine and Israel but can't afford the heavy costs now under consideration. Nor can the U.S. afford a larger conflagration in the Middle East. Already we hear the former Head of NATO suggesting that Ukraine join NATO but only the parts of the country they control. The implication is to leave the rest to Russia. Call it a draw.

The solution is an armistice in Ukraine and having China and Russia stop supporting Hamas, Hezbollah, and a renewed Iranian war on the Sunni Kingdoms. The price will be that the U.S. and China must end their squabbles. When Xi summoned Gov. Newsom to Beijing he lay the groundwork for reconciliation by saying "divorce is not an option". Given that Newsom is Biden's personally preferred running mate, and therefore a possible next U.S. President, this change of tone was very important.

The bottom line is that neither side can afford a messy divorce and both sides now know it. The White House can't raise or cut taxes. Their hands are tied. China can't find a way to stimulate its economy either.

So are we on the brink of a "kiss and make up" photo op?

If so, that would generate a serious rally in the markets and a huge sense of relief amongst the citizens of the world. Maybe the "make up" part won't be as friendly as the photo op would imply. Maybe the U.S. and China will continue to invisibly war against each other underwater, in space and in cyberspace.

But, if this type of conflict is out of the public view, things will get better. A cold war beats a hot war any day. If the two sides must make up a bunch of stories about concessions to get this done, they will. They might now actually make up, but they might make up a story that all is fine. That pushes this whole problem well into the future.

President Xi no doubt is aware that there is a strong desire in Congress in both of the major U.S. political parties for tougher measures against China. Xi's aides have announced that following his meeting with President Biden he will make a major address to both the peoples of America and of China on the world's need for stabilization of relations between the two countries and embarking on a new period of combined efforts to assure a safer and more prosperous world economy.

That San Francisco address may mark an historically important turning point in relations between the two most powerful nations in the world. Or, at least, a worldwide perception that a turn for a better future is not only possible but is under way.

FRENCH AIR FORCE TAKES UP NATO AIR POLICE MISSION ON THE "EASTERN FLANK"

November 29, 2023

By Pierre Tran

The French air force will fly Nov. 28 four Mirage 2000-5 fighter jets to Lithuania in a Nato air police mission in the skies of the allied Baltic nations, amidst Ukraine's concerns on waning Western support for its fight back against Russian forces.

The despatch of Mirage fighters was part of an "air defense on the eastern flank," the French armed forces ministry said in a Nov. 23 statement, pointing up the Baltic Air Policing mission sought to maintain sovereignty of airspace over the three Nato partners - Estonia, Lithuania, and Latvia.

The French fighters will take up the Baltic air operation for four months, taking over from Eurofighter jets deployed by Italy and Spain in a rotating collective security measure aimed at warning off Russian president Vladimir Putin on any move against members of the alliance.

The Mirage jets will take off from the Luxeuil 116 airbase, eastern France, and will be based at Siauliai air base, northern Lithuania, the French ministry said, with some 100 French air personnel supporting Lithuanian forces.

"By committing high level assets and maintaining a regular operational presence in the region," the ministry said, "France shows it is committed to strengthening Nato's deterrence and defensive posture, and acts in a concrete manner to contribute measures of reassurance on the eastern flank of Europe."

The air force invited the press to the Luxeuil air base and attend the despatch of Mirages, which form part of a high-priority mission of air police of the French national airspace.

Meanwhile, Kyiv came Nov. 25 under a six-hour sustained attack by Russian kamikaze drones, raising concern Moscow had replenished its stocks of weapons and was intent on smashing resolve in Ukraine.

Although Ukraine said its air defense had downed 74 of the 75 Russian drones, falling parts of the weapons, reported to be based on the Iranian Shahed drone, wounded five people and   hit buildings in the capital.

The concern in Kyiv was that U.S. political and military attention had turned to the war in Gaza, with Washington switching ammunition supplies to support the Israel Defense Forces, and the White House acting as mediator between Jerusalem and the Hamas irregular force.

The Hamas group agreed to extend by two more days a four-day ceasefire, just hours before the pause in fighting had been due to end on Nov. 27, allowing further release of hostages seized in its deadly Oct. 7 assault on Israeli communities on the border with Gaza.

The Ukraine stock of 155 mm shells was reported to be running low, and the fear was the U.S. has redirected shipments to Israel, now seen as the higher military priority.

There was something of "Ukraine fatigue," with support withering among Republicans in the U.S. Congress, and a general election looming in the U.K., David Manning, a former British ambassador to Washington, Nato, and Israel, said Nov. 26 on BBC Radio 4.

It was likely Moscow "welcomed" the election result in the Netherlands, and the debates going in the U.S., he said.

"This is a real issue," he said, and Western leaders needed to address the Ukraine crisis, which could not be solved by "easy solutions" proposed by populist leaders, and that "Putin can be appeased in some way."

Last week saw the populist, far-right PVV Freedom party led by Geert Wilders win the largest share of votes in the Netherlands general election, allowing him to form a coalition government, ringing alarm bells across Europe.

Western officials such as U.S. defense secretary Lloyd Austin, U.S. secretary of state Anthony Blinken, and British foreign secretary David Cameron, have at various times flown to Kyiv to show support for Ukraine and president Volodymyr Zelenskiy, who is reported to be under German and U.S. pressure to negotiate a settlement with Putin. But the Ukrainian leader has refused to accept Russia hold on to territories seized by military means.

"The stakes are huge," George Robertson, a former Nato secretary general and ex-U.K. defense secretary, said Nov. 26 on Radio 4.

Cameron's visit was all very nice, he said, but there was nothing in the U.K. government's recent autumn financial statement - effectively the national budget - that would replenish U.K. military stocks sent to Kyiv, or send more kit to the Ukrainian forces, which needed longer range missiles, large quantities of ammunition, and more equipment.

"Your visit is not enough," he said, "rhetoric is not enough."

Ukraine was losing kit due to a war of attrition, and British factories needed to be working 24 hours a day, he said. Ukraine was being starved of resources, while the Russian military industry was working at full rate.

If Putin won in Ukraine, the world order would be transformed, he said, with the new rules written by China, Russia, and Iran.

Putin had already failed in his expectation of winning Ukraine in a three-day campaign, he said, and the West needed to "turn the narrative round."

The three Baltic nations joined the transatlantic alliance in 2004, following the collapse of the Soviet Union, and in the wake of the Nov. 9 1989 fall of the Berlin Wall.

Nato allies adopted the enhanced Air Policing (eAP) operation in 2014, in response to Moscow's seizing the Crimean peninsula and taking control of the eastern region of Ukraine.

The French air force has flown 10 times in the Baltic Air Police mission, and has deployed seven times in Lithuania, the ministry said.

The U.S. congress, backed by the senate, has approved the 2024 budget, but the last minute vote left out any fresh financial support for Ukraine, leaving the prospect of Kyiv running out of funds for ordering further arms and ammunition.

Germany has pledged €5.4 billion ($5.9 billion) for its 2023 security capacity building initiative, up from €2 billion last year, with further commitment of a total €10.5 billion in following years, the government said on its military support for Ukraine.

Military assistance to Ukraine mainly accounts for those funds, as well as restocking German inventories for equipment sent to Kyiv.

Among the weapons sent to Ukraine, there were a further 20 Marder infantry fighting vehicles on top of the 60 units already announced, as well as 30 Leopard 1 A5 heavy tanks long sought by the Ukrainian army.

A further 105 Leopard 1 A5 tanks were being prepared to be shipped to Ukraine, in a project jointly financed with Denmark.

Germany will also send over 21,910 rounds of the Nato standard 155 mm artillery shells, up from the 19,530 previously pledged.

IN THE AFTERMATH OF THE OCTOBER 7TH HAMAS ATTACKS: FRENCH "SWATTING" ON THE RISE

November 29, 2023

By Murielle Delaporte

Over the last year, the United States have been experiencing a surge in hoaxes aimed against an increasing number of schools all over the territory.

Such threats usually invoke school shootings and mobilize emergency services and Special Weapons and Tactics police units – the famous SWAT teams – in order to deal with each one of them just in case.

This phenomenon is certainly not new but has been on the rise since the 2000's while the last peak of swatting is revealing a change of pattern that is worrying authorities: they are more sophisticated, more wide-ranging, and in some cases, they are originating from overseas.

France is experiencing a very similar trend right now ever since the October 7th Hamas attacks in Israel in terms of a surge in bomb threat hoaxes. It is too early to know the whole story yet as far as potential foreign interference is concerned, but what is certain is that the fear of an importation of the Israeli-Palestinian conflict in

France is palpable, making the atmosphere far more feverish than usual.

Here is what we know so far and how the French defense and security authorities are coping with this unsettling development, the short term impact of which is not only nerve-wracking but tends to exhaust security and police services.

These services are indeed already far stretched with repeated episodes of unprecedented street violence as well as the dire task of protecting the public during high-visibility events such as the Rugby World Cup last month in France or the preparation of the fast-approaching Olympic games this summer.

So what are the stats as far as bomb threat hoaxes in France are concerned?

Even though actual official figures of bomb threat hoaxes are classified and held tightly by the French Interior ministry and even though the system does not process in real time all the data coming from the field up to the authorities in charge, there is no doubt that ever since the start of the Hamas-Israeli conflict the numbers have ramped up significantly with multiple alerts daily all over the French territory.

Daily local newspapers report on a regular basis hoax by the dozen: 6 schools in Toulouse on October 19th, 3 in Lorient on October 25th, 12 in Mayenne in one week in mid-October and so on. Schools are the main targets, but not only.

Official administrative buildings - like city halls – and cultural sites - such as movie theaters and museums (the Versailles castle has been evacuated seven times in one week in mid-October as well), but also transportation – airports and railroad stations in particular – have all been targeted on a regular basis for more than a month now.

Between the October 18th and the 31st for instance, no less than one hundred bomb alerts have been paralyzing dozens of airports all over France forcing evacuations of thousands of people and the cancellation of 130 flights.

A comparison with past events is hard to do given the lack of exhaustive and precise official data, but we know from the French Justice ministry that in the past two years roughly 700 people were convicted for that type of offense.

Also, the current surge has been confirmed as abnormal by the French government. On October 19th, the minister of Education, Gabriel Attal, was reporting on French television a total of 299 bomb threat hoaxes targeted at schools since September with 75 occurring just that very day.

Several arrests have already been made and multiple inquiries are under way. So far, official police statements mostly point at minors sometimes as young as 11 years old, as well as a copycat phenomenon classic in this type of events especially with the extensive media coverage they tend to generate.

But there is also a lingering fear about the impact of the current developments in the Middle East on radicalized young "lone wolves."

October 7th And The Weaponization of Fear

Traditionally, whenever a conflict involving Israel occurred over the past decades, France has been the theater of terrorist attacks mostly targeted at Jewish institutions. Hence the immediate and systematic enhancement of their protection in the aftermath of the Hamas attacks and the beginning of the war in Gaza.

In this case, a terrorist attack did occur in France mimicking almost to the day the beheading in October 2020 of the history professor Samuel Patty, i.e. another professor teaching French litera-ture, Dominique Bernard, was assassinated in the name of Allah at his school in Arras on October 13th.

In the past weeks, antisemitism has revealed itself in its ugliest way, in particular with the tagging of residences with the David Stars, acts in part attributed to Moldavan illegals apparently paid, according to a November 7th *Le Monde* article, by Moldavan businessman Anatolii Prizenko and relayed by the pro-Russian propaganda network Doppelgänger.

But schools - the place where history is taught - as well as French institutions in general are here the broader and very symbolic target of radicalized terrorists committed to proceed with the same strategy of terror that have led to the massacres of October 7th. That is where the current situation differs from earlier day with a superimposition of factors: the classic ripple effects of Middle Eastern politics and the more recent waves of Islamic terrorism.

This terrorist attack has triggered the government to raise the level of the anti-terror "Vigipirate" plan to its maximum like it did after the 2015 Bataclan events (the November 13th 2015 attacks caused the death of 130 people and injured more than 350). No less than 7,000 soldiers have been deployed to reinforce the security of major sites at risk, such as airports with a 40% increase of patrols in airports and a 20% reinforcement of railroad security staff.

That is one part of the French government's strategy to counter the threat itself and the epidemic of hoaxes, which constant repetition plays with everyone's nerves and exhausts a little more everyday security forces already mobilized by the "Vigipirate" plan. That is the (unfortunately familiar) part of the government toolbox that is meant to protect and reassure the population.

What is different this time is a very firm declaratory policy by the Macron government, by the President himself, but also by the key ministers mostly concerned by the hoaxes, i.e. the ministers of Education (Gabriel Attal), Transportation (Clément Beaune) and Interior (Gérard Darmanin), who have been extremely vocal about the determination of the government to find and punish the perpetrators.

A "Big Brother Is Watching You" message asserting that the latter are always found, and that the punishment can go from 2 to 5 years in jail and a 30 to 45 000 Euros fine depending on if one is only falsely reporting a threat or falsely making it. Indeed, the highest punishment has been extended beyond making the threat to the notion of "premeditated psychological violence" by Paris public prosecutor Laure Beccuau.

This has had an impact on irresponsible "jokers," it seems, as the number of hoaxes did slow down a bit. Indeed, they tend to be traceable even when using VPNs and punishable under EU law. However, in the current cases many emails are coming from Switzerland, according to the French authorities.

But the radicalization of an increasing number of young people in France – whether through the increased "Salafization" of mosques until now moderate, through Ankara's tight control of the French-based Turkish Islamist population, through linguistic or cultural associations or even through sport clubs (as stressed in particular in this year's

French Parliament Delegation Intelligence Report recently available to the public) – and a generational rupture are what worries some analysts and policy makers.,

That part of the puzzle deals with the very touchy subjects of immigration, security, urbanization, education, and so on, all subjects which will be undoubtedly at the heart of the next presidential election campaign.

But swatting also touches upon the issue of potential foreign interference on which the government has been vigorously engaged to counteract especially since the beginning of the war in Ukraine. The eviction of Russian spies has been one of the most visible measure taken at the time, which have actually led Moscow to use illegal immigrants as agents (such as the Moldovan taggers mentioned earlier).

But a more global strategy is emerging in France like in the United States and in Europe in general to identify these new types of interferences and try to navigate better in the famous "grey zone" of hybrid threats.

The creation in France of a specific administration to deal with foreign digital interferences called VIGINUM (Service de vigilance et protection contre les ingérences numériques étrangères) within the SGDSN (Secrétariat général de la défense et de la sécurité nationale) in 2021 is one example of a new toughness and zero tolerance towards those who want to sabotage the cohesion of France, a country hosting the largest Jewish community (500 000 people) and the largest Muslim community (6 million) in Europe.

THE NEW HISTORICAL ERA SEEN FROM SPACE: THE CASE OF THE MIDDLE EAST

December 2, 2023

By Kenneth Maxwell

Looking at Arabia this weekend the little green men in outer space must have been completely flummoxed by what they spied from the heavens.

To the west on the Mediterranean coast of the Arabian Peninsula in Gaza there was a vicious war resumed with both sides claiming biblical authority.

Benjamin Netanyahu, the Israeli Prime Minister, cited the book of Samuel: "You must remember what Amalek has done to you says our Holy Bible." The passage urged the Jews to smite the Amalekites after they launched a vicious surprise attack on the Jewish people. The biblical commandment was to completely destroy all of the Amaleks, including babies, property, animals, everything.

Hamas and Hezbollah also wage Holy War. They also kill babies and destroy property and animals. They also wish to exterminate all Israelis in the name of their God (actually the same Abrahamic God) and drive them into the sea. On 7 October Hamas brutally killed at least 1,200 Israelis and kidnapped 240. After ending the temporary "pause" in the Gaza War on Friday, with 137 Israeli hostages still held by Hamas, Netanyahu vowed to deliver on Gaza and its hapless Palestinians "the mother of all thumpings."

The Israeli military is once again indeed giving Gaza a thumping. Over 15,000 Palestinians have been killed since the war began, among them very many women and 6000 children in the relentless Israeli bombardment and ground invasion. Many more Palestinians are already and will surely continue to die.

Meanwhile on the other side of Arabian Peninsula on the western shores of the Persian Gulf, 167 World Leaders are gathered for the United Nations Climate Change Conference (COP28) in Dubai in the United Arab Emirates (UAE) chaired by Sultan al-Jaber.

They include President Macron, Prime Minister Modi, President Erdogan, President Cyril Ramaphosa, Prime Minister Sunak (for a mere eleven hours), German Chancellor Olaf Schulz, and assorted Middle Eastern Kings, Sultans and potentates, and the vice-president of the U.S., Camila Harris, among others. But not the leaders of the two most egregious global polluters, President for life Xi Jinping of China and President Joe Biden of the United States.

Those who were assembled in Dubai were solemnly admonished at the opening ceremony by none other than the Green King.

King Charles III of Great Britain and Northern Ireland "and of

His other Realms and Territories King, Head of the Commonwealth and Defender the Faith," (faith in the other Abrahamic God that is).

King Charles is famous for his long-term dedication to the environment and to cultivating and talking to the flowers in his garden at Highgrove House in Gloucestershire. His Aston Martin at his vast estate at Balmoral in Aberdeen in Scotland, is run on "a blend of English white wine and whey from the cheese process."

But as a consultant on alternative fuel observed the Kings's car is a "boutique" case and is not "scalable" as a model. The King also said that "I haven't eaten meat and fish on two days a week and I don't eat dairy one day a week." 70,000 people are attending COP28 in Dubai. Getting there by commercial and private jets is estimated to added 210 tons of CO2 to the atmosphere.

King Charles, Rishi Sunak, and Baron Cameron on Chipping Norton (that is former PM David Cameron now the British Foreign Secretary) all flew separately from the UK by private jet to Dubai to join what Bloomberg news called "the celebrity studded gathering of rich people."

But King Charles at least got a respite from the consequences of the publication of Omid Scobie's book on the royal family and the naming of him and the princess of Wales as the people who talked about the skin color of the then unborn first child Prince Harry and Meghan Markel (that is the Duke and Duchess of Sussex) There are it seems some small mercies to be found in hot places, even at COP28.

The immensely rich UAE is of course one the world largest exporter of hydrocarbons. Sultan al-Jaber is also the head of the Abu Dhabi National Oil Company (Adnoc). Last year Adnoc pumped 2.7m barrels of oil and is expected to double this by 2027.

Leaked documents published by the BBC and the Center for Climate Change showed that fossil fuel business was being planned to be conducted in bilateral meetings at the climate summit. China's Ministry of ecology and the environment, Zhao Yingmin, was promoting a "strategic partnership" with Abu Dhabi. As well it might.

Chinese sales and trading with Abu Dhabi last year amounted to $15b. Abu Dhabi was also interested in the Brazilian petrochemical company Braskem where Adnoc is a major bidder in a very controversial potential deal where the support of Lula could well be critical.

Braskem is Latin America's largest petrochemical company and a top thermoplastic resin producer with 36 industrial plants in Brazil, the U.S. Mexico and Germany. Another bidder is JBS which is Brazil's top beef producer whose major customers are China and the Middle East.

On the First of December, moreover, Brazil took over the presidency of the G-20. President Inácio Lula da Silva is attending COP28 in Dhabi. He is a key player in the expanded BRICS which now incorporates the oil producing Gulf States including the UAE. Lula has been an outspoken critic of Israel and of the war in Ukraine. He says the UN general security council is "insane."

Brazil intends to greatly expand its already powerful oil and gas sector by more off shore drilling, including off the mouth of the mighty Amazon river. Marina da Silva, Brazil environmental minister, is also at COP28.

Brazil is doing deals with China which is a major importer of liquefied gas and oil and of Brazilian soya and beef. Former Brazilian president and Lula's key ally and protégée, Dilma Rousseff, is the president of the BRICS bank based in Shanghai.

And in the middle of the Arabian Peninsula, the immensely rich oil rich Kingdom of Saudi Arabia, ruled de facto by crown prince Mohammed bin Salman (MBS) is busy "sports washing." He has invested US$50b in sports since 2016. These investments included a ten-year contract with world wrestling entertainment and a US$332m bid (so far unsuccessful) for the French soccer star, Kylan Mbappe.

When he was questioned about sports washing he replied: "I don't care. I have 1% growth in GDP from sport and I am going for another 1.5%." MSB also knows that sport has much more global penetration than politicians and reaches many more people in Europe, South America and Asia. He learnt this from Qatar's very successful hosting of the soccer World Cup last year.

The Saudi backed LIVGolf is as its Australian promoter, Greg Norman, says "a carrot too hard to resist." Major Golf champions have opted out of the PGA tour for LIVGolf, including Dustin Johnson who pocketed US$18m as a promotion bonus taking his earning to more than US$30m.

The Portuguese world soccer star, Cristiano Ronaldo, has joined the Saudi pro-League and even appeared smiling glad in flowing Arabian gear. In October it was confirmed by FIFA that Saudi Arabia was the sole bidder of the 2024 soccer world cup.

All this a part of MSA's ambitious "Vision 2030" initiatives. Where Saudi money is concerned there is not much room for "human rights" concerns or for the memory of the Saudi backed assassination and dismemberment of Jamal Khashoggi in the Saudi consulate in Istanbul.

Meanwhile up in outer space the little green men observing what is happening in Arabia will be scratching their little green heads and moving on with their UFO's to another planet within the solar system with more promising landing spots.

---

1. https://gaodawei.wordpress.com/2023/02/23/2023-rfi-china-changes-china-russia-border-place-names/
2. https://defense.info/re-shaping-defense-security/2023/03/war-in-an-era-of-intelligent-machines-whats-the-war-medal-of-the-digital-era/.
3. https://sldinfo.com/2022/06/chinas-informal-empire-in-latin-america-the-challenge-for-the-biden-administration/.
4. https://www.jstor.org/stable/2591017
5. https://www.npr.org/2023/02/18/1158169215/south-africa-joins-russia-and-china-in-naval-exercises
6. https://www.aljazeera.com/news/2023/5/19/chinas-xi-presents-development-plans-for-central-asia.
7. https://www.statista.com/statistics/1244339/surveyed-monthly-youth-unemployment-rate-in-china/.
8. https://astanatimes.com/2023/05/president-tokayev-outlines-priorities-for-cooperation-at-china-central-asia-summit-signs-xian-declaration/.
9. https://menafn.com/1106281025/The-President-Of-Turkmenistan-Took-Part-In-The-First-China-Central-Asia-Summit.
10. https://www.silkroadbriefing.com/news/2023/05/23/all-agreements-grants-and-initiatives-approved-at-the-central-asia-china-summit/.
11. https://astanatimes.com/2023/05/kazakhstan-and-china-sign-47-agreements-worth-22-billion-as-tokayev-outlines-key-areas-for-partnership/.
12. https://qazmonitor.com/news/1154/kazakhstan-increased-export-to-russia-by-15per cent-in-2022.
13. https://www.fmprc.gov.cn/mfa_eng/wjdt_665385/wshd_665389/202305/t20230521_11080865.html.
14. https://www.fmprc.gov.cn/eng/wjdt_665385/2649_665393/201509/t20150902_679409.html and https://news.cgtn.com/news/2023-01-06/Chinese-Turkmen-presidents-hold-talks-in-Beijing-1gmYT9zmhDG/index.html.

15. https://responsiblestatecraft.org/2023/05/24/dedollarization-is-here-like-it-or-not/.

16. https://www.state.gov/united-states-strategy-for-central-asia-2019-2025-advancing-sovereignty-and-economic-prosperity/.

17. https://www.state.gov/economic-resilience-in-central-asia-initiative/.

18. https://www.state.gov/wp-content/uploads/2020/02/FINAL-CEN-Strategy-Glossy-2-10-2020-508.pdf/

19. https://en.wikipedia.org/wiki/List_of_international_presidential_trips_made_by_Vladimir_Putin.

20. https://eurasianet.org/china-promises-more-investment-at-central-asia-summit and https://ca-barometer.org/en/publications/iran-in-central-asia-future-obstacles-for-chinese-economic-dominance-in-kazakhstan-kyrgyzstan-and-uzbekistan.

21. https://www.thenationalnews.com/travel/news/2022/10/18/sheikh-hamdan-shares-footage-of-falconry-trip-in-uzbekistan/.

22. https://www.mei.edu/publications/why-gulf-states-are-investing-central-asia-and-south-caucasus and https://www.acwapower.com/news/saudi-arabias-acwa-power-expands-its-energy-portfolio-in-uzbekistan/

23. https://uzbek-travel.com/about-uzbekistan/news/uzbekistan-to-restore-34-cultural-heritage-sites-in-2022/

24. https://www.rferl.org/a/afghanistan-taliban-canal-water-central-asia/32350996.html.

25. https://www.zmescience.com/ecology/climate/turkmenistan-emissions-huge/

26. https://www.atlanticcouncil.org/blogs/new-atlanticist/how-dependent-is-too-dependent-on-china-central-asia-may-soon-find-out/

27. https://www.adb.org/publications/asia-infrastructure-needs.

28. https://rusi.org/explore-our-research/publications/commentary/irelands-defence-deficit.

29. https://www.reuters.com/world/fbi-chief-says-china-has-bigger-hacking-program-than-competition-combined-2023-09-18/

30. https://www.csis.org/programs/strategic-technologies-program/archives/survey-chinese-espionage-united-states-2000.

31. https://www.cnn.com/2023/05/24/politics/china-hackers-guam-microsoft-taiwan/index.html and https://www.cnn.com/2023/05/26/politics/us-chinese-hackers-rob-joyce/index.html.

32. https://www.cnn.com/2023/09/18/politics/2024-republicans-china/index.html.

33. https://www.opm.gov/about-us/our-people-organization/support-functions/chief-financial-officer/cybersecurity-resource-center/

34. https://federalnewsnetwork.com/congress/2022/07/cyber-grades-bring-down-agencies-scores-in-fitara-14/

35. https://www.gao.gov/assets/gao-23-105482.pdf.

AMERICA AND ITS PLACE IN THE WORLD

CAN AMERICA LEARN LESSONS FROM AFGHANISTAN AND UKRAINE?

February 8, 2023

By James Durso

If recent U.S. foreign policy had musical accompaniment it would be "New Person, Same Old Mistakes."

Since 2001, the U.S., while pursuing terrorists and promoting the "freedom agenda" has habitually failed to negotiate before taking up arms, so has wasted a lot of money and lives on failed projects.[1]

In the wake of the 9-11 attacks by al-Qaeda, then-President George Bush demanded the Taliban deliver Usama bin Laden to American justice. The Taliban replied they were ready to negotiate, but Bush wasn't having any of it.[2]

The U.S. invasion of Afghanistan ensued and the cure-all nation-building project (really an effort to reform Pashtun culture) was a 20-year, $2 trillion bust at the cost of almost 180,000 dead NATO troops and Afghans, ending with the live-streamed retreat of U.S. forces from Kabul on 15 August 2021.

Bush may have wanted to not legitimize the Taliban by negotiating with them, but the Taliban have claimed legitimacy by defeating America and its NATO partners in combat, and are back in charge in Kabul while Bush paints watercolors in retirement.

And some countries are hedging their bets as over a dozen capitals still maintain embassies in Kabul (though none have recognized the Taliban government...yet.)

It wasn't the first time the U.S. fumbled seizing bin Laden: The Taliban made the same offer in 1998, but backtracked after U.S. cruise missile attacks, and Sudan, which hosted bin laden from 1991 to 1996, unsuccessfully offered to hand him over to the U.S., according to Dr Gutbi el-Mahdi, the former spy chief.[3]

The fact that Islamist regimes unfriendly to the U.S. were anxious to be rid of bin Laden was both a warning and an opportunity that Washington ignored.

Aside from its penultimate failure, the Afghanistan war caused a refugee crisis, fostered a culture of corruption that fatally injured the central government, failed to stop poppy cultivation, which showed steady growth during NATO's tenure, and dampened economic activity in Central and South Asia.

And it presented Pakistan's ruling generals an opportunity to extend their influence in the region, and make a few bucks, besides.

Iran cooperated with America's punitive expedition against the Taliban and soon an Iranian intermediary was regularly meeting with U.S. diplomat Ryan Crocker.[4] Qasem Soleimani, then-commander of Iran's Revolutionary Guards Quds Force reportedly mused, "Maybe it's time to rethink our relationship with the Americans" but that opportunity, which could have changed the trajectory of Eurasia, was dashed by the Bush Axis of Evil speech.

After that, Iran buckled down and helped usher America out of Iraq in 2011, claimed a pre-eminent position in Baghdad, continued developing its ballistic missile and nuclear power programs, and encouraged its proxies in Lebanon, Syria, Yemen, and the Palestinian territories.

The U.S. retreat from Kabul may have encouraged Russia in December 2021 to make offers to the U.S. and NATO about limiting the expansion of the alliance, but Washington and Brussels showed little interest and two months later Russia's Special Military Operation (SMO) commenced.[5]

The U.S. responded with unprecedented sanctions on Russia's government and private sector, a $100 billion spending spree to support Ukraine, and has been steadily escalating the level of military technology it gives to Kyiv.

This hasn't halted Russia's operation which has already killed almost 160,000 Ukrainian fighters – a fraction of Russia's 16,000 to 20,000 dead – as the Pentagon hints time is short and the State Department signals to Russia that it will soon be time to negotiate, assuming Russia's upcoming offensive fails – a big "if."

The Ukraine war has caused Russia and Iran to strengthen their defense relations. Iran sent Russia drones and experienced Revolutionary Guard troops, and Russia has offered Iran advanced combat aircraft and missile systems.[6]

The Wall Street Journal reports that Russia and Iran are advancing plans for a factory that can produce 6,000 drones for the war in Ukraine, news that brings to mind the warning of Zbigniew Brzezinski, the former National Security Advisor to President Jimmy Carter: "Potentially, the most dangerous scenario would be a grand coalition of China, Russia, and perhaps Iran, an 'anti-hegemonic' coalition united not by ideology but by complementary grievances."

Though China isn't taking an active role in supporting Russia's operation, despite their "no limits" partnership, Chinese defense companies are sending Russia "navigation equipment, jamming technology, and fighter-jet parts," according to *The Wall Street Journal*, and Beijing recently announced mutual political trust with Moscow has deepened after its enjoy met with Russian Foreign Minister Sergei Lavrov.[7]

China should be America's priority #1, not deciding which group of Slavs governs the Donbas. The U.S. campaigns in Iraq and Afghanistan distracted Washington and caused it to waste $4 trillion (most of it borrowed), instead of investing in education, scientific R&D, and infrastructure to better compete with China.[8] In fact, while the U.S. was futilely campaigning in the Hindu Kush, China grew its GDP from $1.34 trillion in 2001 to $17.73 trillion in 2021.[9]

The Russian and Ukrainian leaders view the SMO as an existential conflict: the only way out is through. But it's also reputational life-or-death for members of America's "war party:" government officials and their pilot fish in the media, defense contractors, and think tanks. Another strategic defeat, close on the heels of Afghanistan, may call into question pet projects like NATO's next out-of-area venture: confronting China.[10]

Aside from finally getting that victory over the Kremlin that escaped their grasp when the Cold War just ended one day, a win in Ukraine will hopefully make the public forget about the serial disasters in Iraq, Libya, Syria, and Afghanistan.

Historian Michael Vlahos suggests the war party members are seeking the "emotional uplift" that accompanied World War II and that they see themselves as the "lineal descendants of the people who fought World War II," a comical thought if you compare today's place-men to Marshall, Hull, and Eisenhower.[11]

Is it late for the U.S. to press Ukraine to seek a diplomatic solution? Probably. Ukrainian president Zelensky is refusing to negotiate with Russia's Putin, hoping regime change in Russia delivers a pliable Kremlin leader.

That's no surprise after American president Joe Biden declared, "For God's sake, this man [Putin] cannot remain in power," and Former British prime minister Boris Johnson reportedly scuttled a peace deal between Russia in Ukraine in April 2022 – a move recently confirmed by former Israeli prime minister Naftali Bennet who was then trying to mediate an agreement.

However, Washington may finally be looking for an offramp, as the Swiss German newspaper *Neue Zurcher Zeitung* reported that the U.S. offered Russia 20% of Ukraine as an incentive to cease and desist.[12] Moscow called the report a "hoax" but, following earlier U.S. media reports of an American proffer, it may signal the U.S. is moving away from "no Ukraine without Ukraine" as it moves to clear the decks before the 2024 election season and as popular support slips for the proxy war of choice with Russia.

If America's luck holds and the world survives this crisis, hopefully a wiser U.S. will commit to seeking diplomatic solutions in the future, even if the deals don't deliver 100% of what Washington demands – the traditional U.S. definition of "diplomacy," though others would characterize it as delivering surrender terms.

Other than benefitting defense contractors and Yevgeny Prigozhin's Warner PMC, the Ukraine war has caused higher prices for food, fuel, fertilizer, and industrial metals, fueling world-wide inflation, and lent unhelpful credibility to just about any critic of U.S. foreign policy, regardless of their motivations.

It has also encouraged many African, Asian, and Latin American governments (many of them former colonies) to abstain from the latest iteration of the West's "rules-based-order" as the Europeans are settling their disagreements in Europe for a change.

It is important that the U.S. political class finally realize: (1) negotiating, while not as exciting as warfare, especially when your kids aren't in the military, should be the default reaction to potential future crises, and (2) prudent economic management is more essential to the country's future prosperity (as it stares the abyss of a $32 trillion national debt) than the Pentagon's latest weaponry wish list or quixotic "democracy promotion" crusades, which have failed to secure lasting post 9-11 gains for the U.S., and opportunity for future generations.

THE MEXICAN DRUG WAR AND CONFLICT ON AMERICAN TERRITORY

May 5, 2023

By James Durso

In April, six Republican senators introduced S. 1048 – Ending the Notorious, Aggressive, and Remorseless Criminal Organizations and Syndicates (NARCOS) Act of 2023. The bill would designate the Mexican drug cartels as foreign terrorist organizations and set the stage for military action against them.[13]

At the same time, Republican members of the House of Representatives introduced H.R. 2633: Terrorist Organization Classification Act of 2023, and H.R. 1564: Drug Cartel Terrorist Designation Act

Also in April, the U.S. House of Representatives Committee on Homeland Security voted the Border Reinforcement Act of 2023 out of committee. The act would require the Department of Homeland Security (DHS) to report if any of several identified Mexican drug cartels "meets the criteria for designation as a foreign terrorist organization."

In early 2023, Representatives Dan Crenshaw and Mike Waltz introduced legislation for an Authorization for Use of Military Force (AUMF) to target the cartels.[14]

The legislators' actions in 2023 tailgated actions in the previous Congress, such as H.R.2600 – Drug Cartel Terrorist Designation Act and H.R. 8030: Fentanyl is a WMD Act. (In 2019, DHS considered designating fentanyl a WMD "when certain criteria are met" but took no further action.)

In April 2023, possibly in light of increasing congressional demands for action on the southern border, U.S. President Joe Biden authorized the deployment of military reserve forces to the southern border to assist DHS with the surge of illegal migrants.[15]

The migrants are transported by the same cartels that send drugs to the U.S. so the action is minor pushback against the cartels but it probably won't make a difference to the drug traffic.

The U.S. Attorney General responded to Congress that the Sinaloa cartel was already designated a Transnational Criminal Organization which gives the U.S. government significant authority to attack them.[16]

Why the sudden flurry of action about the cartels?

Its partly politics as the Republicans take advantage of President Biden's lack of enforcement action against illegal immigration in the run-up to the 2024 election.

It's also motivated by concern about the ever-rising number of drug overdose deaths, which passed the 100,000 threshold (to 106,999) in 2021. The climb in overdose deaths is largely driven by synthetic opioids, primarily fentanyl, which caused a 279% jump from 2016 to 2021.[17]

Drug addiction is widely acknowledged to be costly to society, and The Pew Charitable Trust estimates the annual cost of opioid overdose, misuse, and dependence: $35 billion in health care costs, $14.8 billion in criminal justice costs, and $92 billion in lost productivity, all after America spent over a trillion dollars fighting the War on Drugs.[18]

And the cartels have millions of allies in the U.S. Not their members and the independent operators and gangs that move the drugs and humans, but the tens of millions of Americans who consume the narcotics the cartels provide.

According to the 2020 National Survey on Drug Use and Health, "Among people aged 12 or older in 2020, 21.4 percent (or 59.3 million people) used illicit drugs in the past year."[19] Those users, full-time and casual, spend nearly $150 billion annually on the stuff, according to the Rand Corporation.[20]

Everyone agrees that synthetic opioids are a national crisis, but is sending in the Marines the best solution?

The U.S. tends to see the military as the solution to vexing political issues and the military leadership is usually all too happy to go along, but sending troops to Mexico would be an act of folly.

The Americans would be starting a war along the southern border which will have consequences on the home front, unlike faraway wars in Iraq, Afghanistan, and Syria.

The U.S. and its NATO partners had two decades, near-unlimited funding, and loose rules of engagement in Afghanistan but failed to stop the opium poppy trade. One year after the allies departed, the United Nations Office on Drugs and Crime reported in November 2022, "Opium cultivation in Afghanistan increased by 32% over the previous year to 233,000 hectares – making the 2022 crop the third largest area under opium cultivation since monitoring began."[21]

Will the U.S. succeed in Mexico, a country with an economy and population much larger than Afghanistan?

Mexico has the 15th largest economy in the world, is the #2 trading partner of the U.S., and is fully-integrated in North American supply chains.

Military activity across the border would damage legitimate cross-border commerce that totaled almost $780 billion USD in 2022. According to *FreightWaves*, cross border trade will remain steady in 2023, bolstered by "re-shoring and near-shoring of manufacturing operations to North America, particularly Mexico."

The U.S. military was used to not getting local cooperation against insurgent forces in Iraq and Afghanistan and it'll get that in spades south of the border.

Mexicans can be expected to react the same as any other people to foreign troops in their midst, regardless of whatever piece of paper the Pentagon lawyers concoct to make the whole thing legal – at least to Americans.

Americans are pretty well armed but so are Mexicans and the cartels would quickly organize local self-defense units against the *Yanqui* troops. Mexicans will also be motivated by the memory of the 1916 punitive expedition against Pancho Villa (he's the good guy in Mexico) and the Mexican Cession, the 529,000 square miles of land ceded to the U.S. after the Mexican-American War, which was primed by the American annexation of Texas in 1845.

So, will the cartels retaliate directly?

You betcha.

The cartels are well-funded, well-armed, and violent. These guys kill judges and stage mass executions (and share the video) so retaliating against the U.S. military (or American civilians) won't be a stretch.

Retaliation wasn't much of a concern when the U.S. was fighting in Iraq and Afghanistan as the Taliban or Islamic State weren't likely to show up in Fayetteville for a little payback, but U.S. bases on the border like Fort Bliss and Fort Huachuca may be the first to get hit.

The cartels use armed drones to fight each other and they may repurpose them to fight the common American enemy. The Jalisco New Generation Cartel, considered the most violent cartel, used a rocket propelled grenade to bring down a Mexican military helicopter and later repeated the feat with a high-powered rifle.[22]

And if the cartels are now called terrorists, they may link up the real thing, like the Hezbollah operators in the Argentina-Brazil-Paraguay Tri-Border Area, or whatever Islamic Revolutionary Guard Corps representatives are knocking around in Venezuela.

Also, 1.6 million Americans live in Mexico according to the U.S. State Department, which is another way of saying "1.6 million potential hostages." Will the U.S. government be as casual about their fate as it was of Americans in Afghanistan and Sudan?

Americans appear indifferent to the fact that their drug consumption is responsible for over 360,000 deaths in Mexico since the start of the Mexican Drug War in 2006.[23]

This is reflected in political leaders such as Senator Robert Menendez, who said at a recent hearing on fentanyl, "I don't know how many more lives have to be lost for Mexico to get engaged."[24]

This casual rejection of suffering caused, or abetted, by America was also reflected in President Biden's claim that Afghan military and police forces were "not willing to fight themselves' – after over 69,095 Afghan military and police died in the 20-year campaign. (American military deaths were 2,324.)

Unfortunately, if American forces operate in Mexico there will be casualties ("collateral damage") among the innocent Mexican population. The Pentagon will likely respond true to form and conduct an investigation, the results of which will never be made public, that will conclude "mistakes were made but no one did anything wrong," convincing Mexicans that they, like Afghans and Iraqis are expendable in America's pursuit of its objectives.

So, what will the cartels do?

There's direct action against U.S. forces, businesses, and diplomatic facilities in Mexico. Attacking an embassy or consulate is a big international no-no, but if you're now a terrorist what have you got to lose?

Then, the cartels or their surrogates could attack military bases in the U.S. or track down military members or their families for retaliation, which the U.S. government will call that terrorism, but that's what you always call the other guy's weapon of choice.

And, as a state of war will exist, Washington can forget any formal or informal cooperation with the Mexican government which will withdraw support from U.S. facilities and leave U.S. diplomats, military attaches, and DEA agents exposed and on their own, the Vienna Convention be damned.

Mexico may consider political-economic responses like joining BRICS (Brazil-Russia-India-China-South Africa), the political grouping with its own development bank that has seen a flood of interested prospective members (including Mexico) in response to Washington's demand for universal compliance with its economic war against Moscow.[25]

Or it may solicit Belt and Road investment from Beijing, and the resulting increased Chinese presence in North America will set teeth on edge up north.

Will the U.S. military be ready to prosecute the Mexican targets? Maybe, maybe not.

During the Trump administration, then-Commandant of the U.S. Marine Corps, General Robert Neller, even declared the Marines faced "rapidly accelerating risks" from, among other things, Southwest border operations.[26]

And after the loss in Afghanistan, the Pentagon is focused on a high-technology, peer-to-peer fight, not another squalid struggle against angry farmers.

The U.S. military, which has likely spent more time thinking about defending Germany's borders than America's, may be unique in that it considers securing the borders a distraction from its day job.

Military leaders may also be concerned about corruption of the ranks – plata o plomo – and that's understandable after the Fat Leonard scandal, and the corruption of military personnel in Iraq and Afghanistan.

And the drug war "pros," the Drug Enforcement Administration and U.S. Customs and Border Protection aren't immune to bribes, so the Pentagon may be trying to avoid even more trouble in a stressed organization trying to recover from two unsuccessful campaigns in Iraq and Afghanistan.

And, given the NATO-Russia war in Ukraine and rising tensions with China, the Pentagon will likely claim another punitive expedition south of the Rio Grande will make it less ready for its preferred contingencies elsewhere, though American taxpayers are justified asking why are we spending over $800 billion on the Pentagon if it can't be bothered to defend the border.

America's appetite for narcotics and its failure to secure the border are acts of self-harm that are seen as the acts of a sick, corrupt society by the rest of the world.

They are failures that Chinese leader Xi Jinping can highlight as the inevitable end-state of the U.S. political model and "rules-based order" so beloved by U.S. officialdom and its pilot fish in the media, academia, and NGOS.

The Communist Party of China propagandists won't even have to make anything up; they'll just roll the tape.

What could the Americans do?

Just stop buying the damn stuff!

Nancy Reagan was mocked when she said, "Just say no," but demand reduction will crimp the cartels' operations more effectively than the 82nd Airborne Division. But the first step in that process will be an uncomfortable conversation about what in American society makes so many people want to self-anesthetize.

But given that America is all about options, not consequences, Washington will probably default to securitizing a social problem that is better attacked by police, prosecutors, physicians, and intelligence agencies than the army and navy.

TAIWAN, U.S. DEFENSE INDUSTRY, AND THE EVOLVING STRATEGY FOR INDO-PACIFIC DEFENSE

July 9, 2023

Too often, the focus is upon Taiwan as a U.S.-Chinese problem or confrontation. Leaving aside the question of why the Communist Party ruling the mainland has any right to seize a free democracy, such a focus misses the question of who lives in the first island chain. It is not Americans: It is Filipinos and Japanese.

The Chinese threats are not about Taiwan but changing the world in their favor. Forget the "rules based order": welcome the new authoritarian order. There is a NATO-Russian war in Ukraine: are we going to see a similar war in the Pacific?

One way to avoid this is to convince the Chinese leadership that this will never be a clean quick takeover of people who live in a free democracy. It will be the start of a major conflict, similar to what the Japanese did when they slaughtered the Chinese in 1938 at Shanghai.

Taiwan needs to be part of the wider strategic effort of the liberal democracies to rework their defense relationships so that Taiwan is not an isolated tidbit to be eaten by the Chinese dragon.

Ed Timperlake and I wrote about a possible way ahead along these lines in an article we wrote in December 2016. "Both the technology available to the United States and the policy shifts of core allies in the Pacific are enabling the forging of a deterrence in depth strategy.

"As Japan has focused on its extended defense, Australia upon the integration of its forces with a capability also for the extended defense of Australia and with U.S. forces focus on shaping a force to operate over the extended ranges of the Pacific, now is the time for a serious rebooting of the role of Taiwan in extended Pacific defense and security."[27]

As Taiwan looks to build its forces to enhance its ability to be resilient and part of a broader defense in depth strategy of the liberal democracies, the role of U.S. and allied defense industry is important but will only play its expanded role if old limiting practices of defense trade are modified, and the new technologies unleashed by the autonomous revolution are fully embraced.

The question of re-working the role of U.S. defense industry in its cooperation with Taiwan has been highlighted by the first visit of a U.S. defense industrial delegation to Taiwan since 2019. Headed by Lt. General (Retired) "Stick" Rudder, a group of defense industrialists visited the island in May 2023 to support a broader conversation and cooperation between Taiwan and the United States in the defense industrial area.

An AP article published on 3 May 2023, highlighted the visit. "Speaking at a public forum in Taiwan's capital Taipei, retired Lt. Gen. Steven Rudder said the U.S. wants to be part of the defense capabilities of Taiwan and improve the supply chain resilience of the island. He also emphasized how critical the island's position is for security.

"For the Asia-Pacific, I would offer there's not another more important area in the world to maintain peace," Rudder said Wednesday morning at the Taiwan-U.S. Defense Industry Forum.

"So (when) you hear 'a free and open Indo-Pacific,' this is a small part of ensuring that shared vision remains intact. We want to be part of the self-defense capabilities of Taiwan," he said."[28]

But what has been missed in the coverage of the visit was the broader point that the U.S. and the allies are changing their military strategy to one of distributed operations and are embracing new technologies, such as next generation autonomous systems to defend their nations and their forces dispersed and distributed throughout the Pacific.

In other words, instead of looking at Taiwan with the eyes of the 1950s as an outpost to be defended, it is part of the first line in a defense in depth strategy for the liberal democratic order in the Pacific.

I talked with Rudder on 21 June 2023 about his take-aways concerning the current state of the relationship.

One the one hand, there is the focus on FMS or foreign military sales efforts such as with the F-16 which are subject to slower than desired implementation and spare parts supplies.

On the other hand, there is the possibility of expanded cooperation of asymmetric capabilities such as UAVs, and USVs in the self-defense of Taiwan. As the U.S. and its allies are working to build such capabilities, Taiwan could be an important partner in this effort.

This is not radically dissimilar from Australia as I write about in my new book on Australian defense. The Australians have favored FMS buys, but they are slow to roll out and the supply chain issue is crucial. Yet the Australians are looking to dramatically increase their ability to deploy the asymmetric weapons and platforms which Rudder highlighted.

When one looks at the defense of Taiwan, East of Taiwan, the democracies have significant defense capability. But west of Taiwan is void of such capability.

That is why one should look to sea denial as a key aspect of the defense of Taiwan and the role, for example, of wolfpack USVs in disrupting the battle rhythm of the PRC forces can be facilitated by such weapon systems. Taiwan could well be the showcase of something which other liberal democracies in the Pacific might emulate.

This also raises an aspect of the defense challenge facing the democracies, namely, how do we collectively build an arsenal of democracy?

This requires multiple production lines spread throughout the democracies, and certainly one should consider Taiwan as part of such an effort.

Rudder agreed. "What we really need more than one line for the systems that we're building. And right now, our defense department acquisition laws mean that we down select one winner. And usually, one winner means one production line."

We won't get an arsenal of democracy this way. In other words, instead of thinking of Taiwan as a country of last resort in selling whatever FMS systems we are willing to sell, why not make them a player in building the new arsenal of democracy in the Pacific, certainly with regard to asymmetric or autonomous systems?

THE ECONOMIST LOOKS BACK AT THE OBAMA ADMINISTRATION

August 23, 2023

In this week's *The Economist*, the lead article addresses what they call "Obama's Biggest Mistake." The article focused on Obama's red line in Syria that was not. They then ask; "How much was his red line in Syria to blame for America's lost credibility?"[29]

Because we essentially are being governed by Obama III, the question needs to be extended to how realistic and effective is American leadership following the traditional liberal path?

The question of course is even broader: Given where the world is and has been evolving, what is a realistic view for America and its place in the world?

I would argue that neither Obama III or the Trump "Make American Great Again" perspectives are realistic in terms of the world in which America finds itself, nor it is capable of navigating.

The world has changed dramatically beyond what either liberals or neo-cons contemplate when considering American policy or anything remotely realist in terms of what America can "lead" in terms of the West.

I agree with *The Economist t*hat going back to the 8 years of the

Obama Administration is a good place to see the disconnect between strategic policy and strategic reality.

And I have recently edited a book on the Administration which provides a year-by-year account of an Administration which could not come to grips with the rise of China or the imperialistic appetite of Putin.

As I put it in the introduction to the book:

The United States does not have the resources, or capability, to remake the countries into which it has inserted itself, and in trying to do so, it has undercut its own geopolitical interests.

Or put another way, American diplomatic and military approaches have reshaped U.S. tools to do things like stability operations, rather than investing in relevant air and naval systems to defend the United States directly and to be able to compete with a rising China more effectively or a resurgent Russia.

As Mearsheimer put it: "Liberals tend to think of every area of the world as a potential battlefield, because they are committed to protecting human rights everywhere and spreading liberal democracy far and wide.

"They would naturally prefer to achieve these goals peacefully, but they are usually willing to countenance using military force if necessary. In short, while realists place strict limits on where they are willing to employ force, liberals have no such limits. For them, vital interests are everywhere."

Even though this quote highlights liberals, the liberal hegemonic approach he is discussing has been at the heart of the past three Administrations' policies, whether driven by neo-cons or liberals.

With the Soviet Union gone, and the working assumption that the Chinese were being assimilated into the global order, the United States was free to work with its allies to reshape the troublesome Middle East and to deal with "Islamic terrorism" as the key strategic threat.

Donald Trump began to change course. His Pentagon released a new national security strategy, which focused on the return of Great Power rivalry and the need to reshape U.S. policies and capabilities to make such a strategic shift.

"It is an open question of whether the Administration was really reorganized to do this or whether the United States can easily shift course. In essence, Trump recognized the shift but provided tactical adjustments rather than a

coherent strategy to deal with the strategic shift and transition to a new historical era.

What is not in question is that the rise of China and the resurgence of Russia have put in play 21st century authoritarian powers directly challenging the United States and the liberal democratic allies whose challenges need to be met.

"Put bluntly, the collapse of the Soviet Union and the end of the Warsaw Pact was seen to open up a new period of domination by the liberal democracies. New states would be added to the EU and to NATO, and the globalization of the economy was seen as inextricably intertwined with the ascendancy of liberal democracy.

"What was lost in this euphoric way forward was the rise of the 21st century authoritarian capitalist powers, Russia and China, and their ability to challenge the ascendancy of the liberal democratic European and American regimes, both at home and abroad.

In this book, we take the reader year by year from 2009 through 2016 to examining the global shifts and how the Obama Administration saw these shifts and dealt with them.

DAUNTING FISCAL RISKS: THE MISSING U.S. GOVERNMENT STRATEGY

August 24, 2023

In a recent paper released by Malmgren-Glinsman Partners, the difficult situation in which the United States Government finds itself financially was underscored.

Their white paper argued: Over and above the concerns surrounding inflation and the economy, there are also daunting fiscal risks facing the U.S. government. And this situation will be aggravated by spending needed for new global commitments, the Ukraine War and spending for U.S, military operations.

They highlighted the factual situation as follows:

While financial market news is currently preoccupied with the inflation rate and possibility of recession, an entirely different policy challenge is emerging: How will mammoth U.S. Government debt be managed in the next 15 months before 2024 national elections?

The bipartisan Congressional Budget Office (CBO) estimates that the *federal budget deficit for the first 10 months of the current fiscal year (which runs from October 2022 to September 2023) is $1.7 trillion. This is more than twice the deficit for the same period in the preceding fiscal year.*

To put this escalating figure in perspective, government debt as a percent of GDP in the year 2000 stood below 50%, whereas U.S. government debt today stands at 118.6%, and is projected by the CBO to go even higher.

At the end of July, the U.S. Treasury announced that it expected to need to borrow $1,007 trillion from private markets in Q3 (July to September), and another $852 Billion in Q4 (October to December).

It was not made clear what assumptions had been made in these estimates.

It should be noted that the all-time high for quarterly borrowing of almost $3 trillion was hit in April-to-June 2020, thanks to the pandemic crisis.

In early August, several days after these numbers were announced, a Treasury spokesman said the Treasury was no longer assuming a recession in 2023. No recession is a growing financial market view. No recession would mean no large decline in tax receipts or rise in counter-cyclical spending such as unemployment compensation.

However, tax receipts have slowly been declining in recent weeks, suggesting sagging economic activity.

Falling measures of physical economic activity, such as declining volume of shipments of goods by sea, rail and trucks, are suggesting significant slowdown.

If, as we expect, recession begins to erode GDP growth, then the July 31 borrowing estimates would have to be revised to take into account rising unemployment benefit expenditures and falling tax receipts, resulting in larger numbers for the remainder of this year, and of course, higher numbers well into 2024.

They then reviewed the global situation and how the Administration is spending defense money, notably in Ukraine, and argued that the global situation will likely accelerate the debt problem.

They highlighted the various commitments the Biden Administration is making globally which require increased defense spending and then underscored that the Ukraine aid added to these commitments and increased spending necessary for operations short of the beginning of armed conflict with a peer competitor. These actions all argue for increased defense spending ON TOP of the current debt structure.

They noted: *Enhanced integration of U.S. military responses with Japan,*

Australia, South Korea, and possibly other like-minded nations is being actively pursued.

As part of U.S. military conflict contingency planning, the U.S. military is likely considering wider dispersion of its military presence in other locations in the neighborhood of the South China Sea, Sea of Japan and the Pacific Island rings.

If an armed conflict between the U.S and China were to happen, there is no doubt that management of the U.S. government budget would be dramatically affected. Wars are brutally expensive. Moreover, the costs of conducting an armed conflict are invariably underestimated when political decision makers decide to act without elaborate analysis by the military in advance.

How viable is such a situation?

And where is the strategy to deal with it?

They argued: *If the U.S. did find itself entangled in an armed conflict, the U.S. Treasury would have to develop an emergency debt management program that would entail massive new borrowing.*

This possibility has been given virtually no thought in Congress or mainstream journalism.

Even if no armed conflict took place, a process of preparing for conflict would inevitably entail dramatic escalation of the defense budget to cover widespread deployment of U.S. forces throughout the Indo-Pacific Command.

A new National Defense Activity Authorization would have to be enacted.

With that, new Treasury operations scenarios would have to be developed, and the Federal Reserve would have to reconsider the changed financial market parameters posed thereby.

2024: AMERICA AT A CROSSROADS IN THE WORLD

September 4, 2023

As the United States faces its presidential election in 2024, there seems to very little consideration of how the United States has changed and its realistic place in the world. No longer is the United States the leader of the "free world" and the guardian of the "rules-based order."

The rise of the 21st century authoritarians, the growing significance of global players working congruent actions rather than forming classic alliances, budget deficits out of control, a migratory upheaval in the United States and core allied states and a strategic system which can not take realistic decisions in terms of the world as it is and becoming rather than what a nostalgic view of America and its role in the world after the collapse of the Soviet Union has created a situation where key decisions about the future need to be taken.

Now let us look at the 2024 Presidential election.

Does anyone really suggest that the "debate" about the Presidency has any relationship with framing the tough choices America needs to take and to do so in a way that its closest friends and allies need to take account of and increase their capability to defend common interests?

The illusion of the NATO-Russian war in Ukraine is that the United States leads and the allies follow and that the United States has a military capability of underwriting the Western global order.

The Ukraine adventure is the latest manifestation of the Iraq-Afghan syndrome of making commitments with no clear consideration of what the American interest realistically is and an inability to calibrate a realistic American and allied termination point. Only this time we risk nuclear war.

As James Durso has noted: "The United States has expended "$2.26 trillion for the Afghanistan misadventure that put the Taliban back in charge in Kabul, and another $2.21 trillion to destabilize Iraq and deliver it into the hands of Iran."

We also have built a military to fight in such wars and face an upheaval battle to build the military which we now need, and even more important we need a fundamental debate precisely about the question of what kind of military we now need to protect American core interests.

Let me be clear: it is about not intervening everywhere to protect American interests based on the ubiquitous global commons: it is about much clearer recognition that the United States needs to focus its resources on protecting its core interests.

Again, as Durso noted: "Unique in the world's militaries, the Pentagon doesn't think it is responsible for defending its country's borders. Instead of defending America, it defends American interests, which are mutable and can change with a new administration and are not viewed overseas as positively as they are in Washington, D.C. green rooms."

The budget crisis highlighted by Malmgren-Glinsman Partners suggests clear limits on American options for action in the world. They highlighted the various commitments the Biden Administration is making globally which require increased defense spending and then underscored that the Ukraine aid added to these commitments and increased spending necessary for operations short of the beginning of armed conflict with a peer competitor.

These actions all argue for increased defense spending ON TOP of the current debt structure.

They noted: "Enhanced integration of U.S. military responses with Japan, Australia, South Korea, and possibly other like-minded nations is being actively pursued. As part of U.S. military conflict contingency planning, the U.S. military is likely considering wider dispersion of its military presence in other locations in the neighborhood of the South China Sea, Sea of Japan and the Pacific Island rings.

"If an armed conflict between the U.S and China were to happen, there is no doubt that management of the U.S. government budget would be dramatically affected. Wars are brutally expensive. Moreover, the costs of conducting an armed conflict are invariably underestimated when political decision makers decide to act without elaborate analysis by the military in advance."

How viable is such a situation?

And where is the strategy to deal with it?

They underscored: "If the U.S. did find itself entangled in an armed conflict, the U.S. Treasury would have to develop an emergency debt management program that would entail massive new borrowing. This possibility has been given virtually no thought in Congress or mainstream journalism."

There is also a core question facing the future of the volunteer military. And it is not just the impact of the Biden Administration social preference policies, it is the decreasing population pool and the clear need to much more rapidly incorporate automated technologies in the military to compensate for reduced manpower.

Durso provided significant insight with regard to a number of aspects of this challenge: "The military isn't the only public institution suffering a bad reputation, but it is used to basking in public esteem so it may not know how to recover.

"A public defeat in Afghanistan, commanders prioritizing woke social programs over battle skills, epidemics of sexual assault and suicide, substandard housing, exposure to dangerous chemicals and hazardous materials...no wonder the services are in danger of missing their recruiting targets, which will further weaken support for big defense budgets as a family with someone in uniform is more likely to both support a big defense budget and encourage their children to join the military.

"Calls for a "limited military draft" when Congress has not declared war will be rejected by the public, and a proposed "national security strategy for military recruiting" will occupy a panel of worthies for several months but will it come up ideas that escaped the military recruiters?

"Probably not. There are fewer young Americans eligible to serve, due to physical fitness standards and prohibitions on drug use, and only 9% of 16-21 year old Americans have an interest in putting on the uniform.

"And when the Pentagon asked young Americans, "What would be the main reason(s) why you would NOT consider joining the U.S. Military?" 70% replied "Possibility of physical injury/death" and 65% replied "Possibility of PTSD or other emotional/psychological issues."

"Those distressing numbers are likely due to the well-known epidemics of suicide and sexual assault in the military, and the promotion of "wounded warrior" charities has probably made more prospective recruits aware of the severe injuries they may suffer. In short, is the GI Bill worth losing your legs?

"And "the kids" may be on to something: a recent report published by the Journal of the American College of Surgeons says that in a war against a near peer adversary, i.e., Russia or China, U.S. troops will suffer injuries more severe than those in Iraq or Afghanistan, that is "multiple high-velocity penetrating injuries, barotrauma, and blunt injuries from being thrown during the explosion, and traumatic brain injuries."[30]

"In addition, U.S. forces won't command air superiority so evacuation from the battlefield will be difficult if it is even possible.

"The military has traditionally relied on military families to provide recruits for the services, but the Secretary of the Army isn't helping matters by declaring she wants to avoid relying on a "warrior caste" of families with a military tradition.

"It is commendable that she wants to broaden interest in military service but not clever if it will discourage the ready pool of volunteers before she has alternates signed up. The Army Secretary has her work cut out for her as even military veterans are less and less likely to recommend military service to their kids."

As United States hard and soft power instruments are under significant pressure to shape much more realistic global goals for the country, the nature of global competition is changing beyond the usual American interpretation of the world in which it has had such a central role creating after World War II.

That world simply no longer exists.

An example of the change is the expansion of the BRICS organization. What holds this group together is a common interest in secure acquisition of energy while the United States turns from such a policy towards a "green future," something the BRICS don't seem focused on as a core interest.

In Ken Maxwell's assessment of the expansion of the BRICS he underscores a critical point with regard to how the evolving global system works – not by states forming alliances but finding partners to pursue congruent interests limited in scope, time and purpose.

"Is it any surprise that the Sheikhs in the Gulf and the potentates in Beijing and Moscow (let along the rulers in Brasilia and New Delhi) draw their own conclusion. The issue is not whether the BRICS+ will form a coherent block. What matters is that are a congruent bloc where they may agree on some questions but not on all.

"And that does not matter. What matters is they are a forum of nations which are not automatically in favor of the West, and many are hostile to the institutions which have defined the international order since WW2, and they going about consciously to create alternatives."

The presidential campaign of 2024 is not likely to raise these issues and to frame a core debate on the reality of America in the world and how can the United States shape expectations about its behavior symmetrical with success.

Being successfully globally has not been an important part of national politics for some time – just making commitments and being engaged globally seems to be the mantra.

But the world is moving on – how can the United States find its realistic place in the evolving world?

THE U.S. MILITARY AND ITS FUTURE: SIZE THE FORCE TO MATCH THE NATION'S WILLINGNESS TO PROVIDE SERVICEMEN

October 3, 2023

By James Durso

Next year, the U.S. military will spend an unprecedented $900 billion dollars of the taxpayers' money but it continues to fail to interest young Americans in military service.

"Gen Z is unpatriotic!" and won't join the military we're told, but are they really?[31]

If so, why?

It's partly poor health and an inability to pass the qualifying physical exam, which has nothing to do with patriotism, but also an increase in mental health disorders and more common casual drug use. These are problems the military can't fix, and the Pentagon will probably try more money and social media outreach on the latest China-owned short video app but that's a band-aid fix, not a real solution.

Zoomers may be wary of American institutions, but they are not alone in that regard as it is a long-term trend in the U.S. A 2022 Gallup poll found, "Americans are less confident in major U.S. institutions than they were a year ago, with significant declines for 11 of the 16 institutions tested and no improvements for any."[32]

And considering how the military and national security establishment has performed since 9-11, what do they have to be patriotic about?

The country has been at war their whole lives, and for no discernible reason other than bureaucratic momentum and President George W. Bush's vacuous claim about the motives of the 9-11 attackers: "They hate our freedoms."

Since the 9-11 attacks, which no official was disciplined for, the country started a war based on a lie (Iraq) and suffered a humiliating loss (Afghanistan).

The U.S. green lighted the NATO attack on the internationally-recognized government of Libya that caused an ongoing civil war and a refugee surge that upended politics in Europe, and may be partly to blame for the deaths caused by the recent flood.

U.S. officials knew things were going badly in Afghanistan but lied to the American people that NATO forces were "turning the corner" almost up to the day of the live streamed retreat from Kabul.

The Southern border is no more, and the biggest threats to America are the national debt and drug addiction, not Vladimir Putin and Xi Jinping.

Either U.S. leaders are unable to recognize real problems or they are gaslighting Americans while they try to improvise their way out of problems they helped create.

The military's problems weren't cooked up in the Kremlin, they are home grown.

To start, there is a plague of sexual assault in the ranks. According to the Pentagon, "the Department received 8,942 reports of sexual assault involving Service members as victims and/or subjects in Fiscal Year 2022, an increase of 1 percent from the 8,866 received in Fiscal Year 2021," but at least the risk of sexual assault is no better or worse than in the civilian population, so there's that.[33]

However a 2022 Pentagon briefing disclosed that "Sixty percent of female service members also did not trust that the military would ensure their safety after reporting a sexual assault" so the real number of sexual assaults is likely under reported.[34]

The suicide rate is likewise a blot on the services.

The suicide rate for young service members in 2020 was over

double the rate for young civilians, and higher than all other groups in the civilian population, according to the Pentagon and the Centers for Disease Control and Prevention.[35]

In September, Secretary of Defense Lloyd Austin directed actions to reduce the suicide rate, but it may not be a problem the military alone can solve. That said, it's not the news a parent wants to hear when their child says he's thinking of enlisting.[36]

But there are some problems the Pentagon can control and there it is failing.

The military has been under pressure due to the substandard condition of its privatized family housing. And to add to that, just last month, the Government Accountability Office (GAO) reported that many barracks (that house unmarried soldiers) are unsatisfactory, with broken heating and air conditioning, doors and windows that don't lock, and are infested by mold and rodents. In one macabre case, GAO was told "service members are responsible for cleaning biological waste that may remain in a barracks room after a suicide."[37]

In 2022, *Navy Times* reported that the Navy-run barracks at Walter Reed National Military Medical Center – the President's hospital – lacked hot water and air conditioning, and may rooms had no locks on the doors. One building hadn't had hot water *since 2015*. On a ship underway when the hot water goes out the Commanding Officer is immediately notified and it becomes a priority task for the ship's Engineer.[38]

While the Pentagon is supervising an all-hands effort to reduce suicides it has taken its hands off the wheel on housing for single soldiers. Why? Because it's a bureaucracy that only reacts to bad headlines and congressional pressure. Then there is the "tough it out" aspect of military culture that normalizes dysfunctional practices when everyone knows they are wrong.

GAO helpfully published a follow-on report of recommended fixes to the barracks problem, but the military shouldn't need to be told by a bunch of civilian auditors how to fix the barracks, however that's where we are today.[39]

And the military isn't just failing to satisfactorily house its troops, its failing to properly feed them, too.

In August, *Military.com* reported that at Fort Hood, Texas, only two of the ten dining halls were open and those for reduced hours. The Army blamed a shortage of military cooks, but most every dining hall uses contractor cooks, so the real cause is either bad contract administration or the service isn't paying enough to get better help.[40]

The Army scrambled to open more dining halls, but this is a service-wide issue that may be linked to a 2016 project to reduce the number of dining halls and update food delivery to the troops but efforts like this often fall of the radar when the immediate financial savings are pocketed and the leadership's attention wanders.[41]

The "woke stuff" has been blamed for the recruiting crisis and it is definitely one of the causes, but the military's inability to ensure the safety and welfare of its people will do more damage than transgender bathrooms.

There are fewer young Americans eligible to serve, due to physical fitness standards and prohibitions on drug use, and only 9% of 16-21 year old Americans have an interest in putting on the uniform.[42]

And when the Pentagon asked young Americans, "What would be the main reason(s) why you would NOT consider joining the U.S. Military?" 70% replied "Possibility of physical injury/death" and 65% replied "Possibility of PTSD or other emotional/psychological issues."

Those distressing numbers are likely due to the epidemics of suicide and sexual, and promotion of "wounded warrior" charities has probably made more prospective recruits aware of the severe injuries they may suffer. In short, is the GI Bill worth losing your legs?

And those potential recruits may be on to something: a recent report published by the Journal of the American College of Surgeons says that in a war against a near peer adversary, i.e., Russia or China, U.S. troops will suffer injuries more severe than those in Iraq or Afghanistan, that is "multiple high-velocity penetrating injuries, barotrauma, and blunt injuries from being thrown during the explosion, and traumatic brain injuries."[43]

In addition, U.S. forces won't command air superiority so evacuation from the battlefield will be difficult if it is even possible.

The U.S. Army War College recently published a study that predicts a war with China (over some chip foundries in Taiwan) will see a casualty rate of 3,600 *per day*. At that rate, the U.S. would surpass the casualties in the wars in Iraq and Afghanistan in two weeks. The college opined that it may be time to consider "a move toward partial conscription [the draft]."[44]

The military has traditionally relied on military families to provide recruits for the services, but the Secretary of the Army isn't helping matters by declaring she wants to avoid relying on a "warrior caste" of families with a military tradition. It's good that she wants to broaden interest in military service but not clever if it will discourage the ready pool of volunteers before she has alternates signed up.

However, that "warrior caste" problem may be solving itself as veterans are less and less likely to recommend military service to their kids.

We've all been told, "Live within your means."

The reluctance of young Americans to enlist is a silent vote against putting their life and limb at the disposal of the Pentagon and a national security class that is always eager for someone else's kids to fight in service of the "rules-based international order."

We saw these guys in Iraq and they later resurfaced in Afghanistan: the toadies, wranglers, and intriguers who never seem to run out of at-bats no matter how many times they strike out.

Fewer enlistees may also shape Defense Department choices and recommendations to the President.

An undermanned Pentagon may feel it must take more risk in the early stage of a conflict to make gains before casualties pile up, but a riskier strategy may cause the other side to escalate, making a negotiated resolution harder to achieve.

On the other hand, a fully-manned military may make the brass think they have the support of all Americans when it really may because of a bad economy (which always helps enlistments).

Here's a crazy idea for the Pentagon: size the force (and thus the strategy) to match the nation's willingness to provide servicemen.

Just kidding!

There is a lot the Pentagon can do to make young Americans interested in military service, but first it must:

First, it can end the military's epidemics of suicide and sexual assault, instead of hyping the nuisance of those right-wing extremists in the ranks who never showed up despite Secretary of Defense Austin's extremism "stand down" and General Milley's fascination with "white rage."

Second, they can stop lying and start learning from your mistakes. It's OK, guys; everyone knows we lost in Afghanistan.

After America's defeat in Vietnam, General Creighton Abrams, the Army Chief of Staff, boldly started the 20-year project of rebuilding the Army which was near collapse and haunted by defeat but also wracked by the social disruption of the 1960s.[45]

The U.S. Army War College has published a study of the Iraq campaign, but are the services using efforts like this to reflect, publicly acknowledge their mistakes, eliminate weak programs, and, most importantly, promote the officers who can fight the next war, not the guys who did well in the last war?[46]

Third, they can fix the housing, messing, and the other unglamorous base support functions that are less fun the buying the next major weapon system that will fail to live up to expectations, such as the Navy's Littoral Combat Ship.

The military leadership must prove it is worthy of the men and women it leads, and someday it may resemble what it aspires to be.

And the sooner it gets started the sooner it may have the military the country needs for deterrence and winning future conflicts.

HAMAS, ISRAEL'S GOLEM: THE DANGER OF WORKING WITH RELIGIOUS-INSPIRED PROXIES

November 14, 2023

By James Durso

t seemed like a good idea at the time, they said in Jerusalem on 8 October 2023.

Israel's national security leaders were caught flat-footed by the 7 October attack by Hamas launched from the Gaza Strip, and you'd have to feel sorry for the poor saps if you were willing to overlook their hubris and gross negligence.

Norman Mailer explained how it probably went down: "We all

congregated in the Director's meeting room on the seventh floor for a bit of summitry, all of us, satraps, mandarins, lords paramount, padishahs, maharajahs, grand moguls, kingfish, the lot. And we sat there...It's the only time in all these years when I saw so many brilliant, ambitious, resourceful men – just sitting there."[47]

Hamas is a Cold War creation and was founded by Sheikh Ahmed Yassin (and funded by Israel) in 1987, at the start of the First Intifada, to oppose the secular, nationalist Fatah organization, run by Yasser Arafat.[48] The group is an offshoot of the Muslim Brotherhood.

Hamas then opposed the peace efforts between Israel and the Palestine Liberation Organization, and opposed the Oslo Accords when rival Fatah renounced violence and recognized the existence of Israel as part of a two-state solution.

After 9-11, President George W. Bush, as part of his "Freedom Agenda," supported the "Road map for peace," a plan proposed by the Quartet on the Middle East (the United States, the European Union, Russia, and the United Nations).

Unfortunately, the plan deadlocked and was overshadowed by the Second Intifada. Israeli prime minister Ariel Sharon, frustrated, evacuated the Gaza Strip in 2005 and rocket attacks, which started in 1994 when the Israeli Defense Forces left most of the Strip, jumped.[49]

Bush insisted the 2006 Palestinian legislative elections go ahead and, when Hamas won, demanded it change its policies in exchange for recognition; Hamas refused. Hamas took control of Gaza from the Palestinian Authority and Fatah in 2007, and the U.S. planned a coup to remove it, but failed.[50] Instead of America's Founding Fathers, Bush channeled Turkish president Recep Tayyip Erdoğan: "Democracy is like a tram. You ride it until you arrive at your destination, then you step off."

Somewhere at Hamas HQ there is shrine to Ariel Sharon and George Bush.

According to journalist Seymour Hersh, Netanyahu made a deal with Qatar that it would fund Hamas because "Bibi was convinced that he would have more control over Hamas with the Qatari money" and "you can create a Frankenstein and keep control of it."[51] Netanyahu's plan was to divide power between the Gaza Strip and the West Bank, that was controlled by the Palestinian Authority, and "most of the time, Israeli policy was to treat the Palestinian Authority as a burden and Hamas as an asset."[52]

Qatar was the cutout, but will be hard to attack Doha as the al-Thani have the receipts and, if necessary, will disclose *everything* via Al-Jazeera which is more credible in the region (and much of the world) than any American or Israeli spokesman sputtering, "It depends on what the meaning of the word 'is' is."It was good while it lasted and, in 2019, Netanyahu put it out there: "Anyone who wants to thwart the establishment of a Palestinian state has to support bolstering Hamas and transferring money to Hamas," Netanyahu told his Likud party's Knesset members in March 2019. "This is part of our strategy."[53]

And don't just take BiBi's word for it.

Israeli historian Adam_Raz reports that Netanyahu's policy from 2009 is "on the one hand, bolstering the rule of Hamas in the Gaza Strip, and, on the other, weakening the Palestinian Authority."[54]

As a result, he turned Hamas "from a terror organization with few resources into a semi-state body." To that end, Netanyahu allowed cash deliveries by Qatari envoys to Gaza (especially important after the Palestinian Authority cut off Hamas from further funding), leaked a top-secret military report on the potential repercussions of conquering Gaza to derail the diplomatic strategy of the previous Israeli government, and "continuously thwarted all the targeted assassinations [of Hamas leaders]."

Netanyahu's strategy was similar to Iran's strategy as Tehran pays over $100 million a year to Palestinian groups, including Hamas, Palestine Islamic Jihad, and the Popular Front for the Liberation of Palestine-General Command, according to the U.S. State Department.[55]

And the Hamas charter is clear about its goals, so a violent confrontation was inevitable, despite Hamas's double-dipping.[56]

Israel should have learned from America's experience with the Afghan *mujaheddin* where a useful, well-funded vessel turned on its creator.

When the Red Army invaded Afghanistan on 24 December 1979, Zbigniew Brzezinski, the U.S. national security advisor, saw a chance to weaken the Soviet Union. In fact, on 3 July 1979 – five months before the Soviets intervened – President Carter authorized secret aid to the opponents of the pro-Soviet regime in Kabul.[57] That day, according to Brzezinski, "I wrote a note to the president in which I explained to him that in my opinion this aid was going to induce a Soviet military intervention."

In December, he got his wish and on the day of the Soviet attack, Brzezinski wrote to Carter, "We now have the opportunity of giving to the USSR its Vietnam war."

The war in Afghanistan ended on 15 February 1989 when the final Soviet forces withdrew across the Friendship Bridge into Soviet Central Asia. On 26 December 1991, the Soviet Union dissolved and Brzezinski, a son of the Polish aristocracy, had his revenge on the Reds.

The true cost of Brzezinski's adventure was 14,453 dead and over 53,753 wounded Soviets, and at least 800,000 dead, about 2 million wounded or disabled Afghans. 5 million Afghans (one-third of the prewar population of the country) fled to Pakistan and Iran.[58]

The U.S. and its allies were left to deal with the economic and social impact of the war, worsened by Western sanctions, when they invaded after the 9-11 attacks and started the unsuccessful twenty-year reconstruction project that, at its heart, was about reforming Pashtun culture to Western standards.

In 1998, Brzezinski declared, "What is most important to the history of the world? The Taliban or the collapse of the Soviet empire? Some stirred-up Moslems or the liberation of Central Europe and the end of the cold war?"

The Soviet Union probably would have probably collapsed from its internal contradictions in a few years, anyway, and a few more years of economic stagnation in the USSR and satellites might have been worth it if it meant Osama bin Laden would only be known as the pious son of a Saudi construction magnate.

And those stirred-up Moslems are still a problem, especially for the Moslems of the non-stirred-up persuasion.

And after the Soviets left Afghanistan, the U.S. ignored the country, leaving Pakistan to create a settlement. Pakistan did so by helping the Taliban, former *mujahideen* that emerged in the early 1990s, to seize control of the country. In 1996, former *mujahid* bin Laden fled from Sudan to Afghanistan where he was welcomed by the Taliban.

So here we are: America's bad choice in 1979 to support the *mujahideen* bit it twice – on 9-11, and on 15 August 2021 when the U.S. and its NATO were routed in Kabul. Israel's bad choice of 1987 bit it on 7 October 2023 when Hamas attacked Israel, and is also biting the U.S.

The U.S. is staring at a string of strategic losses: the 2021 NATO defeat in Afghanistan; the stalemated NATO-Russia war in Ukraine, that will probably end in a negotiated settlement in 2024 in Russia's favor; and a "defeat by association" with Israel as the televised razing of the Gaza Strip is viewed negatively by most of the world, resulting in protest marches and recalls of ambassadors from Jerusalem.

Though U.S. president Joe Biden says "We will continue to have Israel's back," the U.S. is looking increasingly isolated as it was one of only 14 nations that voted against a United Nations General Assembly (UNGA) resolution calling "for an immediate ceasefire in Gaza, the release of all civilians, the protection of civilians and international institutions, and ensuring the safe passage of humanitarian aid into the [Gaza] Strip."[59]

The vote in the UNGA came after the U.S. vetoed two Security Council resolutions on the humanitarian situation in Gaza as they failed, it said, to affirm Israel's right to self-defense.

U.S. Secretary of State Antony Blinken was recently admonished by Middle East leaders that Washington's acceptance of Israeli attacks on refugee camps, hospitals and apartment buildings "could shatter American influence for years to come."[60]

And China and Russia could not be happier; their diplomats are no doubt reminding all and sundry that American weapons are killing innocent Palestinians, while they marvel at how easy their jobs have become.

And the Global South was always with the Palestinians as they think Israel is Britain's colonial project to settle Europeans in the Muslim Middle East. It's not about anti-Semitism, but long experience at the sharp end of the West's *mission civilisatrice,* and Israel's history of friendly relations with the South African *apartheid* regime.[61]

And U.S. diplomats are sounding the alarm in interval channels that America's policies will isolate the U.S. from the Arab and Muslim worlds, which may make for a less cohesive response to rapidly unfolding events in the region, and dilute Washington's ability to rally opposition to Russia and China, the latter being the leading trade partner of much of the world.[62]

Winston Churchill said, "You can always count on the Americans to do the right thing, after they have exhausted all the other possibilities."

It has been a long, expensive lesson for America, but hopefully the political level will finally absorb the lesson that the bill for its decision to use a religious militia to push over a faltering Soviet Union came due on 9-11, when 2,977 Americans were killed, and on 21 August 2021, when American power was publicly humiliated by that same militia.

And Washington needs to stop deferring to local judgement and start giving some orders to ensure its allies in Jerusalem never again do something as stupid as supporting their sworn enemies, hoping they really don't mean what they say.

---

1. https://georgewbush-whitehouse.archives.gov/infocus/freedomagenda/
2. https://www.theguardian.com/world/2001/oct/14/afghanistan.terrorism5.
3. https://www.theguardian.com/world/2001/nov/05/afghanistan.terrorism3 and https://www.theguardian.com/world/2001/oct/17/afghanistan.terrorism3.
4. https://www.washingtonpost.com/politics/2020/01/03/when-united-states-qasem-soleimani-worked-together/
5. https://www.brookings.edu/articles/russias-draft-agreements-with-nato-and-the-united-states-intended-for-rejection/
6. https://edition.cnn.com/2022/11/05/middleeast/iran-drones-russia-intl/index.html and https://www.forbes.com/sites/pauliddon/2023/01/22/beyond-su-35s-the-russian-helicopters-and-missile-systems-iran-might-soon-acquire/?sh=1318457c4465.
7. https://www.reuters.com/world/china/china-says-political-trust-with-russia-has-deepened-after-envoys-visit-2023-02-04/ and https://www.msn.com/en-us/news/world/russia-is-aiming-for-200-billion-of-trade-with-china-as-it-backs-no-limits-partnership-with-beijing/ar-AA16X7xV.
8. https://watson.brown.edu/costsofwar/files/cow/imce/papers/2021/Costs%20of%20War_U.S.%20Budgetary%20Costs%20of%20Post-9%2011%20Wars_9.1.21.pdf.
9. https://data.worldbank.org/indicator/NY.GDP.MKTP.CD?locations=CN.
10. https://www.atlanticcouncil.org/in-depth-research-reports/report/implementing-natos-strategic-concept-on-china/
11. https://www.youtube.com/watch?v=58uQZJfQIJQ.

12. https://english.almayadeen.net/news/politics/kremlin-denies-claims-that-cia-chief-offered-russia-20-of-uk.

13. https://thehill.com/homenews/senate/3924590-gop-senators-introduce-bill-designating-mexican-drug-cartels-as-terror-organizations/

14. https://crenshaw.house.gov/2023/1/reps-crenshaw-and-waltz-introduce-aumf-targeting-mexican-drug-cartels.

15. https://www.borderlandbeat.com/2023/05/us-reserve-troops-being-sent-to.html.

16. https://eu.usatoday.com/story/news/nation/2023/04/16/mexican-drug-cartels-terrorist-organizations-senators-fentanyl-mexico-border/11666432002/

17. https://www.zerohedge.com/medical/fentanyl-overdose-deaths-skyrocket-279-2016-amid-nationwide-drug-crisis.

18. https://www.pewtrusts.org/en/research-and-analysis/data-visualizations/2021/the-high-price-of-the-opioid-crisis-2021.

19. https://www.samhsa.gov/data/sites/default/files/reports/rpt35325/NSDUHFFRPDFWHTMLFiles2020/2020NSDUHFFR1PDFW102121.pdf/

20. https://www.rand.org/news/press/2019/08/20.html.

21. https://www.unodc.org/documents/crop-monitoring/Afghanistan/Opium_cultivation_Afghanistan_2022.pdf.

22. https://www.borderlandbeat.com/2015/05/jalisco-cjng-used-rpg-to-bring-down.html.

23. https://www.cfr.org/backgrounder/mexicos-long-war-drugs-crime-and-cartels.

24. https://www.npr.org/2023/02/21/1158300583/fentanyl-smuggling-border-mexico-overdose-drug-war.

25. https://www.ndb.int/

26. https://www.military.com/daily-news/2019/03/21/top-marine-border-missions-storm-damage-causing-unacceptable-readiness-risk.html.

27. https://sldinfo.com/2017/01/taiwan-in-pacific-defense-turning-a-new-page/

28. https://apnews.com/article/taiwan-us-defense-contractors-56701cc96df33999d1a6b6f524086f47.

29. https://www.economist.com/international/2023/08/22/reassessing-barack-obamas-red-line-in-syria

30. https://www.ncbi.nlm.nih.gov/pmc/articles/PMC10344429/.

31. https://nypost.com/2023/09/07/military-faces-recruitment-crisis-as-unpatriotic-gen-z-fails-to-join-up/

32. https://news.gallup.com/poll/394283/confidence-institutions-down-average-new-low.aspx.

33. https://www.sapr.mil/

34. https://news.usni.org/2022/09/01/latest-military-sexual-assault-report-shows-tragic-rise-in-cases-pentagon-officials-say.

35. https://taskandpurpose.com/news/military-suicide-double-rate-civilians/

36. https://www.hstoday.us/subject-matter-areas/mental-health-resilience/dod-announces-new-actions-to-prevent-suicide-in-the-military/

37. https://www.gao.gov/assets/gao-23-105797.pdf.

38. https://www.navytimes.com/news/your-navy/2022/02/09/hellish-walter-reed-base-barracks-now-in-congress-sights/

39. https://www.gao.gov/products/gao-23-107038.

40. https://www.military.com/daily-news/2023/08/08/fort-cavazos-soldiers-have-been-without-proper-access-food-months.html.

41. https://www.armytimes.com/news/your-army/2016/02/08/army-1-in-3-dining-facilities-will-close-or-shrink-within-three-years/

42. https://jamrs.defense.gov/Portals/20/Documents/YP54Fall2022PUBLICRELEASE PropensityUpdate_20230713_v1.pdf.

43. https://www.ncbi.nlm.nih.gov/pmc/articles/PMC10344429/

44. https://press.armywarcollege.edu/cgi/viewcontent.cgi?article=3240&context=parameters.

45. http://armedforcesjournal.com/rebuilding-the-army-again/

46. https://press.armywarcollege.edu/monographs/386/.

47. https://archive.org/details/harlotsghost00mail_0

48. https://theintercept.com/2018/02/19/hamas-israel-palestine-conflict/.

49. https://www.israelhayom.com/2023/10/15/912423/.

50. https://www.theguardian.com/world/2008/mar/04/usa.israelandthepalestinians.

51. https://www.theinteldrop.org/2023/10/13/netanyahu-is-finished-seymour-hersh/.

52. https://www.france24.com/en/middle-east/20231014-qatar-iran-turkey-and-beyond-the-galaxy-of-hamas-supporters.

53. https://twitter.com/haaretzcom/status/1711329340804186619.

54. https://www.haaretz.com/israel-news/2023-10-20/ty-article-opinion/.premium/a-brief-history-of-the-netanyahu-hamas-alliance/0000018b-47d9-d242-abef-57ff1be90000?v=1699735825749.

55. https://www.state.gov/reports/country-reports-on-terrorism-2020/.

56. https://www.middleeasteye.net/news/hamas-2017-document-full.

57. https://www.counterpunch.org/1998/01/15/how-jimmy-carter-and-i-started-the-mujahideen/

58. https://en.wikipedia.org/wiki/Soviet%E2%80%93Afghan_War#Impact.

59. https://www.cnn.com/middleeast/live-news/israel-news-hamas-war-10-18-23/h_44fe066c239c32a2ec4fdf7cf08cbb97.

60. https://www.msn.com/en-us/news/world/u-s-is-warned-about-its-global-standing-as-gaza-suffering-persists/ar-AA1jLrSX?ocid=NL_ENUS_A1_00010101_1_1.

61. https://imeu.org/article/an-overview-apartheid-south-africa-israel.

62. https://www.politico.com/news/2023/11/06/u-s-diplomats-slam-israel-policy-in-leaked-memo-00125538.

❀ 3 ❀

COMMANDER'S PERSPECTIVES ON SHAPING A WAY AHEAD

THE PERSPECTIVE OF THE U.S. NAVY AIR BOSS

January 18, 2023

Recently I visited San Diego and had chance to discuss with Vice Admiral Whitesell the work the Navy is doing in terms of introducing new capabilities and training for high-end operations.

The Navy is introducing new capabilities onboard the large deck carriers, focusing on new concepts of operations captured in part by the notion of distributed operations and are working new ways to train for high-end operations.

We discussed all of these themes during our meeting in his office on January 4, 2023. I had last visited that office when Vice Admiral Miller was the Air Boss and we discussed during my meetings with him the process of change as the air wing of the future or as I prefer to call it the shaping of the integratable air wing comes to the large deck carrier and does so as the Navy is working new ways to integrate fleet, joint and coalition operations.

When I was last there, Vice Admiral Miller discussed the coming of the first package of capabilities associated with the new air wing coming to the USS Carl Vinson. Now it has done so along with the USS Abraham Lincoln. This is where we started the conversation.

Whitesell underscored that when he came aboard, they were preparing to deploy the F-35C, the CMV-22B and the Advanced Hawkeye as a new package on board the Vinson and then the Lincoln. This meant that the first steps towards integration of the new capabilities onboard the carrier and then working with the fleet was the first task.

These initial operations are always a learning process, but it was one where the early findings were significant with regard to ramping up the operational capabilities for the carrier and the fleet.

The advanced sensing and targeting capabilities of the F-35 (along with its ability to work across a joint F-35 force), the advanced C2 capabilities of advanced Hawkeye (which can seamlessly connect with other naval, joint and coalition assets to have an enhanced ability for the carrier force to work in an extended battlespace) and the CMV-22 (with its ability to operate beyond simple point to point logistics and to support contested logistics ops) are significant expanders of fleet operations.

And has been noted by a number of F-35 operators, the aircraft makes the other strike aircraft more lethal and survivable. This is true not just for the evolving Super Hornets, but the Growlers as well. He noted that "the Growler when operating with the F-35 creates some incredible synergistic capabilities."

With the deployment of the new "module" of air wing capability comes a new approach to training as well. The capabilities unleashed by fifth generation aircraft lead to the need to train in a way that the blue side needs to understand how to master advanced tactics without letting the adversary see this capability. The introduction of live virtual constructive (LVC) training is a keyway to do so.

Vice Admiral Whitesell noted that a LVC terminal was onboard the Lincoln which allowed for such training at sea. Of course, Naval Aviation Warfighting Development Center (NAWDC) with its enhanced training facilities is leading the way in terms of LVC training for the Navy. He described his own experience at Navy Air Station Whidbey, where he flew a Growler in a LVC training event.

"I was up in Growler about six months ago, flying a high-end event with another aircraft. We were just two aircraft, but on the display and with the weapons we had simulated on the aircraft, we simulated flying in a high-end fight. The sweat pumps get running. You're running a high-end scenario with multiple Red and Blue assets engaged."

He underscored that at NAWDC, the training along these lines have added a week to the basic training scenario which enables enhanced high-end training. The USAF is now fully engaged with NAWDC in the last week module of what used to be a four-week syllabus but now is a five-week module.

Vice Admiral Whitesell added that the F-35 pilots through their basic training are already understanding training for the high-end threat. As he commented: "The level of training and the skill of the kids nowadays means they can handle high end training early on. We're just taking it to another level."

He underscored as well that during his time at U.S. Pacific Fleet, just prior to taking his current job, there has been a major shift in USAF and U.S. Navy joint operational cooperation and integration.

"We train now with the Air Force at NAWDC, and we run long range maritime strike missions together. That's why that extra week was added on to the NAWDC syllabus. They are working on joint long range maritime strikes against the priority targets that an Indo-PACOM has assigned us."

We then discussed the coming of the CMV-22 to the carrier air wing. When I was last at NAWDC, I asked about where the new aircraft fit into the curriculum.

The answer was: they were not sure for the C2A Greyhound was a point-to-point logistical delivery system. The CMV-22B is not – it can operate with significant flexibility and as a kill web support capability and thereby can expand the Navy's development of distributed operations.

I asked the Vice Admiral about how the Navy was now addressing the arrival of this new aircraft to the fleet. He emphasized that the baptism of the CMV-22B in its first two deployments, the first aboard Vinson and the second aboard Lincoln, allowed the Navy to certify that it was "going to be a successful maritime aircraft and to execute the COD mission."

But now the kid gloves were off. "What is our concept of employment for this aircraft? To answer this question will require a mindset change within naval aviation and the COD community. The expeditionary nature of the CMV-22B expands the possibilities for successful distributed maritime operations and we are determined to get full value out of the aircraft in terms of its synergy with con-ops evolutions for the fleet."

He added: "Under distributed operations, the carrier strike group is deployed differently. We are shaping a completely different way of thinking about that and the CMV-22B can be used is part of that mindset change."

Vice Admiral Whitesell assured me that when I would go back to NAWDC, I would get a very different response to my question of where the CMV-22B fit into the syllabus. "They are looking at how you would use the CMV-22B, notably in the Western Pacific. The CMV-22B is an all-weather, day and night aircraft that doesn't need a runway. How can we best utilize such an aircraft as we work contested logistics? And does how does it empower the way ahead for distributed maritime operations?"

My own sense is that the fighting Navy is focused on distributed operations as an operational experiment and are working to shape different ways to work the problem of prevailing in the expanded battlespace with both enhanced lethality and survivability.

Vice Admiral Whitesell concluded: "We are in an experimentation phase. We are working force distribution and integration. We are experimenting like Nimitz did in the inter-war years. We are working from seabed to space with regard to force integration. It is a work in progress. But being successful in operating in an environment where logistics are contested, where getting weapons to the fleet in conflict, is not just a nice to have capability but a necessary one."

THE PERSPECTIVE OF LTGEN BRIAN CAVANAUGH

March 8, 2023

I had a chance to meet with LtGen Brian Cavanaugh at his office in Norfolk on Friday February 24, 2023. He is Commanding General, Fleet Marine Force, Atlantic; Commander, Marine Forces Command; and Commander, Marine Forces Northern Command.

As LtGen Cavanaugh has spent many years in the Pacific, he comes to the Atlantic area in a period of change and under the impact of the war in Ukraine. He argued that the Marines are in a process of transformation which can be understood as one affecting all of the joint forces.

As he put it: "The joint forces have acquired their equipment and training in the past twenty hears focused on a capability, not necessarily specific threats. This clearly has changed as we recognize specific threats to which we need to modernize equipment and train our forces."

"The joint forces have acquired their equipment and training in the past twenty hears focused on a capability, not necessarily a specific threat. This clearly has changed as we recognize specific threats to which we need to modernize equipment and train our forces."

The updated National Defense Strategy and National Security Strategy undoubtedly identify the primary threat from the People's Republic of China and the CCP. The Corps has taken this task head on as evident in the Commandant's Planning Guidance and the past few years of Force Design.

However, from his seat on the Atlantic coast, where his headquarters sits abreast the Navy's U.S. Fleet Forces Command, Cavanaugh explains the Corps' support to National Defense is more than just a focus on the Pacific.

"We know the PRC is operating globally and competes with the U.S. and our allies across all domains. The Corps, and the greater Naval force, is looking at how we address security issues globally," said Cavanaugh.

His command is co-located with U.S. Fleet Forces Command, and he works closely with this command to support the Marine Corps'

Naval Integration efforts. Cavanaugh emphasized that they are working together to meet the evolving threat envelope facing U.S. and allied forces.

The Marines are the smallest of the joint forces but are very adaptable. Cavanaugh is focused on transitioning advanced Marine Corps capabilities and joint concepts to enable the Navy and the joint force to meet these emerging challenges across all global regions.

He argued that the current command structures along geographical lines needs to adapt as technology and our Nation's threats do not subscribe to those geographical boundaries. The Marines are working to re-shape and re-define how they tailor their forces to work the defense problems posed by the newly evolving threat envelopes.

Cavanaugh explained that concepts like Expeditionary Advanced Base Operations and Littoral Operations in a Contested Environment address global security threats in support of Fleets and Combatant Commands.

"We are focused on shaping different ways to use our tools to adapt various force packages to get the desired joint effect. In my discussions with fleet commanders, I focus on our complimentary capabilities. Marines can provide fires and sustainment in the broader Naval campaign.

"The Corps provides commanders across the globe with expeditionary, joint force enabling capabilities. Our air, land, and sea capabilities facilitate integration with our fellow services and allies. That's why we train and equip to enable the operations of the broader Joint Force, our allies and partners, and the NATO construct."

As I have argued in my book on USMC transformation, the Marines are in the process of transformation from the land wars to shaping a more mobile force, one that can provide tailored force to provide payloads designed to deliver the kind of effect desired by the joint commander.

In an interview I did recently with Colonel Marvel, the CO of MAG-39, he described how his command was working the evolution along these lines.

As he commented: "The Osprey provides unique speed and range combinations with an aircraft which can land vertically. It is a very flexible aircraft which could be described as a mission-kitable aircraft. The Osprey has big hollow space in the rear of the aircraft that can hold a variety of mission kits dependent on the mission which you want the aircraft to support."

I discussed with LtGen Cavanaugh a similar process which the latest USMC aviation asset, the CH-53K, is bringing to the East Coast Marines. Cavanaugh has many operational hours in the legacy aircraft the CH-53D/E. He spoke about how he saw the new aircraft operating in the dynamic context he described for the Marines, the Navy, and the joint force.

He argued that the CH-53K is very different from the legacy aircraft in terms of physical attributes of lift capacity and ease of flight operations. But it is a digital aircraft which he anticipates will be part of the overall transition of the USMC in providing tailorable capability to the joint force.

This is how he put it: "Because it is a digitally enabled aircraft, the CH-53K can both operate within the mesh network as user and provider. It's a part of a broader interoperable kill web. It can pass data to other parts of the kill web to enable the joint sensor-shooter relationship.

"I can see the CH-53K as leading with UASs in a mesh web and passing data to an Aegis ship to provide information enabling Aegis operations. It is not just a muscle platform. It is part of the digital interoperability revolution affecting our platforms and allowing them to be part of a joint kill web."

We discussed the importance of the process of Northern European integration and the opportunities this opens up for the Marine Corps as part of naval integration in support of the region and of the innovations of our Nordic allies.

The East Coast Marines will receive the CH-53K first among Marine Corps forces and bringing them into the Northern European area of operation while our allies are shaping new con-ops means that Marines can work with that new aircraft to shape its own path of innovation along with our allies as well.

This type of win-win integration is what LtGen Cavanaugh is focused upon.

THE PERSPECTIVE OF AIR MARSHAL CHIPMAN, RAAF

April 1, 2023

The Sir Richard Williams Foundation Seminar held on March 30, 2023 focused on the next phase of ADF and Australian defense development from a whole of government and society perspective.

How can Australia as a middle power deter a major power like China from the use of force against Australia and to undercut Australian interests and way of life?

This is a challenging question to pose as the world is changing significantly in the post-pandemic world and with it the evolution of the relationship among authoritarian powers and the dynamics of change within the liberal democratic allies of Australia as well. The technologies of war are in the process of significant change although the basics of war and conflict persist.

At the seminar, Air Marshal Chipman provided his perspective on how the ADF and the RAAF will evolve with the deterrent challenge in the evolving context. His focus was upon deterrence from the perspective of a middle power and its ability to deliver a deterrent effect.

At one point in his presentation, he highlighted a way to understand deterrence. "ADM Harry Harris, the former Commander of INDOPACOM, explained deterrence with a simple mathematical equation: deterrence = capability * resolve * signalling. If anyone of these is zero, then the product, deterrence, is zero! Resolve and signalling are orchestrated through diplomacy, but they are underpinned by military capability.

"We influence the calculus of our potential adversaries in all that we do. Force generation is not just the act of preparing for war, it also signals our preparedness for war, and therefore serves to deter it. We should think strategically about our force generation signalling."

If we examine these three aspects – capability, resolve and signalling, we can look at Chipman's presentation in terms of how he dealt with each of these elements of deterrence.

Capability

The question of capability must be determined in relationship to whom you are trying to deter. Given the growing capability of our authoritarian adversaries for precision strike and magazine depth, we have focused on greater ability to disperse or disaggregate force and to work ways to integrate the effects which a distributed force can deliver even though distributed. This is what I have underscored as the shaping of a kill web force.

Chipman emphasized in his presentation several aspects of this trajectory of change. "We are also sharpening our deterrence capability by strengthening our resilience to military coercion and intimidation. A resilient Middle Power will minimise the consequences of adversary actions, through passive measures such as hardening, deception and dispersal.

"And by refining our agile fighting concepts to manoeuvre across our network of northern bases, through all domains; complicating and obscuring the adversaries' targeting options.

"Active measures that protect critical infrastructure and vulnerable supply lines, that strengthen our national resilience, will also help convince potential adversaries of the futility of their action."

Working air assets with ground and sea assets to deliver a combined effect, often referred to as multi-domain effects, is a key focus of attention for the RAAF as well. As Chipman put it: "We have successfully transitioned to the F-35, with its world-leading ability to achieve surprise, gain access, sense and share targetable data, and deliver lethal effects both in offence and in defence.

"Integrated with the Super Hornet, Growler and E-7A Wedgetail, our air combat team is formidable. And they're ready. We test them regularly, through exercises such as TASMAN SHIELD, which recently teamed our full air combat system with two Air Warfare Destroyers to practice high-end, integrated, multi-domain warfare."

"We are investing in long-range weapon systems, capable of striking well-defended warships on the move at great range from Australia. This will be an important complement to our maritime and land forces. Together, we'll present a complex, integrated, multi-domain challenge for potential adversaries to penetrate."

This trajectory of change has taken a decade to achieve. In January 2012, I published an article in *The Proceedings* entitled "The Long Reach of Aegis" which projected how the F-35 and Aegis destroyers could create the kind of combat effect Chipman talked about. It was not exactly a best seller at the time.[1]

Resolve

With regard to resolve, the challenge is for deterrence to be a whole of government and whole of society effort. This is hard, particularly after the land wars which have largely been experienced as a boutique military engagement.

This will require taking serious looks and change with regard to economic and cultural relationships with China, sharpening realistic energy policies, shaping cyber and information resilience at home, and other macro-economic changes far beyond the ability of the ADF to generate.

Chipman did not speak to these aspects of resolve in any depth but focused on what resolve meant in terms of the ADF itself. Chipman spoke to the general issues of resolve in these terms: "it is also in our strategic culture to stand defiant when subject to coercion or intimidation. There is a role for deterrence here, through our readiness, resilience, and the resourcefulness of our people.

"We generate combat power, integrated across domains, in pursuit of our national objectives, for the purpose of preventing conflict. But we remain resolute to act if our deterrence strategy fails."

As Air Marshal Chipman put it: "Our capability and willingness to stand alongside allies and likeminded partners – with combined diplomatic and military weight. Our readiness to act in unison, with political and strategic alignment underpinned by technical, procedural, and human interoperability. The threat of responding as an alliance will exacerbate a fear to attack and strengthen our deterrence capability."

Chipman went on to enhance those comments: "It is surely the central pillar of a Middle Power deterrence strategy – to operate in concert with allies and partners in pursuit of common interests. To deter other nations from acting against those interests by presenting strength in numbers, wherever and whenever that is demanded of us. This is not about surrendering sovereignty, but rather sharing it among trusted allies and partners – to advance our national interest. This is the experience of our alliance relationship with the United States for over 70 years.

"But of course, this strategy extends beyond the United States. Through training, education, key leadership engagement, development assistance and crisis response. Building partner capacity, strengthening our partner's sovereignty will help inoculate our region from the predations of others."

Signalling

Now let us turn to signalling. This is key aspect of deterrence but a neglected one during the land wars. It is a forgotten art. In the 1980s, much of my work in Europe and with the Russians during the Euromissile crisis and then the run up to what would become the unification of Germany was in the domain of communication and signalling. We only avoided nuclear war in 1983 by activating communication and signaling networks.

How are we going to do that today? How do we do so with the Chinese? The Russians? The North Koreans? All three are Pacific powers and will shape the play of conflict in the region.

Air Marshal Chipman in his presentation focused on the central significance of thinking through how the adversary might think in a crisis and to calibrate our messages to do so. Messaging obviously comes through actions as well as words, but both are important.

This is how he put it: "Imagine you're leader of one of the most powerful nations on earth – with deep financial resources, extraordinary industrial capacity and an impressive military capability. Power, prosperity, longevity pull on all three strings of Thucydides famous triptych – fear, honour, interest.

"From your vantage point, advantage is easily accrued or coerced. What cannot be coerced can ultimately be compelled. What has long been coveted can now be imagined and may even be within your reach.

"How might your ambitions be deterred? What might make you fear to attack?

"A rational leader might start with a cost-benefit judgement. Relative interest and relative power are the core ingredients that will shape this judgement.

"How important is this interest? Is it a core interest or peripheral to your national objectives? How do your interests intersect the interests of others? How determined, committed, or desperate will they be to defend them?

"What is your military advantage – in technical and numerical terms; your strategic reserve and capacity to absorb counter actions; what about your experience, resolve, fighting spirit.

"Is your force as capable as you believe it to be? Recent expeditions in Europe might give pause to ponder.

"Is your adversary concealing strengths? Will they escalate in ways you can't anticipate? Will they mobilise allies and partners against you?

"These uncertainties will play on your judgement in a military sense, as will relative economic power and international legitimacy. The potential these challenges might present across all operational domains and elements of national power simultaneously, must in itself influence your thinking.

"Surely, for a rational actor, doubt lingers...How might you control your destiny if you choose a path of uncertainty?"

He concluded his presentation with some general observations about what one might call "the practice" of deterrence or what I would call the ability to operate your military force within the general context of the art of statecraft, which in my view seems a lost art but one which we need to recover and to build a credible version for the global order we are living through rather than some kind of net zero utopia.

"Let me finish on a cautionary note. I mentioned earlier that deterrence works on the threat of escalation. But we must be clear, as a Middle Power, this must stop short of actually provoking conflict. Deterrence fails at the point conflict begins.

"Strategic competition is dynamic and unstable: peripheral interests might become core over time. For a deterrence strategy to succeed through a prolonged period of strategic competition, we must also build pathways for de-escalation. This is as important in force design and force posture as it is to campaign design. The capabilities we invest in, where we stage them and how we intend to use them.

"De-escalation pathways restore the pre-crisis or pre-conflict balance of power. Seizing a diplomatic off-ramp too early may cede advantage; too late will cause unnecessary attrition. Our successful deterrence strategy will need to consider escalation and de-escalation in equal measure.

"So let me conclude. Our Middle Power deterrence capability is fixed by relative interest and relative power dynamics. Where a potential adversary's core interests are at stake, deterrence requires strength, and strength comes in numbers. It is axiomatic of Australia's strategic culture, that we seek to work with allies and partners in defence of our common interests, and this will endure."

"Which takes us back once again to the mind of our potential adversaries. To ensure they understand our core interests, and interpret our signals accurately, so that we might compete, deter and de-escalate without provoking conflict."

A FOLLOW-UP INTERVIEW WITH AIR MARSHAL CHIPMAN

April 4, 2023

I have known Air Marshal Chipman since he was the first co-chair of Plan Jericho. My first interview with him was with his co-chair Jake Campbell, now of Northrop Grumman. In that first interview conducted in their offices in 2015, the emphasis was taking the coming of the F-35 as a forcing function of the joint force to create what was identified in later seminars as a fifth generation enabled force.

"In effect, the blending of strike with situational awareness within a distributed C2 environment is one of the key targets of the Plan Jericho effort. And reshaping the template for operations in light of the coming of the F-35 makes sense as a C2/ISR fighter comes into the force, playing a catalytic role for further change, notably in a force which is being reconfigured to a more effective 21st century combat force."

Now as Chief of the RAAF, the challenge is to reap the advantages of that transition to deal with new strategic situation facing Australia and its allies and to build effective short to midterm change for the ADF with its allies but in way that would lead to successful deterrence in the long term. Much like the original focus of Plan Jericho was to work on the foundation of change, that challenge remains central for the RAAF.

After his participation in the Williams seminar on the future paths of deterrence, I had a chance to sit down with Air Marshal Chipman in his office to expand on his views about the challenges and the way ahead for his air force and the ADF.

I started by raising the point that the other air force commander who spoke at the seminar was General Wilsbach, the U.S. Pacific Air Force Commander. I noted that General Wilsbach has come to several Williams Foundation Conferences, the first being when he was 11th Air Force Commander.

His interest in working with Australia is suggestive of the evolving U.S. relationship with the ADF and in particular the RAAF relationship with PACAF. It is not widely known that General Wilsbach has an Australian Deputy Commander, which is more than a symbolic gesture, but one which reflects more than simply working exercise interoperability.

Air Marshal Chipman: "General Wilsbach has been a fantastic partner for Australia. He has been interested in our evolution and commits a lot of his time and his intellectual firepower to working with us. He has created a position for an Australian Deputy Commander in his headquarters. We are very fortunate to have someone who recognizes the value of our strategic partnership."

It also important to respect differences in terms of allied cultures and objectives in crisis situations. I wrote an essay in my new book *Defense XXII* precisely on the question of recognizing differences and working relationships among the AUKUS partners, for example.

Air Marshal Chipman prior to becoming air chief had some experience in Europe working with various allies and organizations and brings that experience to his current job.

He noted: "In terms of our relationship with PACAF, for example, we need to understand what his ambitions are, what his needs are and how we partner to support him. At the same, we need to both understand and convey our requirements for independent operations as well. We need to be clear what part of our defense effort is focused on supporting the alliance and what part is prioritizing sovereign capability."

Alliance relationships are best understood as overlapping circles in a Venn diagram dynamically evolving in shaping capabilities and commitments, rather than being cast simply in historical terms.

I then turned to the F-35 and the question of moving beyond simple interoperability. The promise of the F-35 as an international program has been to operate as a forcing function for a kind of interoperability which we have not seen before. But this promise has not been fully realized. I asked the Air Marshal for his thoughts on this challenge.

Air Marshal Chipman: "The F-35 enterprise has the potential to be a forcing function for working together much more closely and effectively. The common threats we are facing are driving us to work more closely together. We will be incrementally disadvantaged over time if we are not. If the F-35 does play a forcing function, we will see this in our ability to provide collective logistics support and operate the aircraft as a common fleet."

The coalition aspect is crucial for the ADF. But Chipman emphasized that such cooperation was crucial in deterring the big conflict but will not eliminate the need to manage the spectrum of conflict. To operate across the spectrum of conflict requires capabilities across that spectrum to deal with different conflict or crisis situations.

This is how Air Marshal Chipman put it: "As I highlighted in my presentation last week at the Williams Foundation Seminar, there is strength in numbers to deter the worst possible outcome, but such an approach will not by itself prevent smaller scale coercion. We have to be prepared as a middle power to deal with actions from the adversary that will not trigger a broader alliance response, but nonetheless are important to us."

I then turned to the question of what are his priorities for the short to mid-term?

Air Marshal Chipman: "My three key priorities are readiness, resilience, and resourcefulness. We are shifting our focus from delivering new capabilities through a 10-year acquisition cycle, to integrating the capability we have in service today, to deter actions here and now.

"I have to fight with what I have, and that is as much about tactics, techniques, and procedures that we employ as it is about the equipment we buy now. Air Force is in a relatively good position. We have bought good equipment for 20 years, so it is not as if we are starting at a position of significant disadvantage. We now have to make sure we can employ what have, and what we might add, optimally at any moment."

A key aspect of the evolving alliance situation in facing the China challenge is how the core allies Japan, Australia and the United States actually will craft more effective use of the air, maritime and land baes they use over the Pacific thought of as an extended operational space.

If the three countries can work creatively land basing, with seabasing, with air basing with the use of new autonomous systems they can field and evolve an effective force for the long game of competition with China. Certainly, from this perspective, I would view Australia is the strategic reserve of the broader alliance.

As Chipman commented: "I haven't heard it described that way. But I think that's what we are working towards. I think that's the mindset that we have. The idea that Australia provides strategic depth for forces moving forward, is absolutely part of our thinking."

He underscored that an alliance that could take advantage of the multiple basing solutions which I highlighted, noting that would take "distributed logistics to the next level, where we need to be."

THE PERSPECTIVE OF GENERAL WILSBACH, THE PACAF COMMANDER

April 6, 2023

At the 30 March 2023 Williams Foundation seminar which focused on the way ahead for deterrence, one of the most significant of the presentations was General Wilsbach, the PACAF commander. He has come to various Williams seminars since he was the 11th USAF Commander.

At this seminar, General Wilsbach's focus was on integrated deterrence. He discussed the concept by first examining at how he looked about both concepts and how they then came together into a single construct.

"First, let's look at integration. It's useful to sort integration into three tranches: military, interagency, and across Allies and Partners. The military tranche is likely the best understood as we have made tremendous strides towards joint integration in the past few decades. The key to joint integration is command and control. C2 is what separates a professional fighting force from an armed mob.

"The ability to clearly communicate intent and relevant information undergirds armed conflict, and those who have failed in that task have paid in lives. Within INDOPACOM, we recognize the need to enhance our C2.

"What worked in Iraq and Afghanistan is not sufficient for this time or this region and we must adjust accordingly. To that end, we are iterating on a Joint Fires Network that leverages current capabilities while we procure new capabilities designed to flatten network architecture and get data where it needs to go, when it needs to be there.

"This network leverages the best practices and equipment on-hand today to link INDOPACOM together and has created an environment more joint than any I have seen in my 37 years of service. Crucially, it leans on starting our planning process with the joint perspective. PACAF Airmen routinely operate with Sailors at sea, Soldiers on the ground, Marines in the air, and Guardians managing orbital assets— often all at once.

"Here in Australia, you have demonstrated your commitment to joint operations through your Joint Training System and collocating your service joint force contributions under the Chief of Joint Operations. This naturally leads to the main benefit of joint integration— joint fires.

"Each service brings unique capabilities to the fight, and that means that F-35s may not be the best shooter for a target. Maybe a submarine would be a better solution, or an island-hopping Marine force with short-range coastal cruise missiles, or an Army hypersonic artillery battalion far back from the front lines. The point is that it doesn't matter who takes the shot so long as the shot is effective."

General Wilsbach then turned to what he considered to be the second tranche of integration, namely, interagency capabilities. "While our militaries are powerful forces, they are still tools. And like any tool, they are best applied to the range of problems they were designed to address. Thankfully, our governments have agencies purpose-built to cover domains in which the military is not built to operate....

"It also gives us the same opportunity that INDOPACOM has capitalized on with our joint planning—integration by design instead of by accident. National governments have a wide range of agencies for a purpose—each has strengths that complement others to support and defend national interests.

"Aligning those strengths toward a common goal is how that integration best serves its citizenry and is something we as air leaders must be cognizant of how to best utilize our capabilities. All that said, the integration of processes within one country will never be as strong as the integration of those processes across many."

He argued that integration is a key capability which the liberal democratic nations have compared to the 21st authoritarian powers. "Just as it doesn't matter which platform engages a target so long as the target is hit, it doesn't matter who directs what effort supporting the international order so long as it remains stable.

"Our adversaries are incapable of that level of trust, transparency, and integration. Could you imagine a Russian general as a PLAAF deputy commander? I can't! If I were an adversary planner, seeing a host of Allies and Partners moving in concert across every level of government with joint integration would keep me up at night."

Then General Wilsbach turned to deterrence and more to the point to what he considers to be the essence of integrated deterrence. "To me, it comes down to credibility. Our credibility is determined by two things: readiness and willingness. Both our nations are answering whether we can respond to destabilizing actors that choose to defy international norms by increasing our readiness."

He then highlighted the kind of actions which makes deterrence credible. " We can deny adversaries the expected benefits of their aggressions, impose cost on them that they are not willing to accept, or show that we're so resilient, we can overcome any impact they might have on us.

"The first message of denial is, in essence, the will to fight. Investment in modernization is one way to convey this message. More capable platforms allow us to respond to Chinese destabilization efforts across the Indo-Pacific more effectively, whether that's an E-7 providing airborne C2 during an unprofessional intercept by the PLAAF or space assets providing overhead imagery of the PRC gray-zone actors trespassing in a nation's exclusive economic zone.

"The second message of cost imposition is simple on its surface but has layers to consider. First and foremost, we all understand that no one wins if a conflict with China breaks out in the Indo-Pacific. That would be the worst-case scenario for every nation that calls the region home and is the last thing any of us want.

"So if an aggressor chooses to cross that line, they are already willing to bear considerable cost. That's why the deterrence must be credible and convincing. You cannot leave room for doubt that the cost could be tolerable. To do that, you need to know who should receive that message. In authoritarian regimes, it must reach the few people at the top who hold all the decision- making authority. They may never bear the cost personally, but their power relies on the fear and submission of those who will.

"The third message is in line with Secretary Pezzullo's remarks on resilience. Agile Combat Employment is one way we can create a resilience effect in combat. Through dispersal, mobility, and flexible C2, our forces use ACE to create enough targeting dilemmas for an adversary that we'll always have forces in the fight to challenge them.

"As another example, Australia has inspired the region by demonstrating resilience to diplomatic and economic coercion. Similar actions of resilience are occurring in fields as varied as air defenses to industry supply chains."

He concluded with this correlation of integrated deterrence with the kind of global development which liberal democracies favor.

"Denial, cost, resilience. Ideally, our deterrence actions should convey all three messages simultaneously. If I were an adversary planner, seeing capable forces across multiple, like- minded nations committed to action, able to deny my goals at overwhelming cost to me, and resilient enough to weather any of my attacks, that would keep me up at night. Integrated deterrence requires integration, readiness, and willingness, but it also needs one more thing—belief.

"Committing to upholding peace and stability is not an easy path to take. It requires significant investment of both time and resources, constant maintenance, and hard choices by leaders like yourselves. All of that requires a belief that it is worth it.

"I believe upholding the international order that has led to the most prosperous time in world history is worth it. I believe standing as a shield against authoritarianism is worth it. And I believe preserving our shared values of democracy, human rights, and freedom is worth it."

THE PERSPECTIVE OF LTGEN SIMON STUART, AUSTRALIAN ARMY

April 8, 2023

With the Australian Army having been heavily invested in the Middle East land wars and working closely with the U.S. Army in those endeavors, what is role in the enhanced emphasis on the direct defense of Australia?

Of course, each of the services and the joint force itself is facing how to meet the challenge of direct defense, but the question of the relationship of the land forces to the joint direct defense of Australia is especially challenging.

At the Williams Foundation Seminar on deterrence, LTGEN Simon Stuart, COS of the Australian Army, provided a general look at the deterrence challenge, the role of the ADF and of the Australian Army.

Although he noted in his speech "that that there is anything uniquely Australian about deterrence as part of our strategy, or indeed how we might practice it."

But with the emergence of what is often called great power competition, the role of nation has been enhanced and the need to shape national approaches even when interactive with key allies is central to the way ahead for national deterrence.

LTGEN Stuart then addresses the question of an Australian approach from that perspective.

"If there were to be such a thing as a uniquely Australian way of deterring, it would surely be founded by what defines us as a nation and what defines us Australians.

"Who are we as a nation, and who are we as a people in the middle decades of the 21st century?

"A uniquely Australian approach to deterrence would surely be founded in what our national aspirations were, our strategic culture, and approaching the task of deterrence from that perspective. So, the founding question for me is: how do we conceive of and combine our amazing national endowment?

"Our enviable strategic geography, our stewardship of a significant proportion of the Earth's surface – both the land mass and the seas that we are responsible for, and over 40 per cent of the Antarctic continent, which we lay claim to.

"We are among the world's top 15 economies, we have convening power both regionally and globally, we have a vibrant and diverse successful social experiment in our society today, our amazing human capital, and we have a series and a set of alliances and partnerships which are the envy of many.

"We have the capacity to be a global energy and food superpower.

"We have incredible natural resources, both those that have been in demand up until now, and those that will be in demand in the future. And the capacity to draw on 65,000 years of human history and endeavour on our continent.

"So how can we conceive of that wonderful endowment, and how do we conceive bringing it together?

"Are we outwardly focused and engaged, or are we insular and closed?

"And, for everyone who wears or has worn our uniform today – and certainly for every Australian soldier – the answer to the question 'who are we?' is of fundamental importance to service.

"Because we need to understand for whom and for what we are serving. And if we are in the fight, those questions are brought into even sharper relief.

LTGEN Stuart then addressed the key question of the nature of the new strategic context within which Australia or other liberal democracies are now operating.

"Pax-Americana was an historic anomaly. The norm in human history is a violent transfer of power from one empire to another – and 14 of the 16 transitions between empires in human history have involved wars.

"We live in an era that might be described as post-peak globalisation. Understanding how the international system works, what the great economic or trading blocks are, is an endeavour we need to understand.

"There are a range of theories, but personally I like Parag Khanna's new regionalism model because it emphasises partnerships, and partnerships within the context of regional blocks from an economic perspective – but also from the other elements of national power, which are in the ascendancy in the global system today.

"To some of our more recent history and the thinking from the 1980s that shaped our national security and defence policy, strategy, and practice over the last 30 years.

"The thinking that we do today, and the decisions that our elected representatives make today, will influence our policy and practice over the next few decades.

"That thinking, in my view, failed to engage with the world as it was, failed to engage with globalisation, either refused to engage or didn't recognise pretty much everything we've actually been doing these past few decades.

"It was defensive and inward looking.

"And finally, the wars we've been involved in, the wars we've been fighting over the last 20 years, the so-called 'wars of choice', did not touch Australia and did not touch Australians.

"They were a defence endeavour, involving only the military element of our national power, and largely an ADF endeavour. They did not touch the society we live in."

What then shapes a way ahead for the ADF in this new historical era is the importance of being embedded in a broader national approach requiring skill sets beyond those expected of the military

LTGEN Stuart the addressed some of these broader capabilities.

"How does our national aspiration and our national identity find expression in our strategic thinking and our policy and practice. It finds expression via statecraft, which is the mobilisation and orchestration of all elements of national power.

And the key areas of focus are that people like us need to help our elected representatives deal with are founded in national identity, and national unity, and therefore the wellspring of unity and purpose.

"It relies on social cohesion; it relies on the means by which to execute the strategy – that is our economy – the means connote and provide agency for us as a nation.

"It will rely on an involved relationship between the private and public sector, on better harnessing the incredible capacity of our academy.

"It will rely on the practice of statecraft on a more expansive engagement with partners and the development of partnerships."

LTGEN Stuart finally focused on the military element of deterrence. "The military element of national power needs to be four things. Firstly, it needs to reflect our national identity and aspiration.

"It needs to reflect the nature of the challenges, the threats, and the competition. And it needs to reflect the nature of our strategy, which in its broadest terms is shape, deter and respond.

"It needs to respect the arc of human history, and the history of warfare, and respect the requirement to balance between the enduring human nature of warfare and its changing character – which is generally speaking dominated by technology.

It needs to ensure relevance – relevance and credibility that are relative to a pacing threat, and an operating environment, and the opinions of our allies and partners.

"It also needs to be resourced because a strategy without means is an illusion.

"So our strategy today calls on us to shape the environment, deter actions against our interests, and be ready to respond with military force in all five domains when required.

"But shape, deter and respond does not connote a linear progression or the luxury of focusing on one at the expense of others.

"It is all three, all at once and in five domains, in the context of the execution and application of statecraft.

"If deterrence fails, war and its very unpredictability demands an ADF that is relevant and credible in all five domains – a system of systems that has the best chance of mission success whether we are deterring or we are prevailing in the conquest of war.

"To come back to the point about strategy being an illusion is it is not resourced, there are key questions that are being asked today in our nation.

"We have a pretty good sense of what it costs. There is a sharp focus on what we can afford, and then there are choices about what we are willing to pay.

"Each of those price points brings with it a risk profile, and those are the difficult decisions that our government needs to make.

"Those are difficult decisions to which we need to contribute the best advice that we possibly can."

LTGEN Stuart then focused on the way ahead for the ADF and the Army.

"Given the nature of our strategic circumstances, whatever we do requires us to do it quickly. Velocity matters.

"One way we can sharpen the edge of deterrence is by embracing new and emerging technologies and balancing that with the incredible human capital we enjoy in our country.

"I'm going to quote our Chief of Air Force from his excellence speech, which I commend to you, which he gave as a keynote at the Chief of Air Force Symposium in Melbourne as a precursor to the Avalon Air Show recently.

"He said: "It is easy to be seduced by technology; to do so would be to forget that national security is a national endeavour.

"The impediments to boosting capability delivery are often policy related, procedural or cultural. While advanced platforms teamed with cutting edge and disruptive technologies can be game-changes, we won't realise their advantage without evolving our thinking that delivers the military power element of deterrence."

"I think for me that really summarised the set of dilemmas and choices we face today in terms of responding to the strategic environment.

"Another way forward is leveraging the existing strengths of our Defence Force by ensuring we have a sharper focus on how we design our force, which is integrated and greater than the sum of our constituent parts.

"One that is increasingly builds into the architecture a strong and abiding sense of partnership with allies and regional partners.

"Because in an era of great power competition, having more friends is better than having less.

"In our region we have very good relationships with our partners. And the people-to-people relationships we enjoy have been grown and cultivated and reinforced over many, many years and stand us well for the future.

Shared interests' matter, and the many collective agreements like AUKUS and like FPDA and the Quad, and like the support we have of the ASEAN political architecture matter and stand us in good stead for tomorrow.

"From an Army perspective, from the contribution of land power to that integrated force, we offer presence, persistence, asymmetry through first-mover advantage, utility, and incredibly good value for money."

THE PERSPECTIVE OF THE AIR COMMANDER AUSTRALIA

April 11, 2023

My colleague John Blackburn and I met with Air Vice-Marshal Darren Goldie, the Air Commander of the RAAF, in his office on 4 April 2023. One key element which we discussed was the growing significance of agile basing and operations as part of the evolving Australian deterrent posture.

In my earlier conversation that week with Goldie's boss, Air Marshal Chipman, we discussed the new basing and support structure being worked in Australia and across the alliance.

As highlighted in that interview: "A key aspect of the evolving alliance situation in facing the China challenge is how the core allies

Japan, Australia and the United States actually will craft more effective use of the air, maritime and land baes they use over the Pacific thought of as an extended operational space.

"If the three countries can work creatively land basing, with seabasing, with air basing with the use of new autonomous systems they can field and evolve an effective force for the long game of competition with China. Certainly, from this perspective, I would view Australia is the strategic reserve of the broader alliance.

"As Chipman commented: "I haven't heard it described that way. But I think that's what we are working towards. I think that's the mindset that we have. The idea that Australia provides strategic depth for forces moving forward, is absolutely part of our thinking."

Air Vice-Marshal Goldie picked up on that theme as follows: "Our engagement through two decades in the Middle East has arguably driven us down a single service route to force generation, focused on expeditionary operations, hosted from secure bases. We now need to look to evolve our approach to joint force generation from Australian territory.

"We don't have the level of knowledge and normative experience we need to generate regarding infrastructure across Western and Northern Australia for the Australian version of agile combat employment."

He contrasted the Australian to the PACAF approach to agility. The USAF in his view was working on how to trim down support staff for air operations and learning how to use multiple bases in the Pacific, some of which they owned and some of which they did not own.

The Australian concept he was highlighting was focused on Australian geography and how the joint force and the infrastructure which could be built — much of it mobile – could allow for dispersed air combat operations.

This meant in his view that "we need to have a clear understanding of the fail and no-fail enablers" for the kind of dispersed operations necessary to enhance the ADF's deterrent capability.

A key element of this is C2. Rather than looking to traditional CAOC battle management, the focus needs as well to focus on C2 in a dispersed or disaggregate way, where the commander knows what is available to them in an area of operations and aggregate those forces into an integrated combat element operating as a distributed entity.

Goldie commented: "We are developing concepts about how we will do command and control on a more geographic basis. This builds on our history with Darwin and Tindal to a certain extent, although technology has widened that scale to be a truly continental distributed control concept.

"We already a familiar with how an air asset like the Wedgetail can take over the C2 of an air battle when communications are cut to the CAOC, but we don't have a great understanding of how that works from a geographic basing perspective. What authorities to move aircraft, people and other assets are vested in local area Commanders that would be resilient to degradation in communications from the theatre commander – or JFACC?

"We need to focus on how we can design our force to manoeuvre effectively using our own territory as the chessboard."

Air Vice-Marshal Goldie underscored that the ability to work with limited resources to generate air combat capability is exercised regularly by the normal activity of 75 Squadron, flying F-35s in Australia's Air Combat Group. This squadron operates from RAAF Base Tindal in the Northern Territory and as Goldie put it: "they have to operate with what they have in a very austere area."

He highlighted a recent exercise which 75 squadron did with their Malaysian partners. The squadron operated their F-35s, and each day practiced operations using a different support structure. One day the operated with a C-27J which carried secure communication, along with HF communications systems and dealing with bandwidth challenges each bearer posed. Another day they would operate with a ground vehicle packed with support equipment and on another day they would operate without either support capability. The point being the need is to learn to operate in austere support environments and to shape the skill sets to do so.

By learning how to use Australian territory to support agile air operations, and to take those capabilities to partner or allied operational areas, Australia will significantly enhance its deterrent capabilities going forward. This is a key challenge being squarely addressed by the RAAF.

THE PERSPECTIVE OF AIR MARSHAL HARVEY SMYTH, RAF

April 12, 2023

At the recent Sir Richard Williams Foundation Seminar held on 30 March 2023, Air Marshal Harvey Smyth, the Deputy Commander Operations, presented a UK perspective of the challenges facing the UK and her allies in the contentious 2020's.

I first met Smyth when he was the head of the UK F-35 program. In an interview I did with him 2016, Air Commodore Smyth highlighted the coming of the F-35 the UK joint force. In that discussion, he highlighted the importance of the F-35 in enabling coalition operations, which is now considered a key element for integrated deterrence.

This what we emphasized in that interview: "It can be easily forgotten that the USAF and the RAF have not flown the same aircraft for a very long time indeed. The RAF and the Marines have flown Harriers and along with the Spanish and Italians formed a three-decade Harrier community. And Smyth as a Harrier pilot underscored the importance of this shared legacy moving forward.

"As an RAF pilot with significant maritime and carrier operational experience, we are shaping a collegiate and joint way ahead with the Royal Navy which brings the RAF domain knowledge of ways to operate in the extended battlespace with the coming of the F-35B to the new Queen Elizabeth class carrier.

"Being radical, I think it would make sense to put a picture of the Queen Elizabeth class carrier on our RAF recruiting poster: the RAF and the RN are jointly delivering the UK's future Carrier Strike capability, and all RAF Lightning pilots will spend some of their time at sea, as I did throughout my 16-year career in Joint Force Harrier – we are forging an integrated approach together, which is incredibly exciting."[2]

The point simply put is that Smyth has been working integrated deterrence via the F-35 program for several years. But this was before

Brexit, before several years of turbulence in UK and European politics and the return of war to the European context.

But it was also prior to the recognition of the broader challenges posed by the global reach of the 21st century authoritarian powers. When my co-author and I decided to write a book on the return of direct defense in Europe, which we started to write in 2014 and published in late 2020, our original publisher wanted this book to focus on Russia.

We significantly disagreed. We argued that the challenge for Europe's direct defense was posed equally by China as a force within Europe and operating globally. Our view was an anomaly at the time, but it is no longer.

In fact, Air Marshal Smyth underscored that we now face a Euro-Atlantic-Pacific global threat envelope and that the UK is focused on shaping its contribution accordingly within the scope of its means.

He argued that the UK recognized that global deterrence was the critical focus of their defense effort, but such a focus clearly needed to encompass close working relationships will allies going forward. He made the point that even for the United States it was beyond its capability to fight a two-front war.

This meant that shaping more effective allied cooperation through a process of integration was critical and that is what is meant by integrated deterrence. But such an aspiration cannot be realized within the legacy limits on information and technology sharing.

As he underscored: "The key to success will center on our ability to share more of our intelligence, share more of our information, sharing more data, and share more technology.

"We need to work together to identify the gaps and the vulnerabilities in our deterrence posture that an adversary might exploit. And we need to work out how best to work as a collective, rather than as individual nations. This is really, really hard to do."

Air Marshal Smyth emphasized that in spite of its successes, NATO scoped to European defence was not enough for today's UK deterrent structure.

"It is clear that given the changing threat picture, effective defense deterrence will mean working through other groupings further beyond

NATO, and beyond the Euro Atlantic theater, with a renewed emphasis on the concept of strategics, developing and establishing new frameworks, and building a new international security architecture to manage systemic competition and escalation.

"And in today's multipolar environments, the UK will continue to develop a broader deterrence toolkit to include information operations and offensive cyber tools and make greater use of open source information alongside our historically more classified intelligence capabilities."

"We will launch a new economic deterrence initiative to strengthen our diplomatic and economic tools to respond to and deter hostile acts by current and future aggressors.

"On nuclear, of course, the foundational component of UK is an integrated approach to deterrence with our minimal but credible, independent, UK nuclear deterrent. It is assigned to the defense of NATO to ensure that potential adversaries can never use their capabilities to threaten the UK, or indeed our NATO allies...

"We would consider using our nuclear weapons only in extreme circumstances of self-defense, including the defense of NATO allies, and of course, only the Prime Minister can authorize their use.

"But in addition to our nuclear deterrent, the UK's conventional, cyber, and space forces are now becoming sufficiently capable, resilient, deployable, and adaptive, to deter potential adversaries from engaging in conflict and to win if indeed, deterrence fails.

"Beyond these military instruments, we'll also see UK working the much wider aspects of state power to increase the costs of aggression by hostile actors above and below the threshold of armed conflict. The UK will continue to develop such levers to adapt to the changing global threat environments. In particular, we will strengthen our economic capabilities and information statecraft..."

Air Marshal Smyth brought to the attention of the audience, the recent update of the 2021 UK Strategic Defence Review. The Integrated Review Refresh 2023 or the IRR was released last month. And in that review, deter and deterrence was frequently cited throughout and provides a good overview of the current UK government's view of the deterrence challenge facing Britain and her allies.

Based on this document, Air Marshal Smyth discussed the UK

current concept of deterrence.

As Air Marshal Smyth underscored: "We are all very familiar with the three C's of traditional deterrence: capability, credibility, and communication. But in the UK, we're now finding it helpful to consider integrated deterrence through the lens of an additional three C's: comprehensive, coordinated, and coherence.

"First, deterrence must be comprehensive, as discussed in the IRR. This means taking into account all state levers of power and tailoring our approach to maximize use of those levers of power that are best suited to change the perceptions of a specific adversary. The integrated approach attempts to avoid the age-old temptation of over focusing on the military instruments of power... To be truly comprehensive, integrated deterrence must be both multi domain and multi-agency.

"Second, deterrence must be impeccably coordinated with allies and partners so that the impact of our actions are greater than the sum of the parts, from force posturing, all the way to the imposition of economic sanctions. None of us can do this alone.

"And whilst we have all worked hand in glove for many decades in terms of deterrence and defense, in today's information driven, intimately connected, rapidly dynamic but ever shrinking world, there is always more effort required, especially if we are to truly deliver a coordinated, integrated, and determined effect.

"Lastly, we need to take a more coherent approach to developing our deterrence strategies, understanding the complex interplay across the spectrum of conflict, and considering the temporal nature of crises to ensure that our activities remain aligned with the overall objectives and desired end states.

"It is fair to say that capabilities available to state and non-state actors in today's complex world have blurred the traditional thresholds of conflict...And also understanding the role and the impact of strategic or nuclear messaging well below the nuclear threshold, as well as how to manage escalation over time. And this is definitely something Russia's invasion of Ukraine has brought into sharp focus.

"Thus, alongside the long-standing capability, credibility and communication aspects of deterrence, we add three more C's of deterrence: comprehensive, coordinated and preparedness.

"And for me, there's no question that the development of integrated deterrence remains incredibly complex both by necessity and by design across government, and working with allies is challenging enough in the best of times, but for sure, the juice is definitely worth the squeeze."

THE PERSPECTIVE OF VICE-ADMIRAL JONATHAN MEAD

April 13, 2023

In March 2020, I was visiting Western Australia including HMAS Sterling. I was there to visit the HMAS Rankin, one of the Collins class submarines home ported at HMAS Sterling on Garden Island. When I informed a senior U.S. Navy Admiral that I was going to visit the Royal Australian Navy at Garden Island, he wrote: "Awesome, say hello to the fellas down south, incredible team!   And absolutely critical in/out of a fight."

Little did I know at the time of my visit which was 12 March 2020, that in fact I was visiting a future SSN base. I also did not know that I was about to have to escape Australia to get back to the United States with the onset of the pandemic.

In my visits to Australia during the period when Australia was working with France on the build of a new generation diesel-powered submarine, my work with the U.S. Navy, my time in France at my Paris apartment and discussions with the French, and my discussions in Australia gave me a good view of progress on this program.

Then in September 2021, while in my apartment in Paris, the Australian, British and American governments announced that Australia was to cancel the French program in favor of an SSN program which would involve the three countries or the Anglo-Saxons as the French refer to the three, although it is difficult to view the United States or the UK in this light as the two countries change significantly.

Being in France, I certainly had a chance to talk with the French and with colleagues in the United States I could do so by phone and video, and of course reached out to Australian colleagues to sort out an initial read on all of this as well.

I wrote several pieces on this development at the time, but not surprisingly, the most perceptive of the pieces was built around an interview with Vice-Admiral Tim Barrett (Retired).

This is what I wrote in a piece published 19 October 2021:

"During my visit to Europe earlier this Fall, the surprise announcement of the Morrison Administration's decision to shift from their French alliance to deliver a long-range diesel submarine to acquiring nuclear submarine capability through an alliance with the United States and Britain was made. I talked with both French and Australian analysts and provided my initial assessment in a series of articles which highlighted the decision and the dynamics of change associated with that decision.

"But what was clear that the strategic environment has changed dramatically from when the Australian government made its decision to stay with a conventional submarine capability. The nature of the Chinese threat as well as the actions of the Xi Administration has clearly driven a shift in Australian thinking and perceived needs for longer range operational capability in the Indo-Pacific region.

"At the same time, its closest allies in the region the United States and Japan clearly recognize the need to expand their capabilities to operate throughout the region to complicate Chinese operational considerations, and to deter via more capability to operate throughout the wider Pacific as well.

"The announced decision highlighted an 18-month period with Vice Admiral Jonathan Mead in charge on the Australian side of negotiating within the new nuclear submarine alliance to deliver Australian solutions. I interviewed Mead when he was head of Navy Capability in 2016. He then went on to be Commander Australian Fleet and then Chief of Joint Capabilities and Command of Joint Capabilities Group. He has a strong ASW background as well as working closely with the other member of the Quad, namely India. He is now the Chief of the Nuclear -Powered Submarine Task Force....

"I had a chance to discuss these issues on October 14, 2021, in a phone interview with Vice-Admiral (Retired) Tim Barrett, with whom I have had the opportunity to discuss maritime issues since 2015. As the exact nature of what will happen in the program is a work in progress and not really open to public disclosure until that 18-month period is completed, we focused on the context and how one might assess that context.

"Vice-Admiral (Retired) Barrett made three key points. First, the nuclear submarine effort was a strategic one, which was about Australian defense and not primarily focused on a priority on ship building on Australian soil. It is crucial to understand that this is about adding core defense capabilities earlier rather than later and would almost certainly encompass interaction between shaping the eco system for the operation of Australian nuclear submarines and the presence of allied nuclear submarines working with the Australian eco system.

"The second key point was that the priority needed to be focused on adding nuclear submarine capability to the evolving USW or ASW capability which Australia was already building out. The Australian government recently decided to add another squadron of Romeo helicopters to the fleet and has procured P-8s and Tritons as part of an expanded ASW or USW warfighting capability. The submarine is not a silver bullet for ASW or USW mission sets but part of the evolution of the kill web approach to ASW and USW missions going forward....

"According to Barrett: "The submarine decision is part of a broader set of decisions with regard to how the ADF should respond to the challenges in the Indo-Pacific. This was a deliberate and considered position from the Navy's perspective, but the political and geopolitical circumstances have changed. This is not the first time that Australia has sought or considered the acquisition of a nuclear submarine."

"The third key point was that flexibility and innovations will be part of working out a way ahead and he noted that Mead had worked with him previously. When Commander of the Australian Fleet, then Commodore Mead was instrumental in working an innovative plan to manage a temporary capability deficiency for fleet fuel tanking. To shore up a gap, the RAN 'leased' a Spanish Navy oiler for 8 months, and the RAN crews trained on the ship and operated the ship in support of the Australian Fleet.

"Eventually, the RAN acquired two new Spanish oilers, but the kind of innovation demonstrated in this example, will almost certainly be part of the way ahead in meeting the challenges of accelerating the operational acquisition of nuclear submarine capacity in support of Australian defense.

"According to Vice Admiral (Retired) Barrett: "The strategic environment has changed. We need to reconsider the balance between sovereign capability for a thirty-year build and the need for creation of capability in the near term. The earlier 30-year period build approach should not be the dominant approach; the capability and its presence to shape deterrent capabilities is crucial and work out over time how the build side of this effort is clarified and put in place. The program needs to be driven by the need for creative capability options first."[3]

Now after the 18-month period, the three countries announced their joint decision on how to proceed on the Australian approach to acquiring nuclear attack submarine technology and capability. To do so, will require Australia to build a comprehensive enterprise to operate, maintain, to sustain, and build an Australian nuclear attack submarine.

The comprehensive approach to do so was announced in mid-March 2023 in San Diego by the three heads of state. The Williams Seminar was held on 30 March 2023 and is sandwiched between this event and the public release of the strategic defence review sometime in April.

The Australian government released a report laying out how it saw the "partnership for the future" or "the AUKUS nuclear-powered submarine pathway."

In that report, the government describe the advantage of nuclear-powered submarines and why Australia was transitioning to an SSN capability. "In the future security environment of the Indo-Pacific, conventionally-powered submarines will be increasingly less able to meet Australia's needs. The United Kingdom Royal Navy and United States Navy retired their last conventionally-powered submarines in the early 1990s because SSNs have superior stealth, speed, manoeuvrability, survivability and endurance when compared to diesel-electric powered submarines."[4]

At the Williams Seminar, Vice-Admiral Mead provided an overview to the approach being taken to establish a nuclear submarine enterprise in Australia.

In essence, the approach is three-fold.

In the first phase, UK and US nuclear submarines will visit HMAS Stirling, and the Royal Australian Navy will learn how to support these ships during their visits. As part of this standup phase, Australia will work with the United States in operating Virginia class submarines.

In the second phase, Australia will obtain Virginia class submarines and operate anywhere from three to five of these boats going forward.

And in a third phase, Australia will particulate with its partners in shaping a new class of SSNs, which will be British designed but enabled by U.S. technologies. In this third phase, Australia will have built its own submarine yard at Osborne where in effect this would be the fourth nuclear submarine yard in the trilateral alliance. In other words, the notion of building an arsenal of democracy through allied cooperation would be realized.

Vice-Admiral Mead started his presentation by indicating that "in 2027, the U.S. will forward rotate Virginia class submarines to Australia and the UK would rotate one nuclear submarine to HMAS Sterling. The aim of this effort will be to allow Australia to deeply immerse itself in a nuclear-powered program. We will be doing maintenance on Virginia class submarines and will be doing crewing of these submarines out of Western Australia.

"After a period of about four or five years, we will reach the point where our partners and we will be able to ensure that Australia is a safe and secure steward of nuclear technology, of nuclear materials and a nuclear reactor. From that point in time, the United States would offer us for sale or transfer up to five Virginia class submarines."

This would constitute the standup and launch phase for Australia shaping a nuclear submarine exercise, and really the key one to ensure a capability being able to operate to replace the Collins class submarines. This is really the key effort which enables the threshold to be crossed into a period of operating nuclear submarines.

In my view, this also allows Australia to build its con-ops for integrated USW and ASW with the P-8s, Tritons, and various air and maritime assets, including the coming of maritime autonomous systems to build an integrated offensive-defensive capability to protect Australian sea lanes.

What then follows is working through what a follow-on submarine program would look like. And this effort will entail in depth cooperation with both the UK and the United States. According to Mead: "It will be a follow-on to the British nuclear-powered submarine but will incorporate U.S. technology, including weapons, sensors, VLS combat systems and torpedos."

Vice-Admiral Mead then looked beyond the pathway discussion to the broader question of what Australia needs to do for this effort to be successful.

The first element is addressing the strategy and being able to gain support for the effort within the Australian public. "We are going to have to be very clear on our strategy."

Second, Australia must successfully manage the trilateral working relationship. "How can we make the best of Australia working with the U.S. and the UK to deliver this capability?"

Third, creating, training, and sustaining the appropriate workforce for the enterprise is a major challenge within Australia. "We will be the first country in the world to operate a nuclear submarine without having a civilian nuclear industry. This presents some unique challenges."

Fourth, Australia needs to build the appropriate infrastructure both in terms of basing and in terms of the shipyard itself. There will be some unique aspects to the yard including shaping high security protection for the yard as well. "We need to design the yard, build the yard and start building the nuclear-powered submarine by the end of the decade."

Fifth, Australia needs to build an industrial base for this effort which can support and sustain the effort into the indefinite future. Osborne will become the fourth nuclear submarine yard to go with the two in the U.S. and the one in the UK. "Osborne will become one of the most advanced and complex technological hubs in the world."

Sixth, the security of the enterprise is a major element for success. In addition to the physical security mentioned earlier, the IAEA involvement will be significant in verifying the quality of Australian nuclear power stewardship. "If we don't have the international community along with us, the enterprise will fail."

But the point of all this effort was highlighted by VADM Mead at the beginning of his presentation: "there is no more powerful instrument of conventional deterrence than a nuclear-powered submarine capability."

THE PERSPECTIVE OF REAR ADMIRAL JEFFREY JABLON

May 8, 2023

During my visit to Honolulu during the last week of April 2023, I had a chance to meet with Rear Admiral Jeffrey Jablon, the Submarine Force, U.S. Pacific Fleet (SUBPAC) commander. We discussed the evolving role of the submarine fleet in the challenging environment of the Pacific.

In Europe, Russia faces three Western nuclear powers. In the Pacific, the U.S. and its allies and partners face three nuclear powers: China, Russia and North Korea. Any consideration of the nature of warfighting in the Pacific has to be considered in the context of the threat of nuclear weapons use, with three adversaries who do not have the same doctrine.

SSBNs are a key part of any nuclear deterrent equation in addition to the key role which SSNs play in the broader conventional deterrence equation. We did not focus specifically on the nuclear dimension, but it can never be forgotten in the Pacific context.

As I wrote concerning the impact of the war in Ukraine to date on nuclear deterrence: "But the core question is simply put: does the possession of nuclear weapons effectively create sanctuaries in your territory in case of conflict?

"Does this work with regard to extended deterrence as well by the United States with its allies? Would this apply to the defense of Australia as it expands its basing support for the United States? Does this work as well in the Pacific with China, Russia, North Korea and the mainland of the United States effectively sanctuaries? How does the question affect warfighting strategies, multi-domain or otherwise?"[5]

Let me start by clarifying what the role of Rear Admiral Jablon and his command is within the overall submarine contribution to the U.S. Pacific Fleet. As the submarine type commander in the Pacific, he is charged with the task of manning, training and equipping the submarines in the theater. He is also the operational commander of Task Force 34, where he reports to the U.S. 3rd Fleet Commander, Vice Admiral Boyle (whom I meet with in January in San Diego) who has responsibility for naval operations east of the international dateline. The U.S. 7th Fleet Commander owns all operations west of the international dateline.

In his role with regard to training and equipping the submarine force, Jablon is responsible for ensuring that the subs are combat ready: able to conduct any mission, and ready to deploy. Warfighting is his top priority.

The SSNs operate on a Fleet Response Training Plan cycle. The subs go on a 6-month deployment. They then come back for 12 months of training, modernization, and maintenance and then go back on deployment.

The stealth quality of the nuclear submarine and its speed are key elements of its ability to be first to the fight. But as described by Rear Admiral Jablon, the submarine being able to be first to the fight is in the context of moving the joint force into a better position to prosecute the fight.

As he put it: "I would no longer characterize ourselves as a silent service. Deterrence is a major mission for the submarine force. You can't have a credible deterrent without communicating your capabilities; if the adversary doesn't know anything about that specific deterrent, it's not a deterrent."

Part of this deterrent emphasis is upon a more public display of the submarines we have and the capability they can demonstrate. Frankly, what the SSGNs have demonstrated over the years is the versatility of the submarine to contribute range, speed and stealth and then deliver firepower including the Tomahawk Land Attack Missile (TLAM) and special operations forces.

Now submarines are becoming part of deterrent signaling and operating in new ways to enhance their overall deterrent impact.

For example, earlier in April 2023, the ballistic missile submarine USS Maine (SSBN 741) publicly visited Guam for a logistics visit. During that visit, submarine commanders from Japan and the Republic of Korea embarked the Maine. The Navy stated that "The embark was an example of how U.S. forces are advancing the U.S-Japan-ROK trilateral relationship that is forward-leaning, reflective of shared values, and resolute against threats that challenge regional stability."[6]

And recently, the White House announced that an SSBN would make a port visit to South Korea. As a Reuters story published on 27 April 2023 noted: "For the first time since the 1980s a U.S. Navy nuclear-armed ballistic missile submarine (SSBN) will visit South Korea to help demonstrate Washington's resolve to protect the country from a North Korean attack. The visit was announced in a joint declaration during a summit between South Korean President Yoon Suk Yeol and U.S. President Joe Biden in Washington on Wednesday....

"The United States has pledged to deploy more so-called "strategic assets" such as aircraft carriers, submarines, and long-range bombers to South Korea to deter North Korea, which has developed increasingly powerful missiles that can hit targets from South Korea to the mainland United States."[7]

Also, the Navy is stepping up its cooperation with allied submarine forces, as illustrated in Rear Admiral Jablon recently hosting the Submarine Warfare Commanders Conference: a core meeting with other submarine commanders from Japan, the Republic of Korea, Singapore, Australia, Canada, France, and the United Kingdom. As he underscored: "During the conference, the submarine force commanders discussed the coalition approach to interoperability, which is a key part of deterrence."

In an 18 April 2023 story published by the U.S. Navy, this conference was highlighted as follows: "Commander, Submarine Force U.S. Pacific Fleet hosted the 2023 Submarine Warfare Commanders Conference (SWCC) at Joint Base Pearl Harbor-Hickam, April 12-14, 2023.

"The purpose of SWCC, which was first held in 2018, is to strengthen a free and open Indo-Pacific region through expanded cooperation between submarine force commanders of allies and partners.

"When we hold the SWCC each year and come together with our allied and partner submarine force commanders, we demonstrate the strength of our relationships," said Rear Adm. Jeff Jablon, commander, Submarine Force U.S. Pacific Fleet.

"Jablon noted: 'Now more than ever, these strong relationships give us an asymmetric advantage as we work together in this incredibly dynamic region to maintain the international rules-based order.'

"Submarine commanders from the Royal Australian Navy, Royal Canadian Navy, French Navy, Japan Maritime Self-Defense Force, Republic of Korea Navy, Royal Navy, and Republic of Singapore Navy met with U.S. Pacific Fleet commanders on the historic submarine base at Joint Base Pearl Harbor Hickam, Hawaii.

"The U.S. Submarine Force is an indispensable combat capability in our Joint and Combined Force to ensure freedom of the seas in support of defending the security, freedom and wellbeing of our nation and allies and partners through deterrence and upholding the international rules-based order," said Adm. Samuel J. Paparo, commander, U.S. Pacific Fleet. "Our undersea warfare is made up of advanced technology, quality of training and exceptional personnel, but the solidarity of our alliances and partnerships is our asymmetric advantage."

"The multi-day event included briefings from each submarine force commander and discussions which focused on the theme of this year's conference, "Improve Multinational Maritime Domain Awareness and Theater ASW Capability in the Indo-Pacific Theater". SWCC provided an opportunity for commanders to exchange perspectives through an open dialogue and encouraged allied and partner countries to continue to find ways to work together through collaboration and innovation.

"The conversations we had during this conference will collectively strengthen our team, and will maintain our overmatch in the undersea domain," said Jablon. "I look forward to more opportunities for us to work together as a combined force in exercises and real-world operations."[8]

The role of the submarine in the joint and coalition force is being expanded. The submarine force is part of the joint fires solution. The submarine force can operate independently or work with the joint or coalition force in providing joint or coalition force combined effects.

As the joint force works enhanced kill web capabilities, combat clusters can operate together to deliver joint fires solutions. As Ed Timperlake and I have argued in our book on the evolution of the maritime kill web:

"Force packages or combat clusters are deployed under mission command with enough organic C2 and ISR to monitor their situations and integrate the platforms that are part of that combat cluster and to operate effectively at a point of interest. Within that combat cluster, the C2 and ISR systems allow for reach back to non-organic combat assets which are then conjoined operational for a period of time to that combat cluster and becomes part of an expanded modular task force.

"With the right kind of security arrangement, and C2 and ISR capabilities, the presence force, now an expanded modular task force, need not be American to expand the reach and effectiveness of the operational force in the extended battlespace. Such an approach and capabilities are the essence of what a kill-web enabled force is and how such integratability can close the geographical and combat seams which 21st century authoritarian powers are focused on generating.

"This allows for the kind of escalation management and control crucial for the competition with the 21st Century authoritarian powers. It is not about getting to World War III as rapidly as possible or generating nuclear exchanges early in a widening conflict. It is about escalation control and management, and an ability to close seams which adversaries seek to open to gain significant escalation dominance as they expand the reach and range of those 21st century authoritarian powers."[9]

Rear Admiral Jablon underscored the nature of the shift as follows: "The submarine force is now becoming part of the 'combat clusters' that you're talking about instead of an independent operator. In the Cold War, we operated independently, alone, and unafraid. During the land wars, we started becoming part of the joint force as we provided land fires via the TLAM. Now, we are fully integrated with the joint force in terms of targeting and communications. But, of course, we can also conduct independent operations as the 'silent service' when directed."

The broadening of the submarine's role within joint warfighting is being expanded by the arrival and then growth in capability of autonomous systems.

In my own view, rather than seeing autonomous systems in the short- or medium-term creating ghost fleets, their role will be to expand the range, capability, and lethality of capital assets. Rather than looking simply at the organic capability on a specific platform, we will consider surface ships using such capabilities as becoming mother ships and submarines will share in this development as well.

Rear Admiral Jablon specifically mentioned two types of autonomous developments of note for the submarine fleet. One is the ability to operate a UUV out of a torpedo tube, with the UUV coming back after its mission to offload data specifically onboard the submarine.

In article published by USNI News on 2 November 2022, this development was described as follows: "In the near future, the U.S. nuclear attack submarine fleet will be able to launch and recover an underwater robot from a torpedo tube, Navy officials said this week.

"The torpedo-sized Razorback — designed to extend the awareness of a submarine— has been in testing on the Navy's attack boats for more than a year but requires a dry deck shelter and divers to recover the 600-pound UUV. The current procedure has blunted the utility of the system, Submarine Force commander Vice Adm. Bill Houston said on Tuesday at the Naval Submarine League's annual symposium.

"The Medium UUV can go on any one of our submarines. That is a priority for us. We have no problem launching UUVs. That's easy. The recovery part has been the critical aspect," Houston said at the Naval Submarine League's annual symposium.

"The Navy tested a system earlier this year to recover the Medium UUV via torpedo tube and is close to deploying the system in the "very near future," said Rear. Adm. Doug Perry, the director of submarine warfare for the Office of Chief of Naval Operations (OPNAV N97)."[10]

Unmanned Undersea Vehicles Squadron One is under Rear Admiral

Jablon's command and is where UUV solution sets are being worked for deployment. And in February of this year, he visited Keyport, Washington where the squadron is based.

The second autonomous development is the ability to launch a UAV while submerged to enable joint fires. Rear Admiral Jablon said that they had specifically worked this with the USMC as the force develops its Expeditionary Advanced Base Operations (EABO) solution set.[11]

Finally, the joint force, including the submarine force, are working new ways to do expeditionary logistics to enable resupply of the force when operating in a contested environment.

A 23 August 2022 Navy story discussed such VERTREP.

"NAVAL BASE KITSAP – BANGOR, Wash. -- Two Ohio-class ballistic missile submarines demonstrated their ability to replenish while operating at sea during a series of vertical replenishment (VERTREP) exercises off the coast of California July through August, 2022.

"During the exercise, the Ohio-class ballistic missile submarines USS Nevada (SSBN 733) and USS Henry M. Jackson (SSBN 730) operated jointly with U.S. Navy MH-60R Seahawk helicopters, U.S. Marine Corps CMV-22 Ospreys, and U.S. Air Force C-17 Globemaster IIIs.

"Recently the Pacific SSBN submarine force exercised a vertical replenishment capability for at-sea SSBNs to prove our resiliency for worldwide operations and to replenish our ships with materials, food and operational gear," said Capt. Kelly L. Laing, director of maritime operations for Commander, Task Group 114.3. "This allows us to maintain an unpredictable forward presence and continued demonstration of the unmatched strength of our strategic forces."

"The event showcased the submarines' ability to remain on mission and at sea while performing essential replenishment operations.

"Our fundamental mission is to deter a strategic attack, which is an existential threat to the United States and our allies." said Rear Adm. Mark Behning, commander of both Submarine Group 9 and Task Group 114.3. "Testing our readiness ensures we maintain a safe, secure and reliable strategic deterrent force."

"The event was part of a U.S. Strategic Command exercise which highlights the interoperability of multiple U.S. military platforms in order to implement the strategic deterrence mission.

"Exercising these VERTREPs was a joint operation involving Marine and Air Force assets," Laing said. "This shows our commitment to joint operations worldwide and between combatant commanders. This is important so that we don't stovepipe ourselves under one community or brand. We are committed to operating together as a global force."

"This event is the latest in a series of efforts by the United States submarine force to look at alternative operations that previously required a submarine to be pier side to accomplish. For example, in May, the Ohio-class ballistic missile submarine USS Alabama (SSBN 731) conducted an at-sea crew exchange, swapping out the blue and gold crews. This demonstrated the submarine's ability to continuously operate and stay on mission for longer periods of time while sustaining quality of life for the crews and their families.

"What this shows to our allies and adversaries is that we have the ability to keep our boats at sea," Laing said. "This shows them that we are ready."

"Nevada and Henry M. Jackson are two of eight Ohio-class ballistic missile submarines home ported at Naval Base Kitsap-Bangor. The Ohio-class ballistic missile platform provides the United States with its most survivable leg of its strategic deterrent forces."[12]

While a variety of systems could be used to replenish food onboard the submarine, if a critical part is required, the speed, range, and variable path of operations of the Osprey would make this the preferred partner. As the Navy is adding CMV-22bs to its fleet, this is yet another role it could play for fleet distributed operations.

For rearmament, the submarine tenders have been developing various locations from which to re-arm submarines. Obviously, the command element would work submarine operations in such a way that a cascading approach to weapons resupply would be worked in times of conflict.

But the Navy has only two submarine tenders, and both are to be replaced by new versions in the mid-term. But the Navy is working various ways to get best value out of their sub tenders, but as the Navy adds UAVs to the fleet, the demand signal goes up on the Military Sealift Command and upon its sub tenders as well.

We concluded by my asking Rear Admiral Jablon what investments in the mid-term would make a significant contribution to his operational force.

"Having a robust maintenance infrastructure is crucial for us, and the Navy is allocating more resources to this through the SIOP program. When we can get submarines through maintenance periods on time or ahead of time, that translates into more time I can operate these submarines at sea, which increases our presence, and increases deterrence."

THE PERSPECTIVE OF AIR VICE-MARSHAL MICHAEL KITCHER

May 12, 2023

During my March-April 2023 visit to Australia. I had a chance to meet with Air Vice-Marshal Michael Kitcher, Deputy Chief Joint Operations (DCJOPS) and to talk with him about the Joint Operations Focus on regional defence after a long period in the Middle East. AVM Kitcher is responsible for assisting Chief Joint Operations (CJOPS) with the command of ADF joint operations, directing command units and assigned forces in the planning and conduct of campaigns, operations, joint exercises, and other activities.

I last met with him during a 2018 visit to Williamtown Airbase with Murielle Delaporte. He was then the Air Combat Group Commander as Air Commodore Kitcher. During that visit we focused on the transition from legacy aircraft to a fifth-generation force.

We started the April 2023 discussion by focusing on the shift of the Joint Operations Command from the shaping of a joint force for operations in the Middle East to a refocusing on joint operations in the region with core allies to shape more effective coordinated allied operations. Kitcher pointed out that the command had been established in 2007 to plan, execute and optimize the conduct of ADF joint operations.

I noted that during the ADF's participation in the Middle East

Wars, the RAAF for the first time deployed an integrated air task force which included air battle management aircraft, lifters, tankers, and fighters and that this experience laid a foundation for bringing back into the Indo-Pacific region an ADF force that had exercised really for the first time this level of air tasking integration.

But as Kitcher underscored: "The focus in this period, up to say 2017, for CJOPS was on operations in the Middle East whilst managing operations in our region. We clearly have leveraged the earlier experiences in our renewed focus on the conduct of Operations, Actions and Activities, OAA, in the Indo Pacific. We are focused on developing a theatre campaign plan to translate strategic guidance into the OAA we execute in our region to achieve our desired objectives.

"We are focused on ways we can operate as a joint force to optimise our regional OAA to have the maximum positive effect in supporting our theater campaign plan. You don't get the maximum benefits from a joint force unless firstly the services provide you with trained personnel capable of executing joint missions and then HQJOC, through focused joint planning, maximises the potential of the individual components. We have made good progress along this path but still have a way to go."

Air Vice-Marshal Kitcher highlighted that we are "now squarely focused on managing operations in a coordinated fashion in our region." And this means both how to get the best joint force effect but also how to coordinate the ADF effort with core allies in also getting the best proper coalition effect.

Obviously in working with coalition partners, national sovereignty has to be respected but at the same time for effectiveness in operations coalition forces need to operate in an integrated manner. This is a key tension which needs to be managed, notably in crises where the government of the day will make decisions about the allowable operations of their national forces, these individual decisions may challenge the effectiveness of a coalition force.

This is challenge which CJOPS has to be prepared to deal with in both exercises and real world operations. Kitcher underscored: "Planning and exercises prepare the way for joint and coalition capabilities but executing them in an actual operational situation requires agility and flexibility of command by CJOPS and his staff, and our parallel staff in the various coalition headquarters."

Air Vice-Marshal Kitcher emphasized that working with partners to deal with challenges in the region has clearly grown in importance for both deterrent and operational impacts. The relationship with U.S. forces has certainly become closer. He mentioned an upcoming CPX exercise with the U.S. Indo-PACOM command in which the ADF and the U.S. will run a detailed CPX on a regional scenario together. The cooperation with both Japan and India is also growing.

And with Australia's regional defence emphasis, joint operations will need to focus on regional partners in the Australian neighborhood. This will see more emphasis on building regional expertise and continued engagement with regional countries through relationship building, languages, cultural awareness, and local knowledge. This can provide an important aspect of Australian leadership in a regional military coalition but dependent on the crisis, a differentiator for Australian involvement as well.

As Air Vice-Marshal Kitcher summarized their job: "We've got a responsibility to make sure that we optimize how well the joint force works together for the greatest positive effect and present the best possible options to government on how that force might be employed. We've also got a remit to ensure that we can work as closely and as efficiently and effectively as possible with our regional partners in both peacetime HADR situations and potential crisis situations.

"We've got a responsibility to be as efficient and as effective together among like-minded nations militaries. If we are not careful, uncoordinated actions in our region will overwhelm smaller countries and not have a positive effect.

"Planning and conducting OAA together ensures we present a much more credible regional security capability than we do as individual nations. The militaries have a large part of the responsibility to generate how we can do so. And then it's up to individual governments to determine how those forces will be employed at any one time or in any one set of security circumstances."

We closed the discussion by focusing on a question I asked him with regard to how does Australia best leverage its geography in shaping its defence and deterrent structure?

He answered that is a core challenge and question. He noted: "The really good thing about Australia is the size of Australia and the amount of nothing that is in Australia. The really bad thing about Australia is the size of Australia and the amount of nothing that is in Australia."

Australia's population and economic base is in the South and East of the country; the core defence locations for projecting force into the region are in the North, North East and North West of Australia. Northern Australia (especially the North and North West) is lightly populated without significant infrastructure and major industrial base. How does Australia have capabilities which can be used to project force into the region from Northern Australia but the majority of the population and industrial base remains well in the south?

For example, the RAAF has a number of bare bases in northern Australia in addition to their main operating bases. But how can those bases really be used for operations in a crisis, and flexibly use all of the basing options available?

How to support all these locations?

How to move fuel and weapons?

How to ensure the necessary level of resilience and that combat support, logistics and health elements are available?

There are no easy or cheap solutions to achieve a viable outcome.

Air Vice-Marshal Kitcher concluded: "The challenge of how we optimize the Australian geography for defence is real and is quite significant. As is how we use Australian geography for the best effect of allies and partners that we might invite to deploy here. This is an ongoing process and a real challenge."

A FOLLOW-UP INTERVIEW WITH LTGEN SIMON STUART

May 23, 2023

The Sir Richard Williams Foundation Seminar on 30 March 2023 focused on the way ahead with regard to deterrence of adversaries in the region, notably with both the behavior and the capabilities of the PRC in mind.

The question of refocusing the role of the ADF in the defense of Australia and its role in the region was a key element for consideration. Clearly, the joint force focus is significant but is the role of service components in the joint force as it adapts its role in the new strategic context.

At the seminar, LTGEN Simon Stuart, COS of the Australian Army, provided a general look at the deterrence challenge, the role of the ADF and of the Australian Army. He concluded: "From an Army perspective, from the contribution of land power to that integrated force, we offer presence, persistence, asymmetry through first-mover advantage, utility, and incredibly good value for money."

I had a chance to continue the discussion with him on his perspective when we met at his office on April 10th. Here he further elaborated on how he saw the role of the Army within the evolving joint force whose mission was being refocused on the region.

LTGEN Stuart started by focusing on what he viewed as key elements of Army's value proposition for the joint and increasingly integrated force. He underscored in this context Army's key role in C2, logistics, domestic security and providing national infrastructure within Australian territory for regional power projection.

He then argued that Air Force and Army are developing and will do so even more in the future their working relationship at the strike and shield aspect of defence of Australian defence infrastructure and territory. He put it this way: "How will integrated air defense be worked in terms of the overall approach to leveraging our strategic geography and our force projection forces?"

LTGEN Stuart highlighted a key element for shaping the way ahead, namely working force integration, including force design and with allies as well. "We must have an architecture that we are building to in terms of our platforms and systems which allow us to leverage the benefits of an integrated force. This also enables us to better plug into allied and partner forces through exercising rotational forces and where appropriate operating for joint basing."

The geography of Australia is a key consideration in shaping a way ahead for both the direct defense of Australia and the projection of power from Australia. One perspective is clearly to focus on the presence of Army structure throughout the country thought of an archipelago. And second, the role of the Army in working in the region with partners, and exercising on their territory as well, or, in other words, working the neighborhood.

LTGEN Stuart spoke at some length to the territorial presence role of the Australian Army as underwriting the ability for direct defense and shaping an effective foundation for joint force power projection from Australia.

"At the foundation and during my presentation, we emphasized the importance of being able to leverage Australian geographically for strategic purposes. The Army is located in 157 locations around the country, from the most northern tip of Cape York to Tasmania and from the West to the East coast. And our connection into local towns, cities and communities is through these 157 locations where our people are located.

"One of the key design principles for our Army Objective Force is what we call the total workforce system. We have a flexible set of arrangements for people to work full or part time or a combination of both throughout their career in the Army. That helps us have a workforce in 157 locations, as some of these are sparsely populated.

"Our capacity to leverage our total workforce system means we can leverage our part time brigades to project force from the bases South of the Tropic of Capricorn into the northern geography to reinforce and protect our sustainment capabilities in that part of the country.

"We have restructured our 2nd Division to be a division which leverages our total workforce system. Its six formations leverage our part time people in great part."

With recent natural disasters in Australia, such as the bush fires, the Army has been mobilized to help the nation in non-defense crises. This has meant that C2 has been used for national mobilization as well as transport equipment to move force to the point of need.

There is the challenge of overtaxing the Army for such tasks, but it does suggest that mobilization is a whole of nation effort, not simply a tip of the spear warfighting support effort.

Because of concern for overstretching the Army in dealing with national disasters, Australian analysts such as Professor John Blaxton have suggested need for a national mobilization system which engages the citizenry to deal with national disasters and could operate as a reserve for national crises, up to those of war itself.

We did NOT discuss this, but clearly if the government is to consider whole of nation solutions for national security and defense, such ideas need to be considered.

We then discussed one aspect of mobilization which has become clearly evident, namely a relationship between government and industry to provide for war materiel at levels of effectiveness and not just in time efficiencies. Alan Dupont and others spoke at the seminar of the impact of the Ukraine war which has demonstrated the absence of the kind of arsenal of democracy which Australia and the liberal democracies need.

We did discuss the munitions challenge which requires significant investment in development and the buying of weapons stockpiles. With regard to Australia, LTGEN Stuart noted: "We need to the capacity to store, maintain, and perform upgrades on guided weapons in Australia using an Australian workforce. And that is a prerequisite to the capacity to then be able to either provide component manufacture or assembly or actually to manufacture guided weapons and explosive ordnance in the country."

For LTGEN Stuart, the Australian Army has a key role to play in the way ahead for the direct defense of Australia and the role of the ADF and the Australian nation in the region. Doing so will take imagination, resources, and commitment – qualities which are always in short supply, at least in my view.

THE PERSPECTIVE OF THE COMMANDER OF THE PEARL HARBOR NAVAL SHIPYARD

May 26, 2023

As the U.S. Navy works its ability for distributed operations with integrated effects, how will the fleet be supported and sustained? One answer to that question is the major challenge of rebuilding the fleet's maintenance infrastructure.

Years of just-in-time maintenance, supporting wars of choice and not wars of necessity, have highlighted the need to invest in the ability to turn U.S, Navy ships out from maintenance in a timely manner and to have the requisite trained workforce to support enduring operations in a high tempo conflict.

Although increasingly recognized as a key priority, rebuilding the U.S. Navy's maintenance infrastructure takes not only time and money, but the human capital to maintain a fleet built for enduring operations.

Unlike China, U.S. maintenance yards need to be redesigned and upgraded to support comprehensive and efficient operations of a modern combat fleet.

What is the U.S. Navy doing to right the ship, with regard to maintainability?

During my late April 2023 visit to Honolulu, I sat down with Captain Richard Jones, Commander of Pearl Harbor Naval Shipyard and Intermediate Maintenance Facility (PHNSY & IMF), to discuss how they are shaping a way ahead that both enhances near-term capabilities and looks ahead to meet the Pacific's challenging strategic environment .

Simply put, the key metric of a shipyard is the speed at which ships under maintenance are returned to combat commanders. Shipyards must continually look for opportunities and methods to ramp up the maintenance period rate, particularly when considering the possibility of sustained conflict against a peer competitor.

With the recognition that shipyards must become more efficient, the Navy established the Shipyard Infrastructure Optimization Program (SIOP) program office in May 2018.

As the Navy has described this effort:

The Navy's four public shipyards -- Norfolk Naval Shipyard (NNSY), Portsmouth Naval Shipyard (PNSY), Puget Sound Naval Shipyard and Intermediate Maintenance Facility (PSNS&IMF), and Pearl Harbor Naval Shipyard and Intermediate Maintenance Facility (PHNSY&IMF) -- perform a vital role in national defense by executing maintenance on submarines and aircraft carriers in order to provide combat-ready ships to the fleet.

Originally designed and built in the 19th and 20th centuries to build sail- and conventionally-powered ships, the Navy's public shipyards are not efficiently configured to maintain and modernize nuclear-powered aircraft carriers and submarines.

With the Navy's needed focus on operations, the aging shipyards have been unable to adequately sustain and optimize their facilities, utilities, dry docks, equipment and information technology infrastructure. These inefficiencies and obsolete facilities result in higher maintenance costs, schedule risks and reliability issues.

To create the shipyards that our nation needs requires making significant investments to modernize dry docks, optimize industrial processes and modernize standard equipment to bring these critical industrial sites to modern standards.

To meet that mission, the Navy established the Shipyard Infrastructure Optimization Program (SIOP) program office in May 2018. The SIOP Program Office (PMO 555) is under the Program Executive Office (PEO) Industrial Infrastructure (II), which was established in Fiscal Year 2022 as a Naval Facilities Engineering Systems Command (NAVFAC) affiliated PEO and is responsible for the cost, schedule, and performance of SIOP. PEO II reports to the Assistant Secretary of the Navy for Research, Development, and Acquisition (ASN RD&A).

The Navy will ensure that the optimization process fully integrates environmental considerations including natural and cultural resources, water and air quality, and more. During the development of individual shipyard plans, the Navy will develop alternatives for assessment under the National Environmental Policy Act (NEPA), Endangered Species Act (ESA) and the National Historic Preservation Act (NHPA).

The Navy will work with stakeholders as part of the decision-making process and will conduct all appropriate NEPA, natural resource and NHPA analyses; agency and government-to-government consultations and public engagement and obtain all required permits to ensure a proactive approach to environmental protection.[13]

With the breadth and depth of needs, the SIOP program has a significant workload to deliver the critical warfighting infrastructure enabling a distributed fleet to operate effectively in crisis and combat situations.

A Government Accountability Office (GAO) report on SIOP indicated the steps SIOP has taken to recapitalize its shipyards:

The Navy has taken several actions to improve its public shipyards in recent years. In 2018, the Navy began an effort to modernize and optimize its shipyards, known as the Shipyard Infrastructure Optimization Plan (SIOP).

The Navy has also implemented some GAO recommendations in its efforts to improve shipyards, such as creating a program office to manage the SIOP. In addition, the Navy invested in shipyard infrastructure above the minimum level set by Congress. Finally, the average condition of facilities at Navy shipyards has improved at three of the four shipyards from 2016 to 2020. [14]

In addition to the progress enumerated by GAO, SIOP has commenced the second phase of industrial modeling for all four shipyards to provide data for optimized workflows and has begun the project planning studies for Waterfront Production Facility (WPF) at Pearl Harbor.

A task order has been awarded for construction of the new Dry Dock 5 at Pearl Harbor, and multiple Facilities, Sustainment, Restoration, and Modernization (FSRM) projects to maintain the shipyards' mission readiness have been executed.

SIOP will continue to "recapitalize the four public shipyards to optimize maintenance production by correcting infrastructure and equipment condition, configuration, capacity, and resiliency shortfalls," according to Mr. Mark Edelson, the head of the program executive office, Industrial Infrastructure (PEO II):

"The happiest Fleet Commanders have the ships required to fulfill forward presence commitments." PEO II has oversight of the Shipyard Infrastructure Optimization Program, which is a holistic plan that integrates all infrastructure and industrial plant equipment investments at the Navy's four public shipyards to meet nuclear fleet maintenance requirements.

In my discussion with Captain Jones, he identified a number of attributes needed for mission success and how PHNSY & IMF is working to build these areas.

A key attribute – and one he emphasized – was having a skilled, capable, and motivated workforce. He noted that for nearly a decade, the shipyard did not hire new staff, prior to the refocus on the great power competition. This led to a major hiring gap which meant they had an experienced but aging workforce. With the returned focus and renewed appreciation of the yards not to mention an increased workload, the shipyard began bringing many new hires onboard.

With this new workforce, the question became, "how to close the gap and ensure proper transfer of skills to the new hires while simultaneously taking in new types of learning and skills?" The new personnel brought new perspectives, approaches, and techniques. Captain Jones indicated that they have been able to blend the old with the new to create a highly effective workforce.

He noted: "If you look at the people coming in, they see the work differently. We don't accept every idea they propose, but we do we listen and take those ideas into account because they may have a great idea that nobody's ever thought of before."

New teaching approaches have helped as well. Captain Jones highlighted the use of virtual reality training. He gave two examples, welding and crane operations. With regard to welding skills, students wear a virtual welding hood that is a simulator.

"It actually feels like you're holding welding rod. The computer system can tell how hard you're pressing on it and if you're pressing on it at the right angle," Jones said. "When you're looking through the hood, you see what you would see during an actual welding operation."

He also described the crane operation training: "We have a rigging trainer for crane operators. When they have their virtual reality hood on, they are in the cab of the crane and have the same controls.

"When you're wearing the virtual reality hood, sitting in the chair, it's very life-like, similar to being in the crane. It really speeds up the training because it doesn't take a physical crane off operations and it's much safer because the trainees can make mistakes virtually and not damage anything."

While the training the workforce receives is a cornerstone of the shipyard, it is also the workforce themselves both as individuals and as a team which is crucial to the success of the shipyard.

Captain Jones underscored the workforce is motivated to join PHNSY & IMF. Not only do they have many more Apprentice Program applicants than available openings each year, but they are part of the local community through sports teams, teaching in colleges and universities, mentoring young scientists in STEM programs, and volunteerism.

The workforce also knows PHNSY & IMF has been and continues to be a vital asset to the Nation's defense both in the past and today. One example is the significant role the shipyard played in World War II and in the following years, ensuring the Navy had the ships they needed to respond to any situation.

It is indeed gratifying to see a local community committed to the nation and its defense.

A second key attribute is to have the proper tooling and material for the repair process. Here the yard could use more investment in new tools and machinery, but the workers use a mix of the old and the new to good effect. As part of the SIOP program, assessments are underway to evaluate the various equipment throughout the shipyard so that upgrades can be made where needed.

Captain Jones noted, "Our machine shop actually uses some pre-World War II equipment. Some of these machines are extremely reliable and they almost never break down and are very good at doing certain things. For example, if we are only going to do single-type milling, it's much faster to do it on the older machine. We have balance between the new and the old that seems to be working very well."

A third key attribute also linked to the SIOP program is the process for redesign of the shipyard to support modern workflows to optimize the work process to speed up the ability to more rapidly do ship repairs. The need for these upgrades is linked to how the yard was established in 1908 and developed over time to meet the needs of that time.

SIOP has completed one phase of industrial modeling that shipyards can leverage to improve efficiency. Another phase of industrial modeling for Pearl Harbor and each of the other three shipyards has begun that will provide data for optimized workflows at the yards. This work will provide modeling data for workflows inside the facilities and will inform more detailed project level planning and design (P&D) for future SIOP construction projects.

Another element of this challenge is to enhance the digital backbone at the yard. When asked what Captain Jones would like to see in future investments, the digital backbone is clearly one capability which he felt needed to be enhanced.

Retired Adm. James Foggo emphasized the need for such investment in a 6 January 2023 article on the way ahead with regard to the SIOP. Foggo argued: "While improving the physical infrastructure of these facilities will be critical to success, it's equally essential that we take this opportunity to build the digital infrastructure required to accelerate our readiness advantage."[15]

Captain Jones noted that they have established an innovation division within the shipyard which will facilitate the digital transition, such as using 3D printing and other technologies. "I think it's a step in the right direction but we are still in the infancy stage."

A fourth key attribute is simply adding more infrastructure capacity. The main effort of the yard is repair of submarines, but the yard does not have the dry docks it needs. The first SIOP related project is the construction of a new graving dry dock to accommodate for a now obsolete Dry Dock #3, which will be replaced by the new Dry Dock #5.

"Our first major project is a new Dry Dock #3 replacement, also known as Dry Dock #5, which will be deep enough, wide enough, long enough for our current SSNs and any future one that's in the books for planning. There is also a Waterfront Production Facility we are going to put next to it and a pier that we need. We have very little pier space here that meets the requirements," said Jones.

"Then there is this optimization piece. If you look at the shipyard, our first dry dock built in 1919 has all the work shops were right along next to it. Then we built dry docks 2, 3 and 4. But most of the work-shops are still located around the first dry dock.

"This is not optimal for our workflow, and we need to bring workers closer to where the work instead of spreading the work all over the yard. A lot of time is consumed in transit throughout the yard.

"We have 1,000 engineers out of 6,000 civilians roughly, the majority of whom are on the fourth floor of this building which is quite far from the waterfront. Moving them down right above the production shops is key element for optimization."

We also discussed battle-damage repair as illustrated by the yard's participation in the last RIMPAC exercise. PHNSY Navy divers participated in simulated battle-damage repair on USS Denver.

As Edward Lundquist noted in an article on this event:

"Before going down on July 22, Denver made one more valuable contribution to the Fleet. Navy salvage and repair experts set explosive charges aboard the ship that enabled battle damage assessment (BDA) teams to respond to actual damage.

"According to Jamie Koehler a Naval Sea Systems Command spokesperson, the event exercised the capabilities and limitations of an expeditionary group of Reservist and Regional Maintenance Center (RMC) Sailors for emergent repair when paired with an emergent repair container capability.

"The event provided the opportunity to survey realistic blast damage and conduct planning to utilize the Emergent Repair Capability afforded by the Emergent Maintenance and Repair Container (EMARC) along with Surge Maintenance (SURGEMAIN) Navy Reservist Sailors to plan and execute emergent repair," Koehler said. "Divers were offered a realistic training environment to learn how to assess battle damage and how to effectively repair the ship."

"The training simulated exactly how a ship would look after an attack or casualty and offered Mobile Diving Salvage Unit One and Pearl Harbor Naval Shipyard divers a chance to work as a team to assess, repair and return the vessel back to sea," Koehler said.

"Opportunities like this also identify future manning requirements, equipment sortfalls, and medical response preparations that can be measured appropriately."

"Battle Damage Assessment Training aboard ex-USS Denver

- Commander, Navy Regional Maintenance Center (CNRMC) coordinated the availability of the EMARC containers.

- Hawaii Regional Maintenance Center provided Sailors an Engineering Assessment team support to the repair planning effort.
- SURGEMAIN provide Sailors and three Officers to support the assessment, planning and execution of repairs.
- MDSU-1 conducted Battle Damage Assessments (BDA) and notified PHNSY of their findings. Their knowledge of salvage equipment and techniques were used to complete the BDA evolution.
- PHNSY conducted Battle Damage Repair (BDR) and patch work to fix the damaged vessel based on MDSU-1's recommendation. Our knowledge of patches and repair techniques were used to complete the BDR evolution."

Let me conclude with a few final thoughts.

The challenge of ramping up the speed to deliver ships back to the operational fleet is a key part effective deterrence. It is also a challenge which requires strategic attention.

PHSNY & IMF is keenly aware of their strategic importance and the importance of meeting the key metric of the speed at which ships under maintenance are returned to combat commanders.. They are actively working to address the key areas of people, process and environment to successfully meet the nation's needs today and into the future.

DENMARK RECEIVES ITS FIRST F-35S: LOOKING BACK AND LOOKING FORWARD

09/26/2023

Recently, I published my book *My Fifth Generation Journey: 2004-2018* in which I highlighted how a program not supported by three presidents nor actively by any Secretary of Defense became the dominant air combat system being flown in the era of "great power competition."

But a key part of the story is Denmark and for me the very unusual conference held in Copenhagen in 2015 between the Williams Foundation and the Centre of Military Studies of the University of Copenhagen.

One of the key presenters at the Conference was Col. Anders Rex, Chief of the Expeditionary Air Staff of the Danish Air Force, who coined the phrase "coalitionability" to express his focus on the core requirement of allied air forces and defense forces shaping ways to work more effectively with one another in dealing with twenty-first century challenges.

Rex went on to become Major General Rex and head of the Air Force where he organized visits for me in Denmark to their bases and to see first-hand their preparation for the arrival of their F-35s and their preparation for fifth-generation enabled combat operations.

He went on to work at senior positions in MoD and is now based in Washington as the Defence Attache.

Upon my return from the DSEI conference in London which was being held while the first Danish F-35s arrived in Denmark, I sat down with Major General Rex to discuss the way ahead, notably in terms of the drive for further integration of the Nordics in terms of defense capabilities and effort.

Major General Rex noted that of course the Air Force would be focused on the standup of their F-35 force, training, equipping and operating the force.

But with the challenges the West faces it was crucial to integrate the capabilities which we have more effectively, and the F-35 could be an important stimulant to that process or as I have called it a forcing function aircraft.

But this rests upon much more effective integration of the data generated by the force. "We need to be able to much more effectively share data among our F-35s and with other elements of the force as well."

Significant progress in data sharing is a key theme when we last talked.

In that 2021 interview held in Copenhagen, he underscored: "For me, joint all domain C2 is clearly the future. But at the same time we have to work on enhanced capabilities with the current force. We need focus on both in parallel. Denmark does not have the muscle to shape the future of all domain command and control, but we also need to drive the change – we need now to get the job done.

"What I have been focused on over the past couple of years, is to make our force better now. Today. We actually already have the capability to shape more effective networks of ISR and C2 without significant investments. For example, we are leveraging the joint range extension application protocol (JREAP) that requires modest investments, and it is a way for us, our allies and coalition partners to build a modest combat cloud linking our data."[16]

So the coming of the F-35s to Denmark is an important step forward but needs to be part of an allied effort for more effective force integration among the allies, notably those allies flying or going to fly the same aircraft in the region.

Major General Rex underscored: "We put so many limitations on ourselves with regard to data sharing. The first one is policy. The technology is driving greater amounts of data and possibilities of sharing.

"But we need for policy to catch up with technology. There is no clearer case of this than building a global fleet of F-35s and the significant possibility of shared data and integrated operations. We just need to get on with it."

He argued that "if you put F-35 pilots together with destroyer or submarine captains they can figure out how to work together and share information.

"We need to enable their innovation with the emergence of data rich platforms. I think the point is there is a critical need to make the most out of what our force could do better now and not just pursuing future options and dreams."

DETERRENCE AND MULTI-DOMAIN STRIKE: THE PERSPECTIVE OF PACAF

October 1, 2023

What is the relationship among multi-domain strike capabilities, warfighting and deterrence?

Multi-domain strike capabilities can only be done with foundational capabilities which enhance one's viability in warfighting, and by being able to do so to enhance the adversary perceptions of their risk calculus. They need to believe that continuing a conflict is not worth the effort because they can not easily defeat you or intimidate you into capitulating to their demands.

But I would argue that strategically enabled multi-domain strike also requires political-military leadership which understands how to engage in war termination.

And I would argue being able to do effective war termination rests on the adversary's understanding of the robustness of our ability to continue a campaign. And this rests as well on a viable distributed force structure whose continued ability to punish an adversary suggests that war termination is in their interest as well as ours.

The presentations of General Wilsbach at the March and September Williams Foundation seminars provide several insights which suggest the relationships among multi-domain strike, war fighting and deterrence.

At the March seminar, the General argued the following: "The message of cost imposition is simple on its surface but has layers to consider. First and foremost, we all understand that no one wins if a conflict with China breaks out in the Indo-Pacific. That would be the worst-case scenario for every nation that calls the region home and is the last thing any of us want.

"So if an aggressor chooses to cross that line, they are already willing to bear considerable cost. That's why the deterrence must be credible and convincing. You cannot leave room for doubt that the cost could be tolerable.

"To do that, you need to know who should receive that message. In authoritarian regimes, it must reach the few people at the top who hold all the decision- making authority. They may never bear the cost personally, but their power relies on the fear and submission of those who will....

"Denial, cost, resilience. Ideally, our deterrence actions should convey all three messages simultaneously. If I were an adversary planner, seeing capable forces across multiple, like- minded nations committed to action, able to deny my goals at overwhelming cost to me, and resilient enough to weather any of my attacks, that would keep me up at night. Integrated deterrence requires integration, readiness, and willingness, but it also needs one more thing—belief."

In the September seminar, Wilsbach focused then on how multi-domain strike empowered deterrent capabilities. He underscored in his video presentation the following:

"There are many reasons to lean into multi domain operations, but I want to focus on one in particular, multi domain operations allow us to overwhelm and trip the adversary. Historically, warfare carries certain constants.

"One of the most important of these is gaining and maintaining the initiative. A combatant seizes the initiative, not through advanced technologies or superior training, but because they hit the adversary hard enough to knock them off balance, then hit them repeatedly to maintain an enduring advantage. pressure generated by synchronizing operations in time and space creates the opportunities where technology and training can make a difference."

To be able to do multi-domain operations requires a warfighting ecosystem which reflects and embodies effective warfighting and deterrent capabilities, of the sort no adversary could miss. Of course, the failure to build such an ecosystem will mean that multi-domain strike will not be feasible or viable. The adversary understands this and targets force integration across a distributed battlespace, and works to enhance antagonisms among allies in a way to undercut the kind of integration which is both possible and necessary.

Wilsbach emphasized three key elements of the warfighting ecosystem which enables multi-domain strike and deterrence.

"The three angles of attack I've covered today, optimizing internal Air Force capabilities, joint integration, and ally and partner integration are areas we need to push. If we want to execute multi domain operations.

"All three will fail, however, if we don't leverage our decisive angle, our airmen and aviators, our people are the best in the world, something our competitors recognize as they tried to copy our methods and attempt to hire our former members to train their forces...."

He concluded with a fundamental warning regarding the importance of shaping multi-domain strike capabilities throughout an integrated joint and coalition force as a core enabler of warfighting and deterrence.

"As I conclude allow me to make one more pass to stress the importance of multi-domain strike, Seizing and maintaining the initiative remains a key tenant of success in conflict. And you can only do that by hitting your adversary from every angle. The modern battlefield has one overarching rule--overwhelm or be overwhelmed."

THE STRIKE ENTERPRISE AND THE ROYAL AIR FORCE

October 3, 2023

With the signing of AUKUS, Australia certainly closely aligned its way ahead with regard to weapons development and acquisition with the United States and the Britain. While most attention has been paid appropriately to TLAMs and long-range strike, what is Britain doing in the strike area of note for Australia?

At least part of an answer to that question was provided by the presentation by the current head of the RAF, Air Marshal Harvey Smyth, to the seminar.

In his presentation, he focused on the RAF's experience with the evolution of its strike enterprise in terms of the development of its airborne strike force as well as providing a very helpful reflection on what the experience of the current conflict in Ukraine and Russia might mean for working a way ahead in the strike area.

Smyth started his presentation this time as he did the last by citing the importance of the UK's "refresh" of the strategic defence review which was issued in March 2023 at almost the same time as Australia's DSR. The "refresh" reaffirmed the core approach of the earlier strategic review but emphasized that the pace of change was accelerating.

And obviously there was a major war ongoing in Europe, which although referred to often as the conflict in Ukraine, I would label it more accurately as a NATO-Russian war in Ukraine. And given the central impact of this war on British interests, it obviously is having a major impact on British thinking as well.

Indeed, Air Marshal Smyth noted that 80% of his "day job" was focused on Ukraine. The "refresh" underscored that "We are now in a period of heightened risk and volatility that is likely to last beyond the 2030s.

IR2023 updates the UK's priorities and core tasks to reflect the resulting changes in the global context.

"First, IR2023 responds to Russia's illegal invasion of Ukraine. Putin's act of aggression has precipitated the largest military conflict, refugee and energy crisis in Europe since the end of the Second World War. It has brought large-scale, high intensity land warfare back to our home region, with implications for the UK and NATO's approach to deterrence and defence.

"As IR2021 set out, Russia is the most acute threat to the UK's security. What has changed is that our collective security now is intrinsically linked to the outcome of the conflict in Ukraine. We must also analyse, learn from and adapt to the changing nature of warfare – notably in the land domain."[17]

So what is Britain learning?

According to Smyth, the war is proving amongst other things that "possessing the ability to successfully execute deep strike missions in a sustained manner, with precision and pace amongst a very dense and complex defense system, whilst in parallel defending against the enemy's ability to conduct similar operations against you is a fundamental cornerstone to modern high intensity conflict.

"Hence, President Zelensky has continued to campaign around the need to gift additional long-range capability like the Storm Shadow cruise missile.

"This missile is currently being utilized with very positive effect. And we've recently witnessed and many successful Ukrainian strikes against targets like the Russian Black Sea Fleet, deep in Crimea hugely symbolic in terms of Ukraine's ability to reach deep into Russian held territory, specifically in terms of penetrating one of the world's most densely complex defenses to achieve precision effect against strategically important targets.

"This is fundamentally altering their dynamics of this whole conflict."

Smyth's example is an important one.

What exactly is the relationship among an ability to deliver long range strike and war termination, deterrence or "victory"?

The NATO-Russian war in Ukraine is raising a lot of questions concerning the relationship of strike to what kind of warfighting and diplomatic outcomes occur and are desired. And the question of what kind of strikes lead to WMD escalation remains a critical one as well in this war.

It is not an exercise: it is not a drill: it is a war in the center of Europe and is driving significant change in the thinking of a number of European countries bordering Russia with regard to what their strike posture needs to be facing Russia.

A key element of the evolution of strike involved in Ukraine clearly is with regard to land-based operations utilizing drones and a decentralized (to put it mildly) C2 system. Here Ukrainians have used a variety of drones to strike and kill Russian ground forces by a combination of space-based commercial capabilities, cell phones, and localized decision with regard to targets.

The Russians have used their drones to attack infrastructure and inflict civilian causalities. This is a good reminder that authoritarian states and liberal democracies have very different targeting philosophies and any asymmetry in this regard musts be considered in warfighting and deterrent calculations.

This dynamic of strike and defense is a key one and Air Marshal Smyth warns: "We should pay particular attention to Russia's ability to sustain an extremely capable long range attack force, bringing to bear on a routine basis coordinated standoff attacks with cruise missiles, hypersonic weapons, and one way attack drones targeting Ukraine's critical national infrastructure on a very regular basis.

"This is a point that will become ever more important as we enter another winter of warfare, where the targeting of energy and power supplies adds a dramatic humanitarian effect and dimension to the challenge.

"For me, the biggest lesson here is that any discussion about the development of multi-domain strike capability must go hand in glove with the discussion around your own integrated air and missile defense. One must be able to defend against the adversary's ability to strike you once you break through their defenses to strike them."

The remaining discussion by Smyth focused on RAF considerations concerning the evolution of the strike enterprise. Here he focused on the evolution of the Storm Shadow to a new family of strike weapons, which they have labelled Selective Precision Effects At Range (SPEAR).

This family of weapons is being developed by the European company MBDA where especially important is the UK-French weapons cooperation. But these weapons are being developed by a construct created earlier in the UK called the Complex Weapons Project which was set up by Lord Drayson, then the Defence Minister, to build weapons in an era of defence dollar scarcity.

I remember this development well for I was working at the time for the U.S. Defence Acquisition Chief, and then Secretary of the Air Force Mike Wynne. In a 14 July 2008 article by Craig Hoyle, the nature of the enterprise was identified: "Including MBDA, Qinetiq, Roxel, Thales Missile Electronics, Thales UK and the MoD, the partnership was formally launched with a signing ceremony at the show involving Minister for Defence Equipment and Support Baroness Taylor. "Team CW will help to maintain the UK's key skills and technologies in missile development and protect our operational sovereignty in this sector for the future," she says.

"This is a real landmark," says Team CW industrial chairman and MBDA UK managing director Steve Wadey. "It has taken radical change in industry and the MoD to reach this point."

"The new framework seeks to remove duplication, simplify platform integration, encourage modularity and provide planning stability to the UK's guided weapons sector. This has suffered a 25% decline in its business over the last few years, but is expected have a potential worth of £6 billion over the next decade, says Wadey."[18]

With this approach and with a strong partnership with the French MoD, the RAF has benefited from the arrival of Storm Shadow and building the new SPEAR family. But as Smyth notes the time line envisaged for SPEAR pre-dates the new situation, and how do we accelerate building the new generation of weapons?

Air Marshal Smyth also underscored that it was important to work the relationship between high-end precision weapons with less costly and more numerous weapon stocks in equipping the force. What is the right balance? How to fund it? How to deploy it? How to connect strategic and tactical effects from the use of such an integrated weapons enterprise?

He noted: "High tech weapons are of course clearly used (in the war in Ukraine), but all must be defended against and these one way attack drones offer a very significant cost differential compared to defensive systems, sending a cardboard drone to an airfield that's being defended by an S-400s.

"This can potentially induce a critical stockpile imbalance and this means that saturation weapons can draw fires from the defender to create an undefended gap because of stockpile depletion, which risks ultimately a loss of control of the air.

"Based on such experiences from Ukraine, we're looking very closely in UK at our future weapons mix. We are trying to understand this in a number of ways. Again, unfortunately, the details of which becomes very classified very quickly."

But he did underscore two key areas where he saw the need for missile modernization which needed to be made for the RAF going forward.

The first involved providing "a proper long-range strike capability for the F-35." This will be done with the coming of the SPEAR family of weapons.

The second involved "the RAF current lack of a viable standoff anti-ship weapon. This was a very hot topic for our last defence secretary. And at present, we're investigating a range of options to meet this requirement and are working with France on two different missile concepts under a specific program."

Air Marshal Smyth concluded: "An appropriate mix must constitute weapons that contribute to deterrence because of their capability and or their mass, alongside weapons that can be manufactured at a pace to sustain follow on stockpiles, and continue to feed the fight. Getting this balance right is critical, and will undoubtedly be informed by the specific adversity we face."

THE MARINE CORPS WORKS THE NEXT PHASE OF THEIR
USE OF UAVS: THE PERSPECTIVE FROM MAWTS-1

November 21, 2023

I wrote a chapter in the 2018 book entitled, *One Nation Under Drones*, which focused on the experience of the USMC with UAVs to date. I wrote this piece as the Marines were shifting from the primary focus on the land wars and to an enhanced focus on amphibious operations.

During operations in Iraq and Afghanistan, the Marines joined in with the U.S. Army and used the Shadow unmanned aerial system, for similar operations as the U.S. Army was engaged in the land wars.

But concurrently with the introduction of Shadow into the Corps, the ScanEagle was also introduced. And this system would fit the trajectory of the evolution of the Corps as it moved from a primary occupation with the land wars to a "return to the sea" and the joining of unmanned systems to the significant evolution of the Amphibious-Read Group and Marine Expeditionary Unit pairing into a flexible amphibious ready task force, a change driven initially by the introduction of the Osprey but being reshaped as other manned aircraft systems come to the force and unmanned systems woven into the overall force insertion capability of the amphibious task force.

The Scan Eagle-Blackjack transition was part of the shift in focus from the land wars to amphibious at sea operations. When he wrote the essay the focus was upon shaping capabilities to be launched from a ship to support the ground maneuver element. At the time, the Marine Corps leadership was focused on a program called MUX (MAGTF Unmanned eXpeditionary UAS) which the aviation plan at the time projected initial operations in the 2025 time frame.

But as the then Deputy Commandant of Aviation, LtGen Rudder noted in 2020, that the MUX was being shelved in favor of a different approach.

"I think what we discovered with the MUX program is that it's going to require a family of systems. The initial requirement had a long list of very critical requirements, but when we did the analysis and tried to fit it inside one air vehicle," they realized they had competing needs, Rudder said.

"With a family of systems approach, my sense is we're going to have an air vehicle that can do some of the requirements, some of the higher-end requirements, potentially from a land-based high-endurance vehicle, but we're still going to maintain a shipboard capability, it just may not be as big as we originally configured."

"The MUX program – formally the Marine Air-Ground Task Force (MAGTF) Unmanned Aerial System (UAS) Expeditionary – was meant to be a Group 5 UAS, the largest of the categories with highest altitude and greatest endurance. It would cover seven missions: command, control and communication; early warning; persistent fires; escort; electronic warfare; reconnaissance, intelligence, surveillance and target acquisition (RISTA); and tactical distribution…

"Program officials realized they had a huge task ahead of them with so many separate missions, though, and early industry talks showed it may become cost-prohibitive. The seven missions were later sorted into two tiers of priority.

"Still, as Rudder said, it became clear that those higher priority missions were incompatible with shipboard launch and recovery.

"Power output and weight capacity, obviously you get more weight and power output with a ground-based system with a longer runway, expeditionary runway, than you can coming vertically off the back of a ship. Shipboard compatibility continues to be a challenge for all our air vehicles," Rudder said."[19]

What has happened since that time is the USMC is buying into the Reaper program and relying on a land based remotely piloted vehicle to provide the support Marines would require for their at sea and from the sea operations. The Marines leased two Reapers from General Atomics since 2018 but then moved from leasing to buying the aircraft in 2021.

When I visited MAWTS-1 in November 2023, I learned how the force was practically moving ahead. MAWTS-1 is a place focused on training an integrated USMC force, not pursing systems that are simply "fairy dust" as one Marine put it to me. It is about how to make the force ready to fight tonight and to do so more effectively.

I discussed the integration of the Reaper into USMC operations with the LtCol Edgardo Cardona, the Executive Officer at MAWTS-1, who is a former DASC officer and current MQ-9A Reaper pilot [20]

LtCol Edgardo Cardona is one of the pilots where the Marines have created a new MOS, which is the 7318 MOS.[21] The Marine Corps Reaper unlike its Predator brethren is not armed so there is not a competition between remotely piloted or manned systems in terms of being trigger pullers.

It is about enhancing the relevant ISR to provide for more effective insertion of force and enabling that force in terms of their operations. This is notably one the most significant changes since I last came to MAWTS-1 in 2020.

The career of the XO has paralleled that of the evolution of USMC experience in UAVs so that he is both a core officer in the evolution of USMC capabilities but has also embodied the transition from the Middle East and the Marines use of Shadow, Scan Eagle, Blackjack and K-MAX. He has been on the ground floor for the introduction of the Reaper to the Marine Corps.

The XO pointed out that his earlier experience at MAWTS-1 with UAVs, the focus was on deconfliction of the UAVs designed to provide ISR for the ground combat element. Now the focus is upon integration with the air element for the overall integrated operations.

The Reaper is working with the combat air elements in sharing a common operational picture and to enable those aircraft to have a view of the objective area prior to reaching it and to in turn to be able to enhance their ability to support the overall Marine Corps force being inserted into that objective area.

The XO underscored that MAWTS-1 was working closely with the USAF on Reaper operations and sharing experience and understanding their different operational requirements as well.

He underscored: "Our goal with Reaper operations is to create a common operational picture enabling ground force commanders or maritime component commanders to make real time decisions based on a plethora of information that we're providing. And we're also focused on fusing different data links that are coming down from different services together to create that operational picture."

He went to note that "we see the MQ-9 as a good F-150 or a good reliable truck that can operate at long range and is reliable. But it is the payloads that are crucial to us and are ability to take the data generated by the payloads and use our digitally interoperable systems to distribute the data throughout the MAGTF."

When he came to MAWTS-1 in 2020, he underscored: "We needed to figure out how to shape an MQ-9 program within the WTI focus of MAWTS-1. Training is a key piece in standing up a new capability and at MAWTS-1, it is about integrated MAGTF capability. We are not training a stand-alone force."

The XO noted that they reached out to the Air Force to help validate their initial MQ-9 training approach, and now they share lessons learned and share training slots when appropriate.

LtCol Cardona underscored: "We are working with the ACC and Headquarters USMC to set up an exchange program to foster the expertise required.

"Any time I have excess capacity, I will take an Air Force student and make them a WTI. And then they will return to the Air Force community. We have a Marine currently in the Air Force 26 Weapons School training program who will graduate in December.

"So now we have a WTIs in the Air Force, and we're going to have USAF weapons school graduates in the Marine Corps who are Marines. And it fosters a lot of TTP development, a lot of great relationships with the Air Force."

He noted as well that they are tied in with the operational test community via VMX-1. They want to do integrated testing on new sensor suites and to be able to provide user input prior to the decision of what exactly gets produced and acquired.

Personally, I believe that the Marines will need to become major players in autonomous systems – airborne, and surface and below surface systems—but the Reaper is beginning the process. But certainly, the unique integrated mission sets the Marines work through a MAGTF will drive innovation which the joint force needs to note.

REFOCUSING THE FORCE: MAWTS-1 WORKS ON WAYS AHEAD

December 15, 2023

During my visit to MAWTS-1 in November 2023, I had a chance several times to talk with the CO of the command, Col Eric Purcell, about the evolution of the three WTIs he has been in charge of since he took command.

Because I had visited in 2020, when MAWTS began to work on the shift in the USMC associated with the Commandant's guidance which has been embodied in Force Design 2030, it was quite interesting to see how MAWTS has translated that into a force that has to fight tonight.

It is not about wargaming: it is about training for combat in today's world. It is not about imaging new weapons that someday the Marines might have or working with a joint force of the future imagined by strategic planners, it is about engaging in conflict anywhere in the world when called upon to do so.

Thinking about a world with multi-polar authoritarian players does tend to focus your mind when you have to train to fight a variety of adversaries.

And that is where we started our interview. Col Purcell noted that one of the major changes at the command is focusing attention on the developing capabilities of the kind of adversaries the Marines have to face.

Purcell noted that the Marines who come to the WTIs know learn about three categories of threats: those posed by Chinese forces; those posed by Russian forces; and those posed within the context of contingency operations.

The experience of the land wars and the historical legacy of fighting against Soviet equipment does not prepare today's Marines for the conflicts in which they are engaged or likely to have to deal with. It is important to re-shape the curriculum to reflect real world dynamic threats, and Purcell noted that they were focused on doing so.

But major challenges face the Marines in doing so, and MAWTS-1 as the core warfighting training center which standardizes operational preparation needs to adapt its training approach to the evolving threat envelope.

One change which Col Purcell underscored was the need to re-focus on tac air and assault support integration. He noted that in the land wars, the two forces tended to operate somewhat in different spheres, but going forward integration was key.

In part, this is due to the range and speed requirements for a Marine Corps insertion force and the opportunity to leverage the advantages which as F-35/Osprey force provides to the USMC along with the arrival of a new generation heavy lift asset, the CH-53K.

But this also due to the changes within the assault force itself, as the Osprey adds new capabilities carried in the back of the aircraft, or its ability to contribute to new missions for the Marines such as ASW support.

A key focus of attention has been moving beyond the training to establish FARP/EABOs, to working on the more important point – what effect are you trying to create through FARP/EABOs.[22]

With current capabilities, the Marines can create EABOs to provide for sensing capabilities, support for the transition of air elements, C2 node creation and support, but until a new generation of weapons show up, limited ability to provide for fires within a transitory EABO.

Col Purcell indicated that a primary focus within FINEX at the end of the course is bringing the different force elements together to test out their capabilities to deal with an integrated scenario.

Two scenarios were notable in our discussion. The first was working maritime strike and support. Here the Marines would operate from Camp Pendleton with San Clemente being an enemy location which was being reinforced by red combat ships coming from the north.

The U.S. Navy has provided ships for this purpose. Tac air provides the main means for interdiction of enemy shipping but simulate longer range strikes from Pendleton is involved as well.

A key capability of fifth generation aircraft is their ability to manage third party targeting which is a capability which the Marines will leverage going forward in terms of tapping into land-based strike, and one might assume this could by Army or Marine Corps ground strike capabilities.

Under the strike force, a TRAP force enabled by Ospreys operates and in FINEX, the Marines operated such a force and exercised it with the Navy and the USCG.

When the interdiction of the surface fleet threat was attenuated, the Marines shifted their attention to provide ASW support to the Navy, largely by providing sonobuoy deployment support.

A second key approach will be emphasized in next year's spring WTI.

Here the integration of TACAIR and assault support will be the focus of attention against an appropriate scenario for using such a force. With the evolution of tac air capabilities supplemented with data provided from Reapers and other ISR sources, and the evolution of the payloads carried by the assault force, a variety of scenarios can be tested in the next WTI and future WTIs.

A major challenge though facing the USMC is the dynamic changes within the joint force itself.

How does the USMC support the joint force if the Navy is in the thrust of significant change sorting through what they mean by distributed maritime operations?

How does the USMC support the USAF if that force is in the process of sorting out what Agile Combat Employment means in practice?

I would add that the fires challenge is a key one.

Who is the fires authority in a maritime strike scenario? A USAF air wing? A Navy surface action group?

Until this is sorted out land-based weapons whether operated by the Army or the USMC cannot have the desired effect. And having an effective joint force rests on having the fires authority challenge met and managed.

As Col Purcell concluded with this dynamic area of joint force engagement: "Typically, we refer to Target Engagement Authority abbreviated to TEA. In land wars between the Combined Forces Air Component Commander (CFACC) and the Coalition Forces Land Component Command (CFLCC) we typically have this ironed out.

"But it has been such a long time since we have done true Joint Naval engagements that the process for engaging maritime targets and who exactly is the Target Engagement Authority (TEA) or can be the TEA is not as tried and true as it is for land engagements."

---

1. https://www.usni.org/magazines/proceedings/2012/january/long-reach-aegis.

2. https://sldinfo.com/2016/05/shaping-a-way-ahead-for-the-f-35-in-uk-defence-the-perspective-of-air-commodore-harvey-smyth/

3. https://sldinfo.com/2021/10/shaping-a-way-ahead-for-the-australian-submarine-capability-the-perspective-of-vice-admiral-retired-barrett/

4. https://www.asa.gov.au/

5. https://defense.info/highlight-of-the-week/the-war-in-ukraine-and-the-sanctuaries-of-rear-support-the-impact-of-nuclear-deterrence/

6. https://www.c7f.navy.mil/Media/News/Display/Article/3384178/first-of-its-kind-submarine-visit-forges-relationship/

7. https://www.reuters.com/world/us-plans-rare-nuclear-missile-submarine-visit-message-north-korea-2023-04-27/

8. https://www.cpf.navy.mil/Newsroom/News/Article/3367000/comsubpac-hosts-submarine-warfare-commanders-conference/

9. Robbin Laird and Edward Timperlake, *A Maritime Kill Web Force in the Making: Deterrence and Warfighting in the 21st Century* (pp. 41-42). Kindle Edition.

10. https://news.usni.org/2022/11/02/new-torpedo-tube-launched-drones-will-turn-u-s-attack-sub-fleet-into-uuv-motherships-says-navy.

11. https://www.thedrive.com/the-war-zone/39700/the-u-s-navys-submarine-launched-aerial-drone-capacity-is-set-to-greatly-expand.

12. https://www.navy.mil/Press-Office/News-Stories/Article/3136198/ohio-class-submarines-work-with-usaf-and-usmc-during-vertrep/

13. https://www.navfac.navy.mil/PEO-Industrial-Infrastructure/PMO-555-SIOP/

14. https://www.gao.gov/products/gao-22-105993.

15. https://breakingdefense.com/2023/01/navy-shipyard-optimization-must-include-a-digital-backbone/

16. https://sldinfo.com/2021/02/the-future-is-now-for-enhanced-integratability-the-perspective-of-major-general-anders-rex/.

17. https://www.gov.uk/government/publications/integrated-review-refresh-2023-responding-to-a-more-contested-and-volatile-world.

18. https://sldinfo.com/2018/07/new-uk-mbda-facility-infrastructure-for-the-complex-weapons-project/

19. https://news.usni.org/2020/03/10/marines-ditch-mux-ship-based-drone-to-pursue-large-land-based-uas-smaller-shipboard-vehicle.

20. https://www.mca-marines.org/wp-content/uploads/0520-DASC.pdf.

21. https://www.marinecorpstimes.com/news/your-marine-corps/2020/10/12/marine-corps-creates-new-mos-for-mq-9-reaper-pilots/

22. FARP is a Forward Arming and Refueling Point. EABO is Expeditionary Advanced Base Operations.

❦   4   ❦

BUILDING 21ST CENTURY COMBAT FORCES

THE CMV-22B COMES TO THE CARRIER: FROM COD TO FLEET CON-OPS

January 22, 2023

Recently, I have had a chance to meet with Captain Sam Bryant, Commander, Fleet Logistics Multi-Mission Wing in North Island. Just the name of the wing should give one an idea that creativity in thinking about the Osprey was envisaged. Captain Bryant's mission statement for the Wing is: [to] "Man, Train, & Equip all USN VRM Squadrons to provide flexible and agile tilt-rotor options to Fleet Commanders wherever our nation requires us to operate."

We started by focusing on the initial deployments and events during those deployments which already demonstrated the difference an Osprey makes expanding capabilities for the core mission from COD to providing enhanced logistical support.

According to Captain Bryant: "Our deployments to Vinson and Lincoln focused on our peacetime concepts of operations. We did a good job and produced good outcomes with the initial deployments.

We already have demonstrated our ability to operate 1000 mile plus missions over water on a regular basis.

"This is certainly necessary given the distances the carriers need to operate in the Indo-PACOM AOR. And that fact that we can operate at night was a key factor in thinking about enhanced operations for these two carriers."

He provided examples of missions performed during those two deployments that the CMV-22B could do and a C2-A could not.

The first was a medevac mission. Here a sailor had suffered a stroke, and a catapult launch could have proved fatal. Via the CMV-22B they flew the sailor directly to the medical support facility ashore long range at airplane speeds, but were able to land directly there in helicopter mode. The medical support facility was not served by a runway so a fixed wing aircraft would not be able to land directly there.

The second involved a repair to a non-functioning catapult aboard the Lincoln. The CMV-22B was able to get the support element needed directly ashore landing helicopter mode and quickly returning.

The particular support facility was not served by a fixed wing airfield so it would have taken more time to obtain the support necessary for the repair if using a C2-A. Time is safety; time is lethality; time is survivability. The CMV-2B is uniquely suited to meet the "golden mile" of shore-to-ship logistics support, and "golden hour" of medevac support.

Captain Bryant reported that the U.S. Pacific Fleet Commander, Admiral Paparo, was pleased with the initial deployments, but feels that the Osprey can do much more in its role in evolving fleet concepts of operations.

The aircraft provides an important support for, but more than that, stimulant for the shift in con-ops whereby the Navy focus on distributed operations which itself is in an experimental development and growth phase and intersects with the USAF's approach to agile combat employment.

In other words, the reshaping of joint and coalition operations is underway which focuses upon distributed task forces which can deliver enhanced lethality and survivability.

Bryant highlighted that the CMV-22B compared to a legacy Osprey has much more capability. The Osprey is a path-breaking aircraft which breaks the rotorcraft's limits on range and speed.

But Bryant noted about the CMV-22B even when compared with the MV-22: "We have better range. We have much better avionics. We have better communications which allows to connect with the strike groups more securely. We are better suited for long-range navigation operations, and the flexibility required to support a high-end fight in the Pacific.

A con-ops to support the fleet approach instantly raises questions about the numbers of CMV-22Bs the Navy needs.

One aspect is the question of how many aircraft the Navy needs to do even the COD mission. When the Marines were asked during the initial process of evaluating the Osprey for the COD mission, they recommended four aircraft and team of 100 to 110 people to operate and support the aircraft. The Navy is currently using three. So that is the first point at which to raise the numbers question.

A second aspect of the demand for increased numbers of aircraft is to look at distributed ops for the fleet and to realize that the aircraft is a web support asset not a point-to-point load carrying asset. The fleet demand could be high, and demand will rapidly outstrip supply when it comes to these aircraft.

The Osprey is a very flexible aircraft which makes it a high demand aircraft. As more fleet elements want to tap into the asset, the aircraft could see pressure on its availability and readiness. This was what I saw already when working with MARFORCPAC Commander LtGen Robling when the USMC Ospreys were placed in a high demand setting with the shortfall in KC-130s in theater in the 2014-15-time frame.

The need to move weapons around the kill web in a contested environment will make the Osprey a prioritized fleet weapons carrier. The ability of the Osprey through role on roll off capability to play the role of an ISR/C2 quarterback which can play a key role in information logistics could see demand spike along these lines.

Notably with the coming of maritime autonomous systems generating task force ISR in key locations the ability of the Osprey to move that data to the point of attack or defense could prove to be a critical capability for the fleet as well.

The shift from simply being COD to becoming part of the dynamic development of maritime kill web con-ops can be seen in the growing relationship between the command with NAWDC. When I went to NAWDC in 2000, I asked where the CMV-22B fit in. The answer was not clear. But now the NAWDC team is working closely with the CMV-22B command to work answers to that question.

Captain Bryant concluded by emphasizing that there might be a need to build a 21st century version of the Cold War approach the Navy once used. They had intra-theater support squadrons with several types of aircraft to support the movement of maritime forces. Now with distributed forces over significant distances, how might the Navy and the joint force do a 21st century version of such a theater support capability?

AN UPDATE ON THE FUTURE COMBAT AIR SYSTEM: PARIS AIR SHOW 2023 UPDATE

June 22, 2023

By Pierre Tran

Belgium has joined as an observer to the Future Combat Air System (FCAS), adding a fourth nation to a partnership which bears French ambitions to boost European defense, amid perception of a leadership competition between France and Germany.

"The participation of Belgium as observer will increase the European dimension in the FCAS program," the French armed forces ministry said in a June 20 statement.

"France, as the project leader, as well as Germany and Spain recognize the Belgian investment in progress in technology and innovation," the ministry said.

President Emmanuel Macron broke the news the day before, announcing the three partner nations had accepted Belgium's request to join the FCAS project.

The French head of state was speaking at a high level conference on European air defense and anti-missile strategy, after inaugurating the Paris air show under blazing sun. Macron flew to the show in Le Bourget, in the northern suburbs, in the navy's new medium helicopter, Airbus Helicopters H160.

The FCAS program will speed up operational links between the air forces of the four nations, the ministry said, and boost cooperation between the Belgian defense and technology industrial base and the partners working on the combat air system.

Belgium's entry as observer rather than full partner stemmed from being late to the party. The industrial partners signed in December a €3.2 billion ($3.5 billion) contract for phase 1B studies on FCAS architecture, setting out work share for three years to the end of 2025.

There is an option for phase two, bringing the total value of work to some €8 billion, with technology demonstrators for a fighter and remote carrier drones to fly by 2028/2029.

It remained to be seen when Belgium fully joined the project and its aerospace companies   receive some of the highly valued work.

Belgium Seeks Partnership

"Belgium has a strong aeronautics sector," a French defense analyst said, and FCAS offered work to make up for a lack of Belgian work share on the U.S. F-35 fighter. Belgian companies would likely work as subcontractors on FCAS, rather than prime contractors.

Belgium and France were close partners, the analyst said, with the former ordering the French Jaguar combat and reconnaissance vehicle and Griffon multirole troop carrier in a €1.5 billion deal for its CaMo motorized capability program.

Asked about Belgium joining FCAS, the executive chairman of Dassault Aviation, Eric Trappier, said June 20, "That's fine. An observer just looks, but does not touch anything.

"We'll see," he said, when asked about what happens when Belgium won full partnership.

Trappier has made clear his opposition to Belgium joining FCAS, as Brussels had chosen the U.S. F-35 fighter over European rivals, Eurofighter Typhoon and Rafale.

The Dassault chief executive also objected to redistribution of work to Belgian companies once partner status was granted, as that was seen as taking jobs from French firms.

Belgium welcomed the shift in European military and industrial policy, pointing up hopes of support for its arms and aerospace sector.

"As a country with an excellent defense, aerospace and space industry, we could not miss this opportunity," the Belgian defense minister, Ludivine Dedonder, said on Monday evening, Belga new agency reported.

Belgian prime minister Alexander De Croo said, "I am delighted with this decision, which is fully in line with the industrial policy we are pursuing and will also strengthen European defense."

Observer status was due to run six to 12 months, and allowed exchange of information with the partners to allow Belgian companies to fit into the project, Reuters reported June 19.

European Computer Clouds

Trappier was speaking on the sidelines of a press conference on the launch by the aircraft company of a commercial offering of a European sovereign cloud computing service with Dassault Systèmes, its sister company in the family held Groupe Industriel Marcel Dassault.

"France and Europe need to build up a sovereign cloud capability, so that they can develop collaborative defense programs with the best possible functionality," he said.

The sovereignty issue arose from storing sensitive data on secure computer clouds, protected from cyber-attacks, he said, and French and European companies and public institutions should not rely on U.S. firms such as Amazon, Google, and Microsoft to house their data.

The aircraft company was using Dassault Systèmes's 3DExperience software to share data with partners on the new generation fighter in FCAS, Trappier said, pointing up the importance of European autonomy and sovereignty.

Charles Edelstenne, former finance director and executive chairman of the aircraft company, set up Dassault Systèmes, which built computer-aided design and manufacturing software.

Dassault Aviation is prime contractor on the new generation fighter (NGF) in FCAS, with Airbus Defence and Space and Indra as respectively German and Spanish industrial partners.

Airbus DS on Command and Control

Airbus Defence and Space had a small chalet dedicated to FCAS at the air show, the first exhibition after a four year break due to the covid health crisis.

The Airbus DS director for FCAS, Bruno Fichefeux, showed June 19 a video presentation pointing up the importance of the concept for battle management through a distributed network of command and control (C2).

The simulation showed a combat cloud system which linked up fighter cockpit, flying command center on a multirole tanker transport (MRTT) aircraft, the medium-altitude, long-endurance drone dubbed Eurodrone, and remote carrier drones.

These crewed and uncrewed aircraft and drones were plugged into a multi-domain network with an "interdependency" of sensors, and linking up satellite, radar, frigate, and artillery.

A distributed approach would allow the tanker aircraft to withdraw from providing C2, and hand over mission management to a fighter pilot, flying while relying on a "harmonization" of the aircraft's avionics and mission systems, helped by artificial intelligence.

That distributed combat cloud was a "huge challenge," Fichefeux said. Airbus DS, Thales and Indra were working on the cloud project, which should be interoperable with the Global Combat Air Program (GCAP) and the U.S. Next Generation Air Dominance (NGAD) fighter.

Britain, Italy and Japan are partners on the former, based on the U.K. Tempest fighter project.

Airbus had some 400-450 staff working on FCAS and that was expected to rise to 800, following start of phase 1B studies.

Fichefeux, 41, said the company was recruiting young engineers, and there would be 2,000 working in the three partner countries for some time to come.

MBDA and FCAS

Over at the MBDA chalet, there was its Orchestrike concept, which proposed remote carriers (RC) drones capable of switching missions in flight if the enemy "popped up" and destroyed some of the drones. Those RCs still flying would have onboard AI to inform the fighter pilot of options for re-assigning drones to hit the key targets.

Sweden Has Its Own Timeline

Meanwhile for Sweden, the priorities were development and procurement of the Gripen E fighter, with studies due to start soon on the next generation fighter which will succeed the Gripen, said Brigadier General Lars Helmrich, director of the air and space systems division at the FMV procurement office.

That focus on the Gripen E version and upgrades of the present C/D model meant Sweden was "out of the timeline" for joining the FCAS and GCAP projects, he told reporters June 18 at a meeting of the Swedish Air Force Fan Club.

Ramp Up

There has been a "ramp up," major general Jean-Luc Moritz, head of the French air force team on the FCAS project, told journalists June 20 at the air show.

"It's working well," he said.

The operational teams were working on a short list of system architectures, seeking to assign missions to fighters and remote carriers, with a final selection in 2025, he said.

The challenge is to be innovative and disruptive, he said, and achieve superiority not just in technology but tactical combat operations.

In the overall FCAS project, each of the partner nations will take a national approach with the new generation and legacy fighters, while sharing the one combat cloud. For France, the new fighter and legacy Rafale, aircraft carrier, and AWACS spy planes will plug into the cloud system, while Germany will plug its own aircraft into the shared network.

There will be European cooperation in sharing communications, software and AI, while at the tactical level there will be share of data, as seen in the allied Hamilton operation in 2018.

Interoperability could be seen in the Hamilton mission, with two French AWACS planes providing command and control for British, French and U.S. forces to hit Syrian chemical warfare sites with air and sea-launched cruise missiles.

"I have a dream," Moritz said, that the French new fighter would be capable of flying with U.S. collaborative combat aircraft, or combat drones, and Tempest and NGAD fighters.

If there were a lack of interconnectivity, as is the case with the F-35, then the prospect would be allies flying in three combat clouds, "side by side," he said.

The French, German and Italian air chiefs signed June 21 an agreement on collaborative air warfare in the FCAS project, setting out the principle the new generation fighter will be the command fighter, with the pilot having the key role of command and control.

"FCAS is structural, indispensable, ambitious and emblematic," Moritz said. Those initials were also those of salon international de l'aéronautique et de l'espace, the official French name for the Paris air show.

However, there was also downbeat sentiment on FCAS.

"FCAS has been the disappointment of the 2023 Paris Air Show," said a report from equity research firm Agency Partners. "The unattended, rather crude, mock-up on a plinth outside the main halls has given the programme the unfortunate monicker of the "Forlorn Combat Air System" at the show."

Call for a European Approach

Meanwhile, back on air defense and anti-missile strategy, the conference pointed up the importance of a broad European approach rather than a fragmented, national plan, said an analyst who attended the open session at the air show.

Perhaps the real issue was rivalry between France or Germany in taking the leading role in European defense, the analyst said, with that competition for leadership underpinning Berlin's anti-missile project, dubbed European Sky Shield Initiative.

That system will rely on the German Diehl Iris-T, U.S. Raytheon Patriot, and Israeli IAI Arrow 3 missiles for hitting incoming missiles at short, medium and long range.

What irks Paris is Berlin's perceived sin of omission, namely failing to include the Franco-Italian SAMP/T, equipped with MBDA Aster missile and Thales radar.

Macron's holding a conference with the Paris air show, inviting senior European Union and Nato officials, and ministers from some 20 European nations was a call for a European approach to strategy, operations, and industry.

"It (the conference) shows the determination of European nations to conduct a deep reflection on a major issue of strategic importance for the security of the continent," the French defense ministry said in a statement.

The call for a cooperative approach was in part a response to the war in Ukraine but could also be Paris responding to Berlin's perceived break-away move with its Sky Shield, seen as an unspoken claim for European leadership.

On the sidelines of that conference, France signed a letter of intent with Belgium, Cyprus, Estonia, and Hungary for a bulk order of maybe more than 1,000 Mistral short range missiles, worth more than €500 million, the ministry said.

Again, that group order for a French missile could be seen as a riposte to Germany's casting aside the Franco-Italian SAMP/T, a medium range missile.

The conference also pointed up the importance of cooperation between France, Germany, Italy, and the Netherlands on the HYDIS project, the ministry said.

HYDIS is the Hypersonic Defense Interceptor Study, backed by the EU's European Defense Fund, which will provide €80 million for work on a weapon to hit a hypersonic missile. HYDIS is based on MBDA's Aquila missile concept, a three-stage model of which stood on display outside its air show chalet. The missile company has teamed up with 19 partner companies and 30 subcontractors from 14 European nations to develop the Aquila concept.

BUILDING A GLOBAL ARSENAL OF DEMOCRACY: THE TAIWAN CASE

By Steven Rudder

July 9, 2023

There is widespread bipartisan agreement on supporting the Taiwan Relations Act and arming Taiwan to defend itself. Several duty expert authors reference "the porcupine" concept when it comes to arming Taiwan, but very few understand the policy, authority, and industry hurdles to adequately support our national vision.

Since 1979 our Foreign Military Sales (FMS) process for Taiwan has been the pillar of Taiwan defense but in recent years it has been episodic. In some cases, years went by without Taiwan FMS cases being approved. Even when a particular Administration is in full support, the FMS process for Taiwan is slow and complex.

The FMS process to transfer arms to Taiwan in antiquated. The foreign military sales process formally begins when a potential customer submits a letter of request for a given American-made weapon system. Then the Defense and State Department staffs each conduct a series of reviews, assessing a range of issues including the risk of disclosing sensitive, classified technology as well as potential human rights concerns.

With most experts cite the potential of a 2027 invasion scenario, Taiwan continues to be subjected to the FMS process of asking by letter of request and then waiting for DoD, State, and Congressional notification and approvals to be completed. All of this transpiring over months sometimes years even when there is widespread agreement on a particular weapon system.

To streamline the process in the 2023 NDAA, Congress authorized up to 2 billion in annual grants from 2023 to 2027 and an additional 2 billion in loans for Taiwan to use to bolster its military capabilities from the U.S.

It also authorized a regional contingency stockpile for Taiwan of up to 1 billion in munitions a year for use in the event of a conflict. Unfortunately, Taiwan leadership is painfully aware that the U.S. Congressional Appropriations committees did not fund the authorization for 2023.

As another attempt for support Taiwan, the proposed 2024 The State, Foreign Operations, and Related Programs bill included $52.5 billion dollars which includes $500 million in Foreign Military Financing Program for Taiwan.

Near term, the 2023 authorization allows for a Presidential Drawdown Authority for Taiwan. Not ideal and not enough, but it appears to be moving forward.

Meanwhile, as we deliberate on arms to Taiwan, U.S. industry watches by the sidelines with no sure investment way ahead other than the currently appropriated support for U.S. forces, current FMS cases, and the added work contributed by the Ukraine conflict.

Currently, buying defense products continues to be based on the DoD budget process, acquisition laws, an industry production model, and year-by-year appropriations. While the program numbers are mostly known by industry, the ability to react with additional skilled labor, advanced procurement, extra machining, and other investments are based on the budgetary process.

This bureaucratic process creates the widely captured dilemma of not being able to quickly scale U.S. industry to a war footing. As Ukraine expenditure of U.S. munitions highlights, the process of munitions procurement and the acquisition path is insufficient under the most ideal circumstances.

There are several ways ahead to consider in altering the acquisition process to aid in the defense of Taiwan.

First, we need to streamline the FMS approval and funding process.

Congressional defense committees should have sole approval authorities for Taiwan FMS and Grants that support weapons deliveries. Each year the U.S. should commit to an FMS and Grant budget for Taiwan. There were years during the previous administrations where no cases were approved.

The Trump Administration approved over 18 billion dollars in arms sales and thus far the Biden administration has approved just over 4 billion dollars. A streamlined process and yearly budgeted funding would allow for predictability for Taiwanese and U.S. industry.

Second, Congress needs to have oversight of FMS delivers to Taiwan.

As the U.S. offers staunch support for Taiwan's democracy, there is no question that the 19 billion dollars of U.S. sales and associated "late" deliveries is having an impact. The lateness of supply chain deliveries coupled with the drain on U.S. stockpiles by Ukraine is well understood inside Taiwan, but the road to recovery is an unknown.

Third, we need to award multi-year munitions contracts to industry.

Like multi-years procurement of aircraft and block buys of ships, munitions should be procured with multi-year contracts with a minimum of 5-year contracts. This would stabilize industry and negate the historical variations in munitions procurement.

Fourth, we need to have congressional oversight on divestments of extant weapon systems.

Congress should have a say in closing production lines without a suitable replacement. The Stinger may be the best example of this. Was there oversight of this production line and the U.S. or partner nations requirements for air defense?

Services should not be allowed to close production lines or divest of equipment without a suitable transition to a replacement. Divest to Invest without a suitable replacement should be scrutinized.

Once a capability is gone without a suitable replacement, we have not only closed the capability production and supply base but, in many cases, the active-duty expertise and the skilled labor that builds it.

Fifth, we need to avoid single points of failure.

It is unthinkable to believe that a single company in the U.S. holds the keys to a particular warhead, rocket motor, or guidance system. Acquisition down selects should consider a winner but also select co production partners with other U.S. companies.

What we really need is more than one line for the systems that we're building. Currently, our defense department acquisition laws mean that we down select one winner. And usually, one winner means one production line and one point of failure.

Sixth, we need to focus a new arsenal of democracy which sees co-production with global industries.

There are valid reasons to enter into co production with foreign companies. For Taiwan, co-production could be the answer to many of the asymmetric capabilities. In other words, instead of thinking of Taiwan as a country of last resort in selling whatever FMS systems we are willing to sell, why not make them a player in building the new arsenal of democracy in the Pacific, certainly with regard to asymmetric or autonomous systems? There are several historical examples where partner nations successfully added to a production of key capabilities.

And finally, we need to amend the Buy American Act which makes a realistic arsenal of democracy impossible in the real world.

We need to review and consider amending Buy American Act for critical capabilities. The process for fulfilling the additional regulations for key end items hinders industry's ability to rapidly scale production.

In short, as with the Ukraine war, the defense of Taiwan is a wake up to shaping a global arsenal of democracy.

WHEN THE IRANIAN OR CHINESE NAVY COME CALLING WHY NOT THROW THEM A CURVE BALL?

July 19, 2023

We have heard a lot about A2D2 and about the authoritarian powers and their asymmetric threats, Well two can play this game.

The U.S. Navy has within reach a new capability to throw curve balls into the con-ops of an Iranian or Chinese navy approach to challenging the U.S. Navy.

And a recent example comes from an event in the Arabian Gulf which has been relayed to me by a reliable Middle Eastern source, an advantage coming from my years of visiting the UAE and Bahrain.

What is the curve ball?

A highly maneuverable, high speed when needed, high-g capable autonomous asset that can operate up to sea state five and operate 24/7.

I am talking about a maritime autonomous vessel or as it is referred to as unmanned surface vessel (USV) operating today and not in the distant ghost fleet future.

This particular USV operates autonomously for significant periods of its operational time with control of the vessel able to be executed in multiple ways.

According to this source, a slow-moving U.S. Navy ship – not a high value capital ship – was being escorted by this USV in the Straits of Hormuz.

The Iranians sent a drone then a second drone to see what they could see.

Then they sent the kind of fast attack vessel which causes significant challenges to U.S. Navy capital ships. The problem which the fast attack boats cause is precisely around rules of engagement and when is the U.S. capital ship authorized to respond with lethal response.

The Iranians reportedly requested that the U.S. Navy withdraw the USV. Not having gotten the result they wanted they sent more fast attack boats in waves to try to disrupt the USV from its escort mission. Aided by the intervention of a USCG vessel, the USV continued its mission. Later the Iranians sent a warship.

With current capabilities, the USV can provide single ship escort. With further software and C2 development USVs can provide a defensive perimeter for U.S. Navy capital ships and to provide the picket fence for ROE enhancement – you attack my picket ship, and I can sink you.

This is something the Iranians need to experience from my point of view.

Take this capability to the waters west of Taiwan and the Chinese navy now faces a threat to their sea control.

The U.S. Navy does not have to have sea control of the waters west of Taiwan; it simply has to have sea denial.

With the acquisition of USVs and working their wolfpack con ops the Taiwanese and any allied navies who would operate these systems would be delivering a curve ball to Chinese plans for sea control of the waters off of Taiwan.

In other words, it is about time that the bad guys start worrying about our ability to mess with their con-ops.

There is no gray zone if you don't accept it.

MARITIME AUTONOMOUS SYSTEMS AND THE OPERATIONAL FORCE: HOW TO ACCELERATE THE EFFORT?

October 3, 2023

Recently, I had a chance to continue my discussions with CDRE Darron Kavanagh who is Director General Warfare Innovation, Royal Australian Navy Headquarters, concerning maritime autonomous systems. Kavanagh has been one of the most articulate leaders of the development and introduction of maritime autonomous systems in Australia.

It is well recognized that autonomous systems are critical to provide the mass necessary for the kind of multi-domain operations which the ADF requires. For example, as Vice Air-Marshal retired Zed Roberton noted at the 27 September Williams Foundation seminar: Going forward, Roberton argued that "we will see a massive focus on things like uncrewed aerial vehicles, uncrewed sea vehicles or land vehicles, the ability to have pre-positioned missile systems and of course, synchronized with cyber and in space effects."

But how to get the effort started operationally?

We need to move from science projects and exercises to regular use by the combat forces to realize the opportunities inherent in maritime autonomous systems.

But how to do so?

Kavanagh started our conversation by underscoring that it is important to understand what these systems are and what they represent. They are not traditional platforms that you are focused on integrating with the force.

He argued: "They don't replace platforms; they complement the integrated force. They are complimentary to that force in that they interface rather than being fully integrated with the current force elements."

With the introduction of new crewed platforms, one must focus on backward engineering legacy systems to work with the new ones. That takes time and has high costs. This is understandable because warriors' lives are at risk.

This is not the model by which to understand maritime autonomous systems, and certainly not the way to understand how you get them into the hands of warfighters for operations. They are not crewed, and your concern is with efficacy, not a primary emphasis on survivability.

Maritime autonomous systems interface with and complement the existing force to enhance their lethality. They extend the ISR and C2 range of the force and add to the non-lethal and lethal weapons available to the combat force.

Maritime autonomous systems add to the survivability of the force. As CDRE Kavanagh noted: "We have a finite number of crewed exquisite platforms. By leveraging autonomous systems these platforms can extend their defensive perimeter and provide various tools to complicate the adversaries attack profile on those crewed systems."

For example, in effect, USVs can play the role of the picket ships in World War II, thereby enhancing the survivability of the destroyer and carrier fleet.

Or to use a Fifth Fleet example, USVs operating with destroyers can operate as a buffer between these key assets and Iranian patrol boats. The USVs function as the police guard dogs and if the Iranians were to attack them, the destroyer's Rules of Engagement then allows it to destroy the Iranian patrol vessel.

And because of how maritime autonomous systems are developed and built, you can shape the kind of affordable mass which we discussed in the multi-domain strike seminar held by the Williams Foundation on 27 September 2023.

As CDRE Kavanagh underscored: "When you start leveraging maritime autonomous systems that are low cost, you can create affordable mass, and you're setting up a system that allows for resilience. You can manufacture them at mass. Not only can I build them in peacetime but we can keep developing them and delivering them quite quickly during hostilities."

And by focusing on complementarity rather than integration, there can be a much wider search within the commercial sector to adopt the rapid innovations in the commercial sector occurring in terms of autonomous systems.

CDRE Kavanagh specifically mentioned the Australian mining sector as one where rapid progress is being made on autonomous systems. If you are not using unique military specs which are designed in order to integrate with the extant force but rather providing complimentary capabilities which can directed by the force, then there is a much wider canvas of innovation from which to adopt autonomous system innovations.

Because there are a wide range of civilian and security missions that maritime autonomous systems are already being used for and their roles and numbers will increase to do so, the military can dip into this existing and growing capability as well. The protection of undersea infrastructure and wind farms are two examples which are suggestive of a broader trend.

According to CDRE Kavanagh: "We simply will delay adoption of autonomous systems by reducing them to the mantra of integration. By focusing on complementarity and finding ways to use the systems as compliments to the fleet and extending the range of the various effects desired, we can find a variety of missions which these systems can meet now and in the future."

He noted that in the DSR, there is much focus on deterrence by denial. Autonomous systems can clearly help in disrupting adversary operations and deny them quick results against crewed platforms.

Then there is the key question of how maritime autonomous systems are being designed from the outset to operate in clusters or wolfpacks. And by so doing, they can operate as an interactive complimentary buffer force operating with the core integrated combat force to deliver persistent effects.

In short, one needs to focus on the broader con-ops of the operation of the forces, rather than on the integration of autonomous systems within the much more complicated integrated crewed combat systems. If you don't, we simply won't use them in the timely manner as we must in the era of strategic competition within which we live.

And an aspect of con-ops we discussed as well was the relationship of maritime autonomous systems and their operations to deterrence.

On the one hand, maritime autonomous systems can be deployed as part of a deterrence by detection strategy. This can be enhanced by sharing with partners who are not close allies, or the kind of allies you wish to integrate your crewed platforms with.

At the March seminar, Jake Campbell highlighted the importance of deterrence by detection as follows: "Adversaries are less likely to commit opportunistic acts of aggression if they know they are being watched constantly and that their actions can be publicized widely."

On the other hand, when it comes to signalling, a key part of deterrence, sending in a maritime autonomous systems wolfpack simply does not have the same meaning as sending a Aegis led surface action group. It indicates concern, but does not raise the weapons threshold that such SAG is designed to do.

In short, maritime autonomous systems considered as complimentary capabilities which are controlled by but not built to be closely integrated with the combat force can deliver a number of the key capabilities which the DSR has called for.

THE DANES BUILD THE NEXT GENERATION MODULAR SHIP: THE "MOTHERSHIP" AND "PAYLOAD CENTRIC PLATFORM MODULARITY"

October 7, 2023

During my visit to the DSEI conference in London In September 2023, I spent a significant part of my time looking at a real revolution in ship building, maritime automated systems, and the payload revolution underlying the kill web.

I did this in large part by the opportunity to talk with Danish colleagues about their progress in building a next generation modular vessel. A key aspect of this effort was the opportunity to conduct a follow up interview with Rear Admiral Torben Mikkelsen who is Executive Director, Navy Programs, Defence Command, Denmark.

Since we last talked, the Danish government has gone ahead with the design and preparation for the first in class of the new modular ships.

In our last discussions, he described how the modular concept is being worked: "A key focus is upon the desired effects to be created, and the missions to be supported by the desired maritime payloads, rather than upon the platforms as the primary focus. The effects focus means that air and land capabilities which are integratable with maritime platforms is a key focus of attention as well in thinking about the operational ecosystem.

"Rear Admiral Mikkelsen underscored the importance of the following in my interview with him at the Euronaval meeting in October 2022: "What effects do we need to achieve? And how will sensors and the weapons as payloads on the fleet and in the force create those effects? How will autonomous systems play a role? How and where in our battlespace?"

The first ship in the new "mothership" class is a Multi Role Patrol Ship designed to operate in the Baltic and the North Sea. It is being built with a clear eye to building out other types of ships all able to operate common payloads to enable both operational flexibilities, and the possibility of a new approach to the arsenal of democracy.

With the modules being built around the standard 20- and 40-foot container dimensions, Mikkelsen argued that Denmark along with e.g. its Nordic allies, for example, could build modules in common which could be swapped across a wider fleet of modular ships.

This allows not only collaborative production across an allied production base but allows for rapid specialization by a particular ship on a mission by swapping in the relevant modules. And these modules could clearly be shared by nations in the area of operation.

If a similar concept is implemented in relation to future naval home guard vessels , the modules would be standardized and available for the kinds of missions which the Home Guard would most likely perform.

Autonomous systems will operate from these modules or in the case of UAVs from the decks of these ships. The first module ships built by Denmark used modules that met Danish specs; this generation will be built using the standard specs built around standard 20- 40-foot dimensions.

This can trigger a global shift in standardization which allied negotiators have rarely achieved. Standardization of modules and systems to be placed in 20- or 40-foot containers can provide a significant opening to shaping an allied arsenal of democracy, of a kind that simply does not exist now.

"Standardization and adaptability could become a reality to a much larger degree than we traditionally have thought about," Mikkelsen said.

Another way to look at the build approach is to understand the focus is upon significantly enhancing the % of the ship which can deliver security and defense loads as compared to a traditional combat ship.

By building a wide-beam ship, which is being continued from the flex class and the trend nowadays, there is the opportunity with modular standardization to enhance significantly the payloads carried on the particular ship within the overall approach to building a mothership class of ships.

Rear Admiral Torben Mikkelsen argued that the approach allows an ability to deal with the spectrum of security and military operations which underlay maritime deterrence.

"In terms of payloads, we are looking at the mix of capabilities needed in peacetime and through the process of fighting a war. We need to create adaptability on the platform; we need to plan for payload innovation and the ability to upgrade rapidly the capability of the ship as a means to operate the relevant payloads to the operation needed.

"By working with standardized modules one can design weapons, sensors, and systems to be carrier in those modules. They can be handled in ports around the world, and racked and stacked. This allows nations to share payloads and to support one another in a crisis."

The ship is a "mother ship" not just because it is operating with flexible payloads but because it is being built to take full advantage of the autonomous system revolution. It will be able to operate UAVs, USVs, UUVs, and other AI enabled elements.

And according to Mikkelsen: "We will focus as well on how we might be able to operate the ship itself remotely in terms of extreme danger as well."

BUILDING MODULAR MOTHERSHIPS: DENMARK AND SINGAPORE LEAD THE WAY

October 7, 2023

The Danes are shaping a second generation of their modular ships. The first-generation flex ships provided for wide beam ships with enhanced payload for a combat ship and modules for the weapon systems as a means of providing for flexibility in capability by mission set.

The next generation modular ships are being crafted in the new age of autonomous systems, both maritime and airborne. These systems provide for the possibility of a new approach to power projection to the point of operational interest, and with flexible payloads one can use the same hull form for a wide variety of missions.

And in this second-generation effort standardization of modules is a key part of the approach. With the focus on using 20- and 40-foot containers and then working with sensor and weapons manufacturers to build to this common standard, a virtual payload revolution can be unleashed.

But how do you build a ship to do so?

At the recent DSEI show, I had a chance to sit down with Kåre Groes Christiansen, the CEO of OMT Group to discuss their approach to designing this new class of ships, the mother ships enabled by automated systems operating within the new approach to modularity.

The first ship in the new "mothership" class is a patrol boat designed to operate in the Baltic and the North Sea.

It is being built with a clear eye to building out other types of boats all able to operate common payloads to enable both operational flexibilities, and the possibility of a new approach to the arsenal of democracy. With the modules being built around standard 20- and 40-foot container dimensions, Denmark along with its Nordic allies, for example, could build modules in common which could be swapped across a fleet of modular ships.

This allows not only collaborative production across an allied production base but allows for rapid specialization by a particular ship on a mission by swapping in the relevant modules. And these modules could clearly be shared by nations in the area of operation....

But the Danish approach is not only for Denmark – by having a modular approach built on international standardization the approach can be adopted by a wide variety of allied nations. The first to do so is Singapore which is building six new mother ships. The design is provided by Saab-Kockums, based on the Danish design approach.

Christiansen started the discussion by focusing on payloads. In fact, one can characterize the Danish approach of re-thinking shipbuilding from the perspective of "Payload Centric Platform Modularity."

He emphasized that legacy shipbuilding has not focused on maximizing payload flexibility. The float and move function have dominated with only about 15 – 30% of the total displacement open to combat payload. The Danish focus is upon how to ramp up payloads on combat ships and to leverage a new modular payload approach to provide for expanded payload flexibility.

Christiansen also emphasized that the Danish approach is built on a factory system to build ships relaying on extensive use of robots. With a factory system it is possible such as in the F-35 program to have distributed production among allies thereby being able to ramp up production rates.

With the Chinese outproducing the West, he argued that distributed manufacturing might be the only feasible solution to build the numbers of ships the West needs to protect their interests.

The Chinese have created the same shipbuilding eco-system to build military and commercial ships. And this ecosystem allows them to have a steady rate of production. We need to shape a distributed manufacturing model to compete, or put another way, we need to change our shipbuilding eco system.

Christiansen noted that on the Danish class of the mothership approach "we are designing software that basically will allow these modules to integrate into the ship systems. For example, if you install a new laser gun, the gateway with the ship will allow the laser gun to plug into the energy production on the ship."

The Singaporeans want to build a ship that reduces the numbers of personnel on the ship but expands the payloads to be operated or launched from the ship.

Obviously, the only way to do so is through the ability to manage a variety of autonomous systems. One description of the Singapore Navy (RSN) new Multi-Role Combat Vessel (MRCV) highlighted the modularity approach. According to a 4 May 2023 article by Andrew Wong published in *The Strait Times*:

"The Republic of Singapore Navy (RSN) will acquire six new multirole combat vessels (MRCVs) to replace its ageing fleet of Victory-class missile corvettes (MCVs), which have been in service since 1989.

"The newer vessels will not be a like-for-like replacement, said the RSN."The MCV was designed for the 1980s and served its purpose very well. But the threat environment in the 1980s versus the threat environment in 2040 will be very different," said RSN Major James Lim, the operations lead of the MRCV project, in a media briefing on April 27."[1]

How will they be different?

First of all, they will be designed to operate a variety of autonomous systems. "In addition to being capable fighting ships, the MRCVs will act as a mothership for unmanned systems.

They function as a force multiplier for the navy fleet, as unmanned drones positioned on the ship expand the area that the ship can oversee. The unmanned systems can range from air to surface to underwater vehicles. "But at the baseline, the unmanned systems on board the MRCVs will include surveillance capabilities," the RSN added."

Secondly, they will be built around the modularity principle. "The RSN is building a modular platform that will equip the MRCVs with the capability and versatility to handle multiple situations."

The Australian Navy builds its ships with a common combat system, namely, the Aegis combat system to provide for enhanced integration. What the Danes are doing its building out a new shipbuilding approach built around a new standard of modularity for payloads, which is their approach to enhance integratability and sharing of combat and security functions across a modularity fleet.

What the projected 9,000-ton Singaporean MRCVs are introducing is significantly new capability to what historically have been considered more or less auxiliary ships to the combat fleet. But now with the arrival of the new autonomous systems such ships can add significant combat capability to the feet.

Nothing less than a revolution in shipbuilding and security and military operations is envisaged.

DEFENSE PROCUREMENT AND CAPABILITIES: HOW TO ACCELERATE MILITARY DEVELOPMENT

October 26, 2023

I have just returned from Australia and have finished a projected annual publication embodying the year's two seminars held by the Sir Richard Williams Foundation plus a wide range of interviews which I conducted around the two seminars.

As such, the volume provides an overview on the year concerning the evolution of Australian defense thinking and policy.

I come away from this year's experience with a single thought: How will the ADF effectively transition from the force in being to one considered more capable for the direct defense of Australia and the deterrence of China?

And in that process, how will an acquisition system be transformed that can accelerate such a transition?

Part of the answer to the acquisition bit is provided by an assessment of the state of UK defense procurement provided by a recent UK Defence Committee report. When Bruce George was chairman of the committee from 1998 to 2005, I played a role as an advisor to the committee and was impressed with their efforts.

This report is quite comprehensive and impressive.

In reading the report, I would highlight a few comments that are most relevant to the Australian situation.

The first is simply the impact of delayed procurement on effective transition.

This is what the report said: "Delayed procurement brings operational consequences. New equipment is usually a replacement or enhancement of in-service equipment. As such, there is a winding down and reallocation of personnel and training as the Service prepares for the expected arrival of new equipment.

"Air Chief Marshal Sir Stephen Hillier, former Chief of the Air Staff, explained: 'If it then happens that the new capability gets delayed, you are not going to be able to reconstitute that existing capability. You now have either a capability gap or less capability than you need.

"That is a serious problem, particularly when you are heavily engaged in operations at the time. It also costs, because you are running on that old equipment and all the contracts and support for it are due to run out, so you have to go back to suppliers and ask to keep it going. That results in unexpected costs along the way. At times it is not good for morale, because people want this new capability and equipment, and that causes frustration in their minds as well."

The second was simply to recognize that long term procurement was almost beside the point with the pressures of the current strategic situation.

The report put it this way: "the UK must now be prepared for what the strategists sometimes call a 'come as you are war' and have an effective procurement system to match. This is the crucial, wider context within which this Report has been produced."

The third was that urgent procurements delivered capabilities; normal procurement practices were simply too slow.

The report noted: "It is a fascinating and repeated theme in the Civil Service that when faced with an emergency they are sometimes able to devise mechanisms for addressing the crisis. However, rather than develop these as advances to change the system and to spread best practice the tendency is to revert to the previous failed practice."

The report contrasted "exquisite procurement" to the speed with which the operational forces need to get actual operational capabilities.

The report underscored the problem in this way: 'Exquisite procurement' is the enemy of speed and time. Over-specifying a piece of equipment creates delays and budget pressures. Exquisite procurement also generally leads to greater cost and therefore less mass.

"For the most part, exquisite procurement should be avoided. Instead, The Front Line Commands and DE&S should aim for a 'spiral development' model as a default. This should be enforced through the Joint Requirements Oversight Committee, the Investment Approvals Committee, and ultimately, Ministers.

"Key trade offs between capability, cost, time, and technical complexity should be made much earlier in the procurement process, when requirements are initially being set. As in the French system,

DE&S should be involved at the outset of formulating requirements and disputes should be resolved, if necessary, by Ministers.

"The current procurement system does not place sufficient emphasis on the value of time. Indeed, as the Permanent Under Secretary (PUS) himself said in summarising the problems with the system: 'we should place more value on time and less on money, so [on] the pace of decision-making and pace of delivery.' We strongly concur with PUS' emphasis on the value of time.

"The Ministry of Defence must develop a much greater sense of urgency in its procurement methodologies. At present, the system is far too ponderous and bureaucratic. There must be a much greater emphasis and value on time. The Ministry of Defence should make greater use of the Urgent Capability Requirements (UCR) method in getting the UK Armed Forces prepared for the immediate future and potential near-term conflicts with peer adversaries.

"The Ministry of Defence, the Front Line Commands—and DE&S in particular—should adopt a 'UCR mindset' which seeks to deliver equipment with much less bureaucracy in a far timelier manner and with a greater emphasis on early operational benefit.

"In the longer term, the Ministry of Defence and DE&S should also review whether the standard processes avoided by use of the UCR method could be removed altogether from all defence procurements."

And then finally, the report highlighted one of their critical points which certainly the United States has forgotten. You need to put key players in place to manage a critical capability and give them the ability to be held responsible for delivering that capability. Certainly, the U.S. would not have nuclear submarines or Aegis ships in a timely manner if such a system was not followed.

This is how the report put this core need: "Senior Responsible Owners (SROs) are a critical part of a successful programme. Their knowledge of a programme and the relationships they build theoretically enable issues to be resolved sooner and more effectively.

"Crucially, via their formal letters of appointment, SROs are accountable to Parliament, including its specialist Committees, such as Defence and Public Accounts, for the successful delivery of the programme in their charge. However, the turnover and frequent 'multiple hatting' of SROs can negatively impacts their programmes.

"The Ministry of Defence should endeavour to keep SROs in post for a minimum of five years to ensure continuity. Whilst it may not be possible to mandate the length of the position, the Ministry of Defence should provide incentives to reward length of service e.g. through renumeration packages and subsequent promotion.

"The Ministry of Defence should also ensure that SROs for category A programmes (i.e. those over £400 million) should have 100% of their time doing that specific job, as opposed to balancing a number of programmes or other roles in one appointment.

"In addition, in order to better align accountability (including to Parliament) with responsibility, SROs, who are often at one or two star level, should be able to exercise direct access to the CEO of DE&S (and if necessary to the Minister for Defence Procurement) in the event of a programme for which they are responsible experiencing serious difficulties, which they are unable to resolve on their own.

"Procurement is seen as a step down within many of the Services. Leaving to work in 'Main Building' or 'Head Office' is seen to be leaving the 'warrior race'. The Ministry of Defence should develop a professional career path within the military that enables Officers to specialise in procurement, as a dedicated cadre, at a much earlier stage of their career.

" If the Ministry of Defence is unable to ensure that military personnel are forthcoming to take on SRO roles, it should consider the greater use of civilian SROs in the long term."

Personally, I think this report is a contribution to AUKUS, and has key recommendations which both the United States and Australia need to take onboard.

SHAPING THE ECOSYSTEM FOR DISTRIBUTED OPERATIONS: C2/AI AND TIMELY DECISION-MAKING

October 30, 2023

During my visit to the DSEI conference in September in London, I noticed that Ultra Intelligence and Communications (Ultra I&C) was attending the conference. And one of the subjects that was on offer was to discuss with their executive team integrated tactical networking.

I contacted the company, and they kindly agreed to meet and discuss the topic which in my words is about the ecosystem for distributed operations. I met with Keith Blanchet, VP Business Development, based in Canada, and Clif Basnight, VP Strategic Technologies based near Washington DC.

The discussion focused less on specific products that Ultra I&C was offering than upon how they viewed the evolving challenge of providing for the evolving eco system for distributed operations. They provided the thinking behind Ultra I&C product development and the foci for solutions to their customers.

Blanchet is an experienced expert on artificial intelligence and decision-making and Basnight is an experienced U.S. Army network engineer and expert in tactical communications. What came clearly through in our discussion was that Ultra I&C was bringing together their two types of expertise into a common effort to deliver distributed decision-making across the battlefield from strategic command to the tactical edge.

It is about being able to work in conditions of data scarcity but finding ways to provide for maximum realistically available information for the distributed force to make decisions at the point of operations.

To enable effective distributed decision making requires advanced networking protocol and next gen communications waveforms working with little to no assistance from a uniformed network technician, powered by AI Tools that curate data into relevant information as rapidly as possible in conditions of data scarcity.

Or put in other terms, communications waveform, networking protocol, and AI need to be orchestrated to work together to deliver actionable data to a distributed force operating at the point of interest.

Blanchet explained that often in defense the focus is upon having too much data and how AI could parse data to deliver solutions. But he felt that in a world of distributed decision making, the core problem is rather data scarcity.

He underscored that we make decisions intuitively based on our past experience. He argued that "AI in a dispersed or distributed environment is really about taking incomplete information and extrapolating suggestions or decision aids for a decision to be made in a timely and realistic manner. Ultra I&C is working right now on decision aids for dispersed or distributed decision making."

Basnight focused on his past experience with the U.S. Army in which there were two separate networks in operations which he referred to as the upper and lower tactical network internet. There were bridges in between but often there was breakage between the two networks and the work arounds were time consuming and difficult.

"It could take hours to days to reinsert a piece of the network into another piece of the network. Until 2019, the most common way to do command and control below the battalion level was SINCGARS."

SINCGARS is a very high-frequency radio where the primary role is voice transmission between surface and airborne command and control assets.

"But now using ubiquitous communications leveraging both commercial (5G/LTE, Wi-Fi 6, LORA) and defense specific waveforms (TRILOS, HCLOS), a warfighter can send and receive relevant, high definition voice and data from wherever they are in the fight."

Technology has matured to a point where mission data can be transformed and transmitted in a timely manner to the tactical edge by leveraging every communication channel available and not just the comms link prescribed.

Basnight noted: "The desired end state is for data to be presented to the radio and then the radio makes the decision of how to deliver it. Through better sensing and understanding of the electromagnetic spectrum the radio can determine how noisy is my environment? What kind of jammers are being operated?

"What type of bearer (i.e., a logical entity that represents a specific network service) do I need to get this particular piece of data out?

"Then using AI-Defined Networking, the software-based radio can determine, in realtime, what waveform is best suited to reliable deliver this data.. We wanted to do this 20 years ago but the piece parts weren't there, but now, for the first time in my career, I believe the technologies and the expertise needed are more readily available to implement without increasing the cognitive load of the warfighter."

"Also, entailed is module mission capability whereby we can change the platform's C5ISR mission set by swapping out the combination of Open System Architecture cards in the platform. This will allow you to transition to the right tools for the mission regardless of what phase of the fight you're in from phase zero to five throughout a given engagement without leaving the field."

Blanchet then highlighted the impact of autonomous ground vehicles into the discussion with regard to distributed operations.

"We are introducing ground unmanned vehicles at the tactical edge to do such missions as logistical support. Such capabilities will also have an impact on decision doctrine. These machines will be making decisions on their own.

"The human is simply tracking the decisions of the machines operating in the combat space. We will have to include these entities in the entire decision-making chain as they are sensors and units of actions in the battlespace."

We then moved to a discussion of the training domain which is clearly a key part of working a way ahead for effective distributed decision making. AI tools can certainly help in shaping live virtual and constructive training, but we focused on the need through training to build trust in the TTPs being worked with the use C2 and AI and the inclusion of unmanned platforms into the ground maneuver space.

Blanchet argued that AI was a key part of being able to work with the complex networks being shaped to empower and enable distributed forces.

"AI makes it easier to use the complex networks being put in place and knowing what spectrum is out there and what's available and what's not available and what I can use, and being able to identify what's new, what's friendly is very key. AI is indispensable to such a decision-making process."

In effect, they underscored that AI networking was a key part of shaping the way ahead for decision making for the distributed force.

Blanchet concluded: "a new generation of soldiers and decision makers are starting to shift their focus in this direction. With forces becoming more expeditionary, much more on the move, much more diverse across coalitions, such complexity requires a transition towards the value proposition from industry being more than software but really providing integration capability and simplifying the problems for decision making."

AN UPDATE ON THE FRENCH A330MRTT: OCTOBER 2023

By Pierre Tran

October 31, 2023

France signed Oct. 6 a contract with Airbus Defence and Space to add a secure, high-speed satellite communications link to the A330 multirole tanker transport, a deal the company sees as plugging MRTT jets into a network of a planned European future combat air system.

"The DGA (Direction Générale de l'Armement) awarded Oct. 6 2023 the company Airbus Defence & Space the first stages of work on standard 2 on the A330 Multi Role Tanker Transport (MRTT) Phénix of the French air and space force," the armed forces ministry said in an Oct. 20 statement.

Airbus D&S also signed Oct. 6 a contract for 10 years' service, with option for two more years, for the MRTT, the company said in an Oct. 23 statement, with the standard 2 communications and maintenance deals worth a total €1.2 billion ($1.3 billion).

Airbus D&S is effectively prime contractor for installing standard 2, which relies on a Thales onboard satellite link dubbed Melissa, and service for the French MRTT fleet. A company spokesman declined to say how that total amount was split between the two MRTT deals.

The standard 2 communications upgrade is seen as delivering an entry to a planned combat cloud extended network, for the MRTT, a military conversion of the Airbus A330-200 wide-body, twin-engine airliner.

"This new standard, which will undergo incremental development, strengthens the capability of the A330 MRTT to evolve in contested environments, while providing greater communications capability with other aircraft and command centers," the ministry said.

The DGA procurement office and Direction de la Maintenance

Aéronautique (DMAé), the aeronautics service unit, also signed Oct. 6 with Rolls-Royce a maintenance contract for up to 20 years for the Trent 700 engine on the MRTT, with the British company delivering its MissionCare service.

Lockheed Bales Out

The Airbus D&S Oct. 23 statement on the MRTT deals coincided with Lockheed Martin's announcement the American company was pulling out of the U.S. air force competition for an air tanker.

Lockheed had partnered with Airbus for the European company to pitch its A330 MRTT, and that departure left Airbus flying solo against Boeing, its archrival in the U.S. tender for some 75 inflight refuelling jets, worth an estimated $12 billion.

France attaches strategic importance to its MRTT fleet, which provides inflight refuelling for the Rafale, boosting the range of the fighter which carries the airborne deterrent, the ASMP/A nuclear-tipped missile.

The Phénix MRTT replaced the U.S.-built French air force fleet of 11 C-135FR and three KC-135RG, which dated back to the 1960s, flown by the Brétagne squadron. Those French air tankers supported the Mirage IV and 2000N, and more recently Rafale, armed with nuclear weapons. Phénix also replaced three A310 and two A340 jets flown by the Esterel transport squadron.

The then U.S. president, John F. Kennedy, authorized the sale of the C-135 when his French counterpart, Charles de Gaulle, was building an independent nuclear strike, said an analyst at the Institut Français d'Analyse Stratégique, a think tank.

The first phase in the standard 2 upgrade includes equipping the MRTT with a defensive aids sub-system, the ministry said, without giving details. The Airbus D&S spokesman declined to comment.

The French authorities see selection of the defensive sub-system as highly sensitive and has that wrapped up in strict confidentiality. U.S. and Israeli companies lead the market for defensive sub-systems.

The Nato multinational fleet of nine MRTT, backed by six member states, is fitted with a direct infrared countermeasures (DIRCM) system from Elbit Systems, dubbed J-Multi Spectral Infrared Countermeasure or J-Music. The German Air Force has also equipped its A400M airlifters with J-Music kit. The system aims to protect aircraft from ground-based, heat-seeking missiles.

Meanwhile, talks are being held for selecting subcontractors for service support, an industry source said. Companies such as Collins Aerospace and Sabena Technics are active in the French service market.

Maintenance, repair and overhaul may be low key but that business offers a steady flow of income, while requiring technical skill. The risk and reward of service contracts could be seen with the French fleet of C-130 Hercules airlifters, which in the past suffered from low availability, stemming from what the then head of air force special operations command said was due to industrial problems. A Portuguese company, Ogma, previously provided service for the French C-130 fleet.

The separate and complementary service contracts for the MRTT airframe and aero-engines reflect the "vertical" approach of the DMAé, the ministry said, and the commitment of work for at least 10 years gave reassurance for the companies to invest €30 million in infrastructure around Istres air base.

Changes The Game

Standard 2 is a "game changer," the analyst said, as the MRTT aircraft adds "multimission" to its support for the French strategic airborne force and flying logistical support for overseas deployment.

The defense ministry gave no details on the value of the standard 2 contract. The DGA was not available for comment.

The satellite communications link will be retrofitted to the 12-strong MRTT fleet flown by the French air force from Istres air base, close to Marseille, southern France. A further three MRTT jets are due to join the fleet by 2030, with the 15th unit to be the prototype for standard two, due for certification in 2028.

Standard 2 aims to plug MRTT into the planned combat cloud, one of the critical technology pillars being developed for the European future combat air system.

"With this new capability of the aircraft, we are preparing the future by transforming the MRTT into an in-flight communications node, as the first building block of the Multi Role Tanker Transport of tomorrow, embedded in the Future Combat Air System (FCAS)," Jean-

Brice Dumont, head of military air systems at Airbus Defence & Space said in the Oct. 23 statement.

Connectivity through telecommunications is seen as a major capability, and the MRTT will be fitted with a satellite communications link, dubbed Melissa, allowing the tanker-transport to hook up to the French Syracuse IV military satellite network.

The Melissa satcom will allow the MRTT to be connected at all time, beating enemies' jamming attempts and extreme weather, the company said. The MRTT standard 2 will deliver "high-bandwidth communication, sovereign and secure," to boost links with the airborne deterrence, the ministry said.

MRTT will hold a "central position in aeronautical connectivity," providing a communications node between C2 command and control and the aeronautic network. The Airbus team in France will be doubled to support the MRTT activities, the company said.

Melissa Boosts Links

On the Melissa communications link, Thales said Feb. 8 2022 the company would deliver the onboard satellite workstation in 2025, offering high bandwidth, high availability, and high performance on large military or government aircraft such as MRTT, A400M, and Awacs spy planes.

The contract for a military system linked to Syracuse IV satellite is for 17 years and is based on a civilian system, which has shown reliability with more than 30,000 flight hours, the company said.

"This military version is specially designed to maintain connectivity with commanders in a jammed environment or in very poor flight or weather conditions," the company said. The link can work with "the sovereign Syracuse IV satellites and is also compatible with other allied military or commercial satellites."

The present French MRTT fleet uses Link 16 for communications with Nato allied aircraft and commanders.

The air force flies 12 MRTT tanker transports, and three more aircraft are due to be delivered by 2030 under the 2024-2030 military budget law, adopted in July. Development work on standard 2 will lead to the qualification of the prototype, the ministry said, with the remaining fleet retrofitted as they undergo routine service over the 10 years contracted with Airbus DS.

The first MRTT to be converted to standard 2 will be number 15 for the French air force, with the conversion to be made at the Airbus Getafe plant, in Spain, Airbus DS said. That MRTT is due to be qualified in 2028. The other MRTTs will be retrofitted at Istres air base.

The MRTT, which entered service in 2018, also serves as a flying hospital for medical evacuation missions.

In the air force's Pegase 23 mission, the service flew five A330 MRTT, along with 10 Rafale and four A400M airlifters to the Pacific region in 72 hours. The service plans for the next air deployment to consist of a full 20-strong Rafale squadron, supported by 10 A330 MRTT tankers, reaching the Pacific in 48 hours.

FROM DISTRIBUTED LOGISTICS TO DISTRIBUTED MANUFACTURING: THE 3D PRINTING REVOLUTION GOES ON

November 2023

By Murielle Delaporte

An interview with Tali Rosman, Start Up Advisor in Miami, Florida, and EIR at Toronto Metropolitan University, Canada

Tali Rosman was born and raised in Israel, studied economics and political science at the University of Tel Aviv and did her military service in the Israeli Air Force.

She has since then pursued a brilliant international career starting with a MBA at INSEAD in France & Singapore, as well as developing extensive strategy, corporate development and new venture experience ranging from large corporations to early-stage startups in London, Geneva, Israel, Singapore and the United States.

She has been in America since 2014, where she works at Stratasys – the leading player at the time in the additive manufacturing market, then NICE, and more recently at Xerox, where she was CEO of Elem Additive.

A well-known expert in digital manufacturing and 3D printing, Tali is today a startup advisor at Miami-based RHH Advisory and an Entrepreneur in Residence (EIR) at the Metropolitan University of Toronto.

In this interview, she focuses on what she describes as her "most significant achievement", i.e. her experience at Xerox where she was in charge of building and launching an entire new company from the ground up, Elem Additive.

Known in the military field for having worked with the Naval Post Graduate School to test the very first Liquid Metal Jetting Printer installed in July 2022 on a U.S. Navy ship, the USS ESSEX, while at sea, Elem Additive has been a major success and acquired by ADDiTEC last summer.

The ElemX Adventure: Successfully Delivering Parts on Demand
The Search for Deployability

Having previously worked at Stratasys' Corporate Development, Tali Rosman knows the Additive Manufacturing (AM) market right and left *"from hardware, to materials, to software and services."*

When she was hired in 2020 to set up Elem Additive with a small team of researchers, the market was dominated by plastic 3D printers and by powder-based metal printers.

Her task was to shift from the latter technology towards safer and deployable metal printers by using wire-fed liquid metal technology: *"The challenge was multifold, as we needed to get away from powder-based technologies considered toxic for the environment and highly explosive, therefore unsafe and not easily deployable."*

Tali Rosman and her team managed to develop a new technology used today by the U.S. Navy, the U.S. Department of Energy and Siemens, based on aluminum wire as opposed to powder.

"Wire is safe, non-toxic and non-explosive. While it is not plug and play, it's as close as you are going to get to it in order match the "just in time/where you need it" requirement," she underscores.

Another key advantage driving the ease of deployment is the straight-forward, much simpler post-processing.

Powder-based metal manufacturing requires post-processing equipment often delocalized to external suppliers, such as HIP, therefore increasing delays of delivery and limiting the ability to produce parts on demand, in remote locations.

"Post-processing for metal printing is cumbersome and expensive. What people want are parts on demand, so it is one thing to print in a few hours, but if post-processing takes weeks, it defeats the purpose, because it is not on demand."

The faster time-for-part is therefore not only due to liquid metal technology, but also to reduced post-processing time allowing the full manufacture of parts the same day on site.

Same Day Turnaround

The ability to deliver a new part usable right away, the same day that a part broke or was lost, changes the game of logistics and inventories in both the civilian and military sectors.

While Tali estimates that the majority of needed parts could be printed that is not to say additive manufacturing will be cheaper than traditional manufacturing, but in times of need, time-to-part might be a greater consideration than part manufacturing cost.

"All you need is space to install the printer – while the ElemX is pretty large, newcomers on the market, such as the Belgian company Valcun, now propose similar products with a lesser footprint and lower energy consumption.

Other than the printer, you only need spools of metal wire (currently both the ElemX and the ValCUN solutions are focusing on aluminum) that you can buy off the shelf and that can be stored without special treatment, and the post-processing equipment, which is minimal when compared to powder-based technologies.

It depends on the parts of course," explains Tali Rosman, *"but most of the time the part comes out of the printer in good shape, and post-processing will primarily include milling for surface finish to make it perfectly smooth, or a simple heat treatment in a regular over to strengthen the part. No need for a proprietary furnace, powder removal equipment, HIP, etc."*

Because the process has been so simplified, another advantage of liquid metal printing is that it is therefore less labor-intensive and the training of AM engineers and mechanics is much easier and faster.

Also, the impact on the supply chain in general could become quickly noticeable for two reasons: *"First you don't have the material complexities posed by powder-bed metal technologies, you just need to buy spools of wire easily accessible off the shelf.*

It is worth noting that all emerging liquid metal printers, from the ElemX, through GROB, to ValCUN, are initially focusing on aluminum, which is 25% of the global market for metal spare parts (steel is another 25% and the rest is spread across a few other materials).

Secondly, you do not need that much material since you just use what you need to produce the part, as opposed to subtractive manufacturing, such as machining, where you take material from a block of material. By definition, because you substract, you are going to have tons of waste. Less material organized by blocs means less inventory headaches: you do not need to store multiple parts anymore, just the material you need to produce them."

Less than a network of warehouses, an AM supply chain may increasingly rely on a *"network of local vendors across the world."*

A few hurdles to overcome, case-by-case

For Tali Rosman, the relationship of 3D printing, or additive manufacturing (AM), to the global supply chain can be compared to the relationship of a back-up generator to the electricity grid: *"If the regular system works, then it's probably better to use it, but if there is a supply chain disruption, then your back up generator is needed and that is what 3D printing can offer and can do.*

For some parts, AM will always be used as a backup generator, but for a few parts it might be the default form of manufacturing. This is the way it is currently on the frontlines of Ukraine, where many parts cannot be shipped, or no ready inventory exists."

At this point in time, there are two major hurdles making it difficult for 3D printing to be used more generally as a "default form of manufacturing."

The first is the technical difficulty to mass produce. ElemX is used for a low-volume and diversified mix of products on a deployed ship or forward base, not for mass production at depots.

"Although, this might change as more non-powder solutions keep emerging," notes Tali Rosman. *"For example, the Israeli company Tritone is using a new process consisting of filling a wax mold with metal paste allowing a production of parts in the thousands, if not tens of thousands. While it is not made for millions of parts, it is already a different market than Xerox – or ADDiTEC today – and Vulcan."*

The second hurdle has to do with the certification and qualification process which is especially cumbersome in the military field. There are many debates going on about that particular issue which does slow down the extension of the use of 3D printing in the armed forces.

One solution is to certify the parts in advance; the other is to reflect on the level of quality one does need for non-critical or non-primary structure parts.

"The question is "do you really need that part certified? For instance, the handle of washing machines on board military ships can, if broken, become an incredible hazard. However, does it need to be of absolute perfect quality?

This brings us to the "good enough to function" argument vs the "top notch quality" requiring a rigorous process of certification making sure the printed part exactly matches the initial part."

From AM (Additive Manufacturing) to PM (Predictive Maintenance): A Revolution In Military Maintenance

A rigorous certification process or in-situ quality control could very soon be greatly facilitated by the current exponential use of artificial intelligence (AI): *"A few months ago, I would have told you that AI was nothing more than a pie in the sky, but today we are all experiencing the ChatGPT effect at multiple levels: for quality insurance, but also in terms of the degree of trust people are now having in these new tools."*

AI can actually contribute to predictive maintenance (PM) by increasingly incorporating quality control and end-users inputs or feedback and accelerating the whole process.

"I've seen a couple of new startups that are starting to close this loop on generative design, and of course Nvidia recently announced the launching of an AI model for 3D design".

In addition, the security issue both in terms of cyber security and IP (intellectual property) protection is now solved by technological breakthroughs:

"There are startups, such as Israeli based Assembrix, that are already successfully working on the secure digital transfer of files, so much so that the actual AM personnel in charge of the printing might not be able to access the proprietary information. So these concerns are starting to be resolved in the field already..."

ADDITIVE MANUFACTURING: REDEFINING U.S. SHIPBUILDING

November 2023

By Murielle Delaporte

Additive manufacturing (AM) technology exists since the end of 1980's, but the last years have seen a quantum leap in the numbers of applications and progress being made, so much so that entire ships can now be 3D printed as a whole.

AM could contribute to alleviate the shipbuilding manufacturing crisis Western nations have been experiencing while enhancing their sovereignty by redefining the rules of the game as far as manpower is concerned. The Unites States is certainly investing in such a future.

ELEM X Lessons Learned: "Enhancing Expeditionary Maintenance"

The ability to easily train AM mechanics is one of the many lessons learned from the Elem X deployment on the U.S Navy amphibious assault ship USS Essex. A sign of the times, the U.S.. Navy now specifically recruits and trains "AM Technicians".

If there has been regular trials of 3D printers on board military ships – the USS Essex already in 2014, but also for example the French Navy amphibious assault ship Dixmude in 2018 and the Charles de Gaulle aircraft carrier in 2019 .

They were done with plastic 3D printers. The Elem X was indeed the first experiment with a metal 3D printer at sea in 2022, during the multinational naval exercise RIMPAC 22, in partnership with the Naval Post-Graduate School (NPS) and the Pacific Fleet (COMNAV-SURFPAC), a relationship initiated in 2020. It was then transferred to LHD4 USS Boxer for more evaluations.

Lieutenant Commander Nicolas Batista, the Essex's Aircraft Intermediate Maintenance Department (AIMD) officer, is quoted as saying about the experiment: "AM will enhance expeditionary maintenance that contributes to our Surface Competitive Edge."[2]

Simplicity and supply chain resilience seem to be key assets of the Xerox technology that was commercially introduced early 2021 and kept improving with the establishment in particular of an AM center of excellence in Cary, North Carolina.

What made the Elem X viable in various sea states was the fact that it was operating in and protected by an industrial shipping container.

The printer itself is 9 by 7 feet, but the container is 20 foot long. That container system also allows the 3Dprinter to be deployed ashore on the ground by deployed USMC units, if need be, since it can be plugged into any kind of power outlet, such as a field generator.

Elem X is meant to produce small volume of aluminum parts up to 10 inches square allowing to reduce the inventories of components such as for example "Common Valve Hand Wheels, Antenna Seal Band Brackets, Fire Hose Spanner Wrenches"[3]

Other metal parts that can be printed at sea are the following: "heat sinks, housings, fuel adapters, valve covers and other small items", as described in a July 11th, 2022 article.[4]

The certification process both for military and civilian purposes is what takes time at first of course, as explained in the same article :

"The U.S. Navy has been testing 3D printing for the last few years in a variety of different applications. In 2018, they installed the first prototype 3D-printed metal part aboard the USS Harry S Truman for a one-year test and evaluation trial.

"By October 2020, U.S. Navy and Naval Sea Systems Command (NAVSEA) reported it had approved a total of 182 3D printable parts in its database and had more than 600 additional parts undergoing engineering review.

"Those tests were being conducted onshore at fabrication plants with the Navy now looking at the capabilities of extending small part manufacturing to the ships.

"The advantage is a major simplification in inventory management since the difficulty is of course to forecast with accuracy which part will break or will be lost once at sea or deployed in general.

"The commercial industry has also been exploring the use of 3D printing. Early in 2021, for example, 3D-printed mechanical parts were installed aboard the U.S.-flagged oil tanker Polar Endeavor in a test.

"After six months in operation, the parts were retrieved and inspected by the vessel's crew, followed by a remote survey by ABS that confirmed their good condition. ABS approved the spare parts after successful onboard testing on the tanker creating the opportunity for wider applications of the technology."[5]

In the case of the USS Essex trial, the Elem X had its twin based at NPS printing the same parts, so the comparison would be facilitated.

Elem X was sold last August to ADDiTEC, but should keep

working with the U.S. Navy, as well as its other customers such as "Siemens, the U.S. Department of Energy's Oak Ridge National Laboratory, Rochester Institute of Technology, and Vertex Manufacturing"[6]

From Obsolescence to Recruiting: AM to The Rescue

Between Covid and Ukraine, a new sense of urgency has been emulated the AM ecosystem to follow the Elem X footsteps. In November 2022, the USS Bataan installed the first additive hybrid-metal 3D printing solution provided by Phillips with Spanish-based multinational Meltio and California-based Haas.

In this case the deployment is the result of a joint partnership with the Naval Sea Systems Command and the COMNAVSURFLANT on the East Coast, as well as Johns Hopkins Applied Physics Laboratory.

Being able to complement it with polymer printer (like the USS Bataan has been doing it) and to integrate both substractive and additive processes for metallic parts could be the best of both worlds on ships already equipped with traditional repair processes on board (such as "the Haas CNC system which can be upgraded into a hybrid AM system"[7]

Improving self-sufficiency, but also being able to treat obsolescence on long-life-cycle parts no longer made by suppliers or for which the availability is limited are what many other companies and navies are working on.

Here are some examples as described in a January 18th, 2023 article:

"Also, in 2022, SPEE3D's WarpSPEE3D cold spray technology was used to print maritime military parts on demand and in various sea conditions.

"Aside from the U.S. Navy, the maritime industry, in general, has had examples of companies making strides with 3D printing, like Norwegian multinational Wilhelmsen, which disrupted the supply chain for marine parts in 2017 after teaming up with AM company Ivaldi to create micro-factories that 3D print and deliver spare parts within hours.

"Another example is the Danish-funded Green Ship of the Future consortium, exploring onboard printing, large-scale 3D printing, 4D printing or repair, and reconditioning with 3D printing."[8]

The shipbuilding industry has been struggling with labor shortfall for some time. In the military, one area especially worrisome is the submarine segment, which could experience "a labor shortfall of 100,000 workers in the Navy's submarine program," according to Matt Sermon, executive director of the U.S. Navy's Program Executive Office, Strategic Submarines, who believes that "metallic additive manufacturing is the path to the capability and capacity you need for critical materials in the submarine industrial base. And that same holds true for surface ships, and its systems, and for sustainment as well."[9]

The hope is that using AM could keep both the Columbia ballistic missile submarine and Virginia-class attack submarines programs on schedule. The program executive office for strategic submarines' database tracks some 5,500 parts, the goal being to "have 3D printers up and running for the six most important metals by March 2024 and produce five additively manufactured parts that will go on submarines this year" and to "be at maturity in those six materials and be putting them on ships and submarines."[10]

The progress to print more and more complex parts using the key metals the shipbuilding industry needs (as well as their recycled waste), such as titanium which is especially resistant to corrosion, makes possible a "closed-loop" manufacturing process, yielding a fully home-grown manufacturing process, from start to finish."[11]

A 100% re-localization process seems therefore reachable at a time when sovereignty concerns are back on front burner.

The next step is Huntington Ingalls Industry (HII)'s goal to build CVN-80 very first Navy 3D-printed ship breaking with more than two thousand years of tradition forging and casting methods. The gain of processing time between AM and legacy methods is estimated at fifty per cent.

If 3D printing is not yet the holy grail, it certainly makes a difference between life and death when under fire, as even the simplest part can become crucial in war time.

Already, with about five hundred parts certified by the U.S. Navy to be 3D printed, life is easier for many sailors who can now reduce the repair time from weeks to minutes whether having a broken part, a pipe leak or a lost tool.

THE WAY AHEAD FOR WESTERN FIGHTERS

November 15, 2023

I have attended the International Fighter Conference in the past but missed this year's offering. This year's conference was held in Madrid, and I was interested in what was discussed at the conference as I am focused on the way ahead for Western air combat forces in the decade ahead.

First, I scanned recently press reports on the conference and really found two news threads. The first involved the Swedes and the fact that they had dropped out of the British led Tempest program and were now looking at their own requirements for their next combat jet.

I am deliberately not using the characterization of next generation fighter for they may not indeed do such as my own view is that the air combat domain is changing way beyond consideration of a next generation fighter.

Gareth Jennings reported that Sweden had dropped out of the British led program.

"Speaking at the IQPC International Fighter Conference (IFC) 2023 under the Chatham House Rule, an official said that the national work followed the official termination of the country's participation in the UK-led Future Combat Air System (FCAS) in 2022.

"We walked away from trilateral studies with [the] UK and Italy about a year ago, and launched a national study. I will not answer questions why it didn't work with the UK and FCAS," the official said on 7 November at the event in Madrid, adding only that had Sweden known in July 2019 when it signed up to FCAS what it knows now about its requirements, it would not have joined."[12]

Tim Martin in *Breaking Defense* also focused on the Swedish presentation.

"After joining and then leaving the UK-led Future Combat Air System (FCAS), the Swedish military is now holding off on deciding its path to a next-generation fighter jet until 2031, after it can assess the "risks and possibilities" with different approaches, an official said today.

"Three options are on the table for Stockholm: Either "build a system, develop a system with someone, or... acquire a system," said the official, speaking under Chatham House Rules at the International Fighter Conference here in Madrid. "It's an open question."

"We did have both bilateral and trilateral cooperation with Britain and also with Italy on the FCAS program," said the official. "We walked away from that about a year ago and started some national studies... connecting to what capabilities are needed for the future." The official declined to comment on the reason behind Sweden ending collaboration with the UK and Italy.

"A decision has not been made by authorities so far on an Initial Operating Capability (IOC) date for whatever it chooses for a next-gen fighter, but a wide range of planning activities will inform the 2031 procurement decision."[13]

The only other story I found focused on Poland. There the emphasis was on the Polish air force looking at autonomous systems that would fly with the F-35 enabled Polish Air Force.

According to _Shephard News_:

"The Polish MoD has been evaluating the UAS market in search of a loyal wingman platform to work alongside its future fleet of Lockheed Martin F-35A fighter jet, the Deputy General Commander of the Polish Armed Forces has revealed.

"Addressing the International Fighter Conference 2023 in Madrid on 6 November, Maj General Cezary Wisniewski disclosed that the Polish Ministry of National Defence (NMD) was engaged in a comprehensive market assessment of the emerging loyal wingman uncrewed combat aerial vehicles (UCAVs) capability.

"The evaluation has formed part of the ministry's efforts to meet the requirements of the Harpii Szpon (Harpy's Talon) adjunct programme for the F-35 fighters.

'We are not yet at the point of an acquisition,' Maj Gen Wisniewski said. 'We are [now] just waiting for more information to be sure that we don't make a mistake – we just want to join the mainstream approach, [but] we think that industry is not ready to provide the capabilities yet."[14]

My own sense is that discussions of next generation fighters although interesting are a bit premature.

First, the dominance of the F-35 within Western nations will provide a significant input to redefining air combat going forward. And the United States will face a major challenge of adapting its legacy mindset on security to the technological realties of a fleet of aircraft that can move vast amounts of data within a combat area to shape the kind of multi-domain warfare capabilities which are often highlighted but ignoring what the arrival of a F-35 global enterprise could enable.

The key is sensor fusion and the ability to do this as a wolfpack. I was in England for the DSEI conference held in London in early September. One of the discussions highlighted by the DSEI organizers on their content hub was with my guru and guide for many years in the UK's process of adopting the F-35, then Group Captain Paul Godfrey and now Air Vice-Marshal Godfrey. He has moved from dealing with combat air to the new space efforts being worked by the UK Ministry of Defence.

Air Vice Marshal Gary Waterfall (Retired) interviewed "Godders" about the challenges of setting up the new UK space command. As the first commander of UK space command, Godders has brought a wide range of experience in terms of working combat air with the broader force transformation effort being pursued by the UK, through the difficult periods of the Brexit transition.

A key theme which was discussed was the focus on being able to access space to deliver the kind of ISR-T and C2 information to a deployed force. Godders made a key point that sensor fusion from space assets was a key challenge facing the force and in doing so he highlighted a key point often neglected when talking about the F-35 and its impact on force transformation, namely, its revolutionary impact on sensor fusion in the cockpit of F-35s operating as a wolfpack.

This is what Air Vice-Marshal Godfrey highlighted:

"Data validation is key. If we both go back to a previous platform that we both worked with, the F-35, it shows one how it can be done. The data from the various sensors around the airplane are fused in the fusion engine.

"The radar might think that there's a 70% chance it is x. Another sensor might indicate that it is 100% chance, or 99.9%. chance that it's x. And data fusion then can present the pilot with that answer that it is 98% certain that it is x. The legal people have had a look at it and that might be enough for you to shoot at the target.

"That's what I'm looking for in terms of how we bring data together or how we fuse it. When you scale that across the enterprise and pair data sources, where is that done? Do you do all of that at the source on a satellite? That's why we're doing this with some of our operational capability demonstrators. Or do you wait for that information to be sent down? Is your F 35 brain in the Space Operations Center? Is it done at edge processing?

"To provide answers, we're doing experiments over the next couple of years to see what works, what doesn't work for sensor fusion from our space data."

What Godders is talking about is the data ecosystem which is being worked to deliver the kind of ISR-T and C2 capabilities necessary for the kind of force transformation underway. And it should not be forgotten what the F-35 as a global enterprise can provide.

Second, next generation UAVs, autonomous systems, are the other major driver of the dynamics of change for the air combat force. Although referred to as wingman they are not that at all. No fifth-generation pilot wants a wingman, that is legacy thinking par excellence.

The new generation of longer-range UAVs provide significant force multiplier capabilities for the outside force, and with ISR and C2 payloads to the inside force as well. It is not so much manned-unmanned teaming as it is filling gaps that currently cannot be filled or as complements to the crewed platforms in the current force.

With the growing impact of the global F-35 force, the next big thing is almost certainly going to be building up a next generation UAV force that fills the gaps and complements the force.

To get an update on what the news stories from the conference did not focus on, I talked with my colleague Billie Flynn who attended the conference to get his take on the way ahead for the fighter world and how the conference addressed this.

First, Flynn underscored his concern with regard to the future of the Royal Canadian Air Force in which he served for many years.

Given the atrophy of Canadian airpower, the number of pilots has been significantly reduced.

This means that although the CAF is finally to acquire the F-35, the CAF is facing a significant pilot shortfall. He raised these questions with the Canadian speaker who really had no answer as to how they were going to deal with this challenge. There does not appear to be a solution on how to produce enough fighter pilots to man the F-35s when they arrive in Canada which will have implications for NORAD and NATO alliances.

Second, he emphasized that the F-35 global enterprise was gaining momentum in ways that most European political leaders simply did not anticipate. But he saw a divide between the AUKUS three – the U.S., Australia, and the UK – and the rest of the F-35 global enterprise with regard to the kind of collaboration which the jet clearly empowers.

Third, he was very skeptical with regard to the European programs which have been generated, whether the British-led one or the French-led one. Much like the Tornado and Eurofighter programs of the past, the emphasis was on workshare and investment distribution, not lethality, effectiveness, or advanced technology integration.

Where are the export opportunities? And what is their relationship to what the F-35 dominance in European air forces will yield in terms of change in air combat?

And he agreed that the priority impact of figuring out how to use the F-35 and the coming of autonomous air systems would predominate operational realities over projected new fighter projects.

Of course, a major impact will come from the B-21 and the entire process of weaponization which will have a decisive impact certainly on the way ahead for the USAF. A fifth generation fighter global enterprise plus autonomous air systems plus a new bomber plus new weapons will almost certainly dominate the real world of air combat evolution much more than development and acquisition of a new fighter.

COL PURCELL'S PERSPECTIVE ON THE IMPACT OF THE COMING OF THE CH-53K

November 22, 2023

During my visit to MAWTS-1 during the first week of November 2023, I had a chance to talk with Colonel Eric Purcell, the CO of MAWTS-1 about the coming of the CH-53K to the USMC.

This is the third new air system I have seen coming to the USMC since I have been coming to Yuma, but because it doesn't look as different as the other two did from their legacy ancestors, it is often not fully realized how important it will be for the USMC and the joint force.

Purcell is the first CH-53 pilot to be the CO of MAWTS-1 which is propitious as the CH-53K has been part of this year's WTIs at MAWTS-1. He has more than 3000 hours on the CH-53E and 130 hours on the CH-53D. He has had two deployments to Afghanistan and two to Iraq, and additional visits to both countries as well.

He noted that he wished they had not called it the CH-53 for the CH-53K is so different from the legacy aircraft. It is designed to fit into the deck space of an CH-53E and to have a reduced footprint for its maintenance as well.

But the big difference is associated with the broader changes across the Marine Corps. When I was last at MAWTS-1 in 2020, they were starting to work on how to enhance the deployability and mobility of the Marine Corps and to do so in formations smaller than the traditional MAGTF.

During this visit, my discussions with the department heads underscored how much work they have done in terms of doing expeditionary basing, innovations in Forward Refueling and Re-Arming points and ways to reduce the signature of the deployed force.

The CH-53K, in Col Purcell's view, contributed to that in a significant way. He focused on the ability of the King Stallion with its triple hooks to carry significant loads to operating locations without having to land and be on the ground for the time necessary to unload from the interior of the aircraft.

Col Purcell pointed out that the aircraft could carry significant fuel loads – 54,000 pounds of fuel -- to locations the F-35B might operate from and could do so with external lift rather than having to land.

Both the Osprey and the heavy lift helo could carry fuel inside and work as fuel providers to aircraft at a FARP. But being on the ground for significant time to do this exposed the aircraft to much greater risk than coming in and dropping off fuel from their external three hook system.

He pointed out that the legacy aircraft two hook system could lead on occasion to "uncommanded" load releases whereby the system on the aircraft would not be able to judge correctly whether loads on the hooks were compromising the safety of the aircraft. Systems on the aircraft prioritized aircraft safety over carrying loads and might jettison a load.

The CH-53K's systems can correctly determine whether the load being carried by the aircraft affect the center of gravity of the aircraft, which is central to its security, and can make more accurate decisions with regard to the safety of the aircraft.

He noted that the load carrying capacity of the aircraft meant that it could carry an Osprey which might be in a location where it could not get repairs needed to fly safely to a location where it could be repaired. Some of the weight, such as the seats, would have to be removed to do so, but it could be done.

Col Purcell underscored that in Afghanistan and Iraq many of the missions which the CH-53E did were medium lift. The CH-53K is optimized for heavy lift and both the Marine Corps and the joint force need to focus on its unique capabilities to support distributed logistics as no other rotorcraft can do in the force. It is optimized for heavy lift, and it is important to capitalize on its unique capabilities.

The CH-53K can be part of a logistic chain involving cargo aircraft like the C-17, the C-5 and the C-130, in that it can carry 463L pallets and work with fixed wing cargo aircraft to transfer their pallets to the Super Stallion and then deliver them in places only a rotorcraft can go.

The new motors on the King Stallion allow it to operate in conditions where one would not want to operate an aging CH-53E fleet. The power margins of the new aircraft are much greater than the legacy aircraft.

Col Purcell concluded: "The force will see the impact of the revolutionary design of the CH-53K to carry heavy loads long range and to enhance significantly the logistical capability of the force and to move in and out of objective areas more rapidly than the legacy system."

THE TECHNOLOGY IS IMPORTANT: BUT THE CON-OPS AGAINST A REACTIVE ENEMY IS DETERMINATE

December 3, 2023

With the coming of maritime autonomous systems, we are reminded once again about the importance of understanding what a technology does and does not do for an organization. If you keep the structure of the organization the same, you simply wait for the technology to be useful to that legacy organization. Your focus is not upon – how can I use that technology now because it is important I do so?

How do I change the way I operate so I can use it NOW?

There is no better case in point than the conventional thinking about the U.S. Navy and maritime autonomous systems.

To be clear, there are those in the U.S. Navy who get it, such as Vice Admiral Brad Cooper, Commander U.S. Naval Forces Central Command. Task Force 59 within 5th Fleet has provided practical leadership for the way ahead in using (not endlessly developing) maritime autonomous systems.

A good illustration of the challenge was highlighted in a recent USNI piece published on 30 November 2023.

In this piece, the author indicated that the unmanned future of the U.S. Navy is "murky."[15]

I would have used the term "confused" instead.

And the difference gets to a key point about how these systems can be used now and not after China has seized Taiwan.

The story highlights the deployment of four autonomous ships which was a months long deployment at the behest of the PACFLEET commander.

The goal of the deployment was to demonstrate utility of such ships to the fleet, and the commander involved was quoted as saying: "The long-term goal ... is to find ways to integrate these unmanned systems across the continuum – subsurface, surface and air – while having the ability to close kill-chains faster, keep them closed longer and be able to operate in a contested environment."

But this a variant of the vision of a so-called ghost fleet which mimics what a legacy fleet does, only doing so with "unmanned vessels" and doing what is referred to as "manned-unmanned" teaming.

And these larger vessels will cost serious money to build and will almost certainly follow traditional production methodologies.

That is not going to get the Navy where it needs to go and will not keep it ahead of strategic competitors.

A different understanding is required.

First, the new generation autonomous UAVs or the new smaller maritime autonomous systems do not have to be designed to be integrated with the combat systems of the extant manned fleet. That misses the point.

As Commodore Kavanagh of the Royal Australian Navy has put it: "They don't replace platforms; they complement the integrated force. They are complimentary to that force in that they interface rather than being fully integrated with the current force elements."

Second, they are part of a kill web, not an integrated kill chain. They can create a combat cluster rather than part of an integrated task force. You give them specific missions and they perform what that limited mission might be. Their job is fully focused on a specific mission thread not replacing a multi-mission manned system.

Put another way, you change the con-ops of the fleet from a task force manned scoped fleet designed for multi-mission operations to one in which manned fleet assets have at their disposal clusters of autonomous systems to which one can delegate a specific mission which the manned assets does now not have to perform.

This is not manned-unmanned teaming – this is delegation of a mission to a wolfpack of smaller autonomous vessels.

Third, the battlespace is conceived as a chessboard. There are significant gaps on that chessboard which the legacy force can not address.

Autonomous systems – the next generation air or maritime

autonomous systems can fill those gaps – in addition to providing complementary ISR, C2, logistics or strike capabilities.

The article mentions one desired effect from PACFLEET which is to create "hellscape" for an adversary looking to occupy terrain in the Pacific.

The article notes: "To keep sailors and Marines out of the deadliest of the Pacific crucibles, they want to overwhelm the invasion force with lethal drones to create what PACFLEET calls "hellscape." The plan calls for thousands of lethal drones on, above and under the sea, creating chaos for the invaders.

"[Enemy] ships are getting damaged, slowing down, big timings are getting thrown off, some are getting lost, some ships are probably going to get sunk," Clark told *USNI News* last week.

"This hellscape, this churn you cause in the invasion lets you mobilize, get your act together and start delivering the long-range fires that are going to actually take out the larger amphibious ships and surface ships," he added.

"The concept has been taken up by the Pentagon and folded into the overarching Replicator initiative."

To do this in the near term is possible but not by focusing on long-terms LUSV builds.

To do so requires building kamikaze boats with ordinance aboard which can attack the adversaries' assets.

One company, MARTAC, has recently created such a kamikaze boat (the M-18) in five weeks, and could be available in the short term.

There are other ways to use smaller boats to enable a Hellscape con-ops but the point is that the con-ops change to drive the technology you tap.

And associated with that is creating a manufacturing model which could build smaller boats to scale, and such a model has virtually nothing in common with legacy shipbuilding models but can be done through the leveraging of smaller more agile companies that can activate a supplier chain more rapidly than the legacy prime contractors.

And to be blunt, whether you are a legacy prime or a smaller company it is all about the supply chain, and that will not exist at the scale needed without significant demand.

By focusing on a con-ops at hand – a maritime kill web force – one can find the place for maritime autonomous systems ready now for identifiable mission threads – rather than waiting for a ghost fleet that mimics the legacy fleet.

After all you want our sailors not to become ghosts while waiting for that futuristic ghost fleet.

ERIC TRAPPIER'S PERSPECTIVE ON FRENCH ARMS EXPORTS AND COOPERATION: DECEMBER 2023

December 5, 2023

By Pierre Tran

he wars in Ukraine and Gaza have not fueled fresh sales of the Rafale, Eric Trappier, executive chairman of Dassault Aviation, prime contractor for the French-built fighter jet, said Dec. 5.

"These two crises are very hard, very sad, (but) there has been no impact," he told the Defense Journalists Association, a press club, when asked whether the two conflicts had sparked greater interest in foreign orders for the French fighter.

Indeed the fighting in those two regions had "slowed discussions," he said.

Exports are critical to Dassault, as Paris has slowed orders for the French fighter in a bid to control the public purse.

There has been much talk in France of a "war economy," since president Emmanuel Macron used that term following the Russian invasion of Ukraine in February last year. The French head of state and commander in chief brought forward a seven-year military budget law, and parliament adopted in July an increased funding of €413 billion ($447 billion), partly in response to the incursion ordered by Russian president Vladimir Putin.

Trappier pointed out the increased military orders consisted mainly of artillery and shells, and the Rafale did not really feature in that war economy.

Meanwhile, Saudi Arabia has asked France for details of the Rafale, an interest that reflected Germany's problems with an export sale of the Eurofighter Typhoon to Riyadh, he said. Berlin's refusal to give a green light for the Eurofighter stems from Saudi Arabia's ordering the killing of a Saudi journalist, Jamal Khashoggi, in Istanbul in 2018, and support for a civil war in Yemen. The Green party, a key German coalition partner, objects to alleged Saudi failings in observing human rights, and rejects arms sale to Riyadh.

Such German resistance to an arms export deal was not a good sign, Trappier said, raising doubt over foreign sales of a planned fighter to be built by Paris, Berlin and Madrid.

There is an updated Franco-German bilateral treaty on arms exports, but there is concern in French industrial circles over future authorization from Berlin for foreign sales of weapons built under cooperation.

Meanwhile, the Dassault top executive said the Italian government had made an "anti-Rafale" move in blocking a $1.8 billion acquisition by Safran, a French company, of an Italian company building flight control systems. Safran builds M88 engines and other equipment for the Rafale, including the AASM powered smart bombs.

The Italian prime minister, Giorgia Meloni, said Nov. 22, the government was using its "golden share," to forbid Safran's offer for Microtecnica, on the grounds the company was a strategic asset and key supplier to the Italian services. Microtecnica is a unit of the U.S. company Collins Aerospace.

Italy is a partner nation in the Eurofighter Typhoon consortium, along with Britain, Germany, and Spain. Rome is also partnered on the F-35, flying and assembling the U.S. fighter which Dassault sees as its arch rival in the European market.

There is a certain amount of interoperability between the F-35 and the Rafale, Trappier said on the sidelines of the meeting with the press club, with the Nato Link 16 communications protocol, but that allowed a basic exchange of information, and the question was what lay in the future.

France has partnered with Germany and Spain on an ambitious project for a future combat air system (FCAS), which rests on a planned new generation fighter, remote carrier drones, and a combat cloud for an extended network of command and control.

Airbus Defence and Space leads work on that European combat

cloud, while Dassault is architect and prime contractor on the new fighter. Simulation studies are being conducted on the FCAS project at the Dassault head office in Saint Cloud, in the suburbs of the capital, and designing algorithms that support the pilot are part of the work, Trappier said.

"We know exactly what we want to do," he said, with the combat drones flying with the new fighter.

There is a French plan to build a combat drone to fly with the Rafale, separate from the FCAS project, which is due to enter service in 2040. That earlier combat drone will be larger than the Neuron, a technology demonstrator for an unmanned combat air vehicle, which is continuing to be used for flight tests at Istres, a French air base, southern France. The French services initially held Neuron in low regard, something of a "gadget," he said, but grew increasingly attracted to the project, which included the launch of weapons.

Meanwhile, Trappier ruled out any prospect of cooperation with the Tempest-Global Combat Air Programme, as two of the core partners, Britain and Japan, are not "European."

Italy is the third partner nation in that project, which competes with the European FCAS led by France, Germany, and Spain. Belgium expects to sign a formal agreement later this month on gaining observer status on the FCAS, and hopes to join as a full partner in the following phase, building a technology demonstrator to fly in 2029. Brussels is keen to join the FCAS, to win high-value aeronautical work for Belgian companies.

That has irked Trappier, who points out the European project is not to promote jobs, but to meet military requirements, the partner nations will buy the aircraft, and it is not clear Belgium will place orders for the new fighter. Brussels has ordered the F-35, but failed to win work share on that program.

On further orders for the Rafale, Trappier expects France to order 42 units later this month, comprising a planned batch of 30, and 12 to replace those sold second hand to Greece. There are also a further 26 Rafale expected to be ordered for the Indian navy, with Trappier appearing unconcerned India is due to hold general election next year.

Indonesia is also expected to order a further 18-strong batch of the fighter.

Dassault has an order book for the Rafale which runs to 2032-33, he said, and the production rate is due to rise to three per month next year. That compares to a previous rate of one per month, or 11 per year, with the Marignane factory, outside Bordeaux, southwest France, closed for the month of August for the annual holiday.

That production rate of three per month could be increased, he said, if there were more orders.

THE REPLICATOR PROJECT: IN SEARCH OF A CON-OPS AND A MANUFACTURING BASE

December 6, 2023

In August 2023, Deputy Secretary of Defense Hicks announced a new "replicator" project or initiative.

As she said in her speech:

"At DoD, we've already been investing in attritable autonomous systems — across the military services, DIU, the Strategic Capabilities Office, and the combatant commands themselves — and in multiple domains: self-piloting ships, uncrewed aircraft, and more.

"It's clear they aren't just lower-cost. They can be produced closer to the tactical edge. They can be used consistent with our principles of mission command, where we empower the lowest-possible echelons to innovate and succeed in battle. And they can serve as resilient, distributed systems, even if bandwidth is limited, intermittent, degraded or denied.

"So now is the time to take all-domain, attritable autonomy to the next level: to produce and deliver capabilities to warfighters at the volume and velocity required to deter aggression, or win if we're forced to fight.

"Since we need to break through barriers and catalyze change with urgency, we've set a big goal for Replicator: to field attritable autonomous systems at scale of multiple thousands, in multiple domains, within the next 18-to-24 months.

"And the 'replication' won't just be happening from a production standpoint. We'll also aim to replicate and inculcate how we will achieve this goal, so we can scale what's relevant in the future again and again and again.

"Easier said than done? You bet. But we're gonna to do it."[16]

But to "do it," and provide a credible military capability, one needs to evolve con-ops, not just buy stuff.

And this is a major question: how does the military operate across the spectrum of warfare using new autonomous systems?

Remember, the UAVs used largely to date are remotely piloted systems and the U.S. Navy has experimented but not deployed such systems.

As I wrote earlier: "The new generation autonomous UAVs or the new smaller maritime autonomous systems do not have to be designed to be integrated with the combat systems of the extant manned fleet. That misses the point.

"As Commodore Kavanagh of the Royal Australian Navy has put it: "They don't replace platforms; they complement the integrated force. They are complimentary to that force in that they interface rather than being fully integrated with the current force elements."

"Second, they are part of a kill web, not an integrated kill chain. They can create a combat cluster rather than part of an integrated task force. You give them specific missions and they perform what that limited mission might be. Their job is fully focused on a specific mission thread not replacing a multi-mission manned system.

"Put another way, you change the con-ops of the fleet from a task force manned scoped fleet designed for multi-mission operations to one in which manned fleet assets have at their disposal clusters of autonomous systems to which one can delegate a specific mission which the manned assets does now not have to perform.

"This is not manned-unmanned teaming – this is delegation of a mission to a wolfpack of smaller autonomous vessels."

It is not simply buying a lot of cool stuff, it is buying systems available now that the military uses now to support an evolving concept of operations.

And added to this challenge is the absence of a credible manufacturing model.

The "last supper" of Secretary Perry left a small number of primes in control of the defense industrial base.

Added to this, the supply chain atrophied during COVID and now is under pressure to provide for foreign allies, not just the U.S. military.

Se where is a credible manufacturing model that would empower a much wider production base to provide for the U.S. military without going through the archaic Pentagon acquisition system?

To be clear: it is not about simply having a vision — it is about significant change in military con-ops and the so-called defense industrial base. I say so-called because much of the production base relevant to a replicator initiative isn't in the defense sector at all.

Featured Photo: Deputy Secretary of Defense Kathleen Hicks participates in a fireside chat with Editor of Defense News Marjorie Censer during the 7th annual Defense News Conference at the Ritz-Carlton, Pentagon City, Va., Sept. 5, 2023. (DoD photo by U.S. Navy Petty Officer 1st Class Alexander Kubitza)

Note: A crucial question facing the U.S. is the defense industrial base and its limitations..

In an article by Greg Ip published in *The Wall Street Journal* on December 6, 2023, the author highlighted the challenge as follows:

"It isn't just defense; the entire U.S. manufacturing base shrank as labor-intensive production migrated to East Asia. There are fewer suppliers, factories, shipyards and, most important, workers available to meet the rising demand.

"True, civilian and military capacity aren't perfect substitutes; defense products often require specialized systems and skills. That makes the shortfall even more severe. It could take three to five years to train a welder to work on a submarine, said Ronald O'Rourke, an analyst at the Congressional Research Service.

"Echoing the quality problems U.S. manufacturers of semiconductors, autos and airliners have experienced, defense manufacturers suffer from endemic cost overruns and delays. On average, a new lead ship costs 40% more than the Navy first estimates, the CBO says. Delivery times for submarines have grown to nine years from six."[17]

THE RELATIONSHIP BETWEEN NUCLEAR WEAPONS AND THE NEW WAR MACHINES

December 10, 2023

By Paul Bracken

The use of nuclear weapons presents a growing risk in the world today, arising from the increasing number of nuclear-armed countries—now nine and counting. The risk also comes from a less appreciated source: the development of new war technologies. AI, cyber, hypersonic missiles, autonomy, space weapons, network hackers, drones, lasers, robot ships, and submarines all interweave with this thickening nuclear context in complex, poorly understood ways.

Nuclear weapons were used in the first nuclear age as the major threat of the Cold War, and they are being used now, in a second nuclear age. They are being used as threats in the same way a bank robber uses his gun. One need not fire a nuclear weapon to use it.

The relationship between nuclear weapons and the new war machines is often overlooked.

This is because the topic is difficult, unwelcome, and sobering. It is easier to focus on an AI-driven military revolution signaled by advances in computer chips, autonomy, and hypersonic missiles.

Here, nuclear weapons are ignored. Or they are filed to an annex labeled "to be opened only in certain largely unimaginable and highly unlikely circumstances."

Any realistic assessment of the new technologies requires a nuclear frame of reference because it will powerfully influence how—and even if—these new technologies are used. Their impressive performance will be shaped as much by this nuclear context as by their technological potential.

The New Strategic Environment

There are two technology enterprises in the global security environment: the new war machines, and "old" nuclear weapons. New war machines are cutting edge. They bring career advancement, funding, and excitement in the West. Nuclear weapons do not.

The U.S. military, most of it, treats the bomb as a necessary evil. Most officers choose to build their careers around the new war machines. The number of currently serving military officers who have ever seen or handled a nuclear warhead is small. The number who have flown off a carrier with a nuclear weapon is zero.

Something more is that intellectual capital concerning nuclear issues has been hollowed out. The topic no longer draws the creatives, the brains, that it once did. Until recently, many political leaders encouraged this brain drain, in order to stigmatize the bomb, to set an example for other countries that it didn't really matter very much. The United States has nuclear weapons, yes, but only because others have them. So, the argument went, other countries should not be interested in getting "the bomb" for themselves.

Unfortunately, nuclear weapons are not looked at in this way by other countries. To China, Russia, India, Pakistan, North Korea, Israel, and Iran, nuclear weapons are not outmoded. My guess is that they are against nuclear war, too, like a bank robber who doesn't want a shootout.

Yet they are putting an enormous effort into their nuclear programs. They are thinking up ways to incorporate nuclear weapons into their broader national strategies, as the United States once did but no longer does. Their intellectual capital grows while that of the United States has stagnated.

For example, China's military does not see it this way. China's People's Liberation Army (PLA) is building the new war machines *and* nuclear weapons.[18]

Something a lot more subtle and nuanced is going on here. In fact, when the Commander of U.S. Strategic Command, Admiral Charles Richard, described the Chinese buildup, he hinted at this. He called it a *strategic,* not a *nuclear* breakout.

This astute description gets to the unwelcome subject of the purpose of these weapons. People, including many experts, say that the only purpose of nuclear weapons is to deter other nuclear weapons.

But a *strategic* breakout says something different: that there are uses beyond narrow deterrence. Purposes beyond "deterrence of other nuclear weapons" often becomes an emotional topic.

Even so, nuclear weapons must be examined in a clinical way, if for no other reason than that our main rivals in China, Russia, and North

Korea have them, and Iran aspires to them. Moreover, there really are other uses of the bomb beyond narrow deterrence.

One use is to drive a wedge between the United States and its allies over the danger of nuclear war. Another is for brinkmanship, to ratchet up risk in a crisis. Still another is to threaten high-tech conventional war in a thick nuclear context to dissuade the United States from fighting at all.

One more use of nuclear weapons is to bolster the sense that a non-White, post-colonial order is taking shape to stand up to Western dominance and the West's self-serving laws and grandiose declarations of principle. This new order breaks the Western monopoly grip on the bomb and other military technologies. It suggests too that it is the United States that is on the wrong side of history.

All of these uses of nuclear weapons are on the table now. All go beyond the narrow framing of stability defined in terms of second-strike surviving forces, which has so dominated thinking in the United States on nuclear strategy.

Counterforce in the Second Nuclear Age

Overly narrow framing of the use of nuclear weapons was a problem in the past. But the new war machines now give an ability to destroy others' nuclear forces with conventional weapons.

Call it *conventional counterforce*. It combines information from AI, drones, target recognition, satellites, undersea sensors, and cyber hacks with the new war machines, hypersonic missiles, stealth, autonomy, and others.

The result is a conventional kill network that can destroy nearly any target. Moreover, it operates even against moving targets: mobile nuclear missiles, ships, satellites, command posts. This new capability has far-reaching impacts. Yet many studies and war games treat it too narrowly.[19]

I have found that studies and war games frequently have an air of unreality about them. They begin with a strike by one side and a counterstrike by the other. They usually go on to calculate the surviving forces on each side after one or two additional back and forth salvos. Then the game ends.

The problem, the unreality, comes from not including how nuclear threats and counter threats play into political decisions. It's like analyzing a bank robbery shootout by the caliber, accuracy, and number of bullets fired by the robbers and the guards.

These matter, certainly, but real bank robberies are not like this. They go wrong. They get messy, with panicked decisions that make little sense. Things happen that the robber never considered beforehand, and the bank guards, too. There's no icy rational calculation of damage.

Real wars go on much longer than two or three salvos. Years, in fact, when the studies and games predicted they would be over quickly once each side cooly calculated the damages and the gains. Vietnam, Iraq, Afghanistan, and Ukraine are all examples. Will Taiwan be a long war as well?

Take North Korea. The United States threatens to destroy North Korea if they use nuclear weapons. In Cold War terminology, this is a countervalue threat. This is fine, maybe, as a declaratory policy. It shows that the United States is all about deterrence.

Yet it leaves out threats and counter-threats that are likely to arise. The highest U.S. priority must be the hunt for North Korea's nuclear weapons, the bulk of which are on mobile land-based missiles.[20] Destruction of cities and infrastructure directs attention and resources away from this.

If war between the United States and North Korea breaks out, the United States is likely, initially at least, to avoid strikes on civilians, both to not provoke North Korean nuclear retaliation and to destroy its nuclear weapons. This is also to limit damage to allies and to end a war that, in all probability, neither side had wanted or intended. No U.S. leader wants to go down in history as the second president to kill hundreds of thousands, or now millions, of Asians with atomic bombs.

In an intense crisis, North Korea is likely to disperse its mobile nuclear launchers, unlock its warheads, and perhaps pre-delegate launch authority—creating a dangerous situation. What drives the danger is less a U.S. nuclear threat than the enhanced conventional counterforce threat.

So conventional counterforce against a nuclear weapon state brings important decision points to the fore. The United States would be unwise to overlook these—far better to understand them and to play them out in studies and games.

But in-depth study and wargaming is needed for another reason, too: to answer the question a U.S. president will ask: "Am I actually authorizing a conventional start to a nuclear war?" This is not an unreasonable question.

There are foolish answers to it, ones that I have seen in studies and war games. "North Korea will not go nuclear because they know what would happen if they did." Or, "Sir, our AI models say we can destroy 60 percent of their missiles."

These are not discussions about a botched exit from Saigon or Kabul here. These are presidential decision points that would result in the deaths of millions of people with vast consequences. These decision points, if mishandled, could lead to either accommodation or paralysis.

Either would be a national security disaster even if nuclear war is avoided.

Strategist Herman Kahn defined a realistic war plan as one where the president didn't throw you out of the office. If we fail this elementary test of realism, all the AI, cyber, and hypersonic missiles in the world aren't going to matter. Declaratory peacetime statements and doctrine will be tossed out the window in a real crisis.

The first question any president will ask is where a conventional counterforce strike on a nuclear state goes next. Failing to point out that the purpose of the said attack is to disarm the enemy of his nuclear weapons is irresponsible and untenable.

Better options are essential, otherwise the alternative is accommodation or a nuclear war that the United States is ill equipped to fight.

The article is excerpted from the author's broader article entitled "Navies in the Second Nuclear Age" published by the Foreign Policy Research Institute and is posted with the author's permission.

A LOOK AT DEFENSE COMPETITION IN THE ARCTIC REGION

December 15, 2023

By Debalina Ghoshal

In the recent years, the Arctic region has not witnessed militarization and weaponization by erstwhile Cold War super powers, the United States and Russia alone, but also by powers like the People's Republic of China (PRC) that has already declared itself as 'near Arctic state.'

In addition, Arctic countries have increased their military presence in the region with credible modernization of their deterrent and combat capabilities.

The region has become one of the most contested regions strategically with concerns over conventional as well as nuclear developments in the region.

Arctic states are focusing on credible means to bolster their 'defense by denial' capabilities and hence, focusing on robust air and missile defense capabilities.

How might missile defense developments in the Arctic region including the developments in the Arctic countries be viewed from this perspective?

Offensive Developments in the Arctic Region

As global powers tussle for superiority, the region of the Arctic has also faced the brunt of great power politics with weaponization and militarization. Deployment of hypersonic weapon systems which include Russia's decision to deploy Kh-47 M2Kinzhal hypersonic missiles puts pressure on strategic stability. Russia may have tested or planning to test nuclear capable cruise missiles on its own base in the Arctic region.[21]

Nuclearization of the region due to deployment of nuclear deterrent assets make deterrence complex in the region. The Arctic region remains a hot spot for clashes among powers. The ongoing Ukraine War further makes Arctic states apprehensive and concerned about their own security and seek to develop missile defence capabilities.

Missile defense systems in the Arctic region could create strategic destabilization as it could lead to states focusing on offensive means that could defeat air and missile defence capabilities.

Nevertheless, missile defense capabilities seem to be the perfect solution at this moment to strengthen deterrence in the region and also strengthens the deterrence of Arctic countries as intercontinental ballistic missile (ICBM) capabilities, the nuclear deterrence backbone of both the United States and Russia have trajectories that cross Arctic region.

China has also increased its presence in the Arctic region under "Polar Silk Route" strategy. If Beijing deploys SSBNs and SSNs in the region, such deployments will be accompanied by submarine launched ballistic missile capability and sea-launched cruise missile capability.

However, the intensification of missile threats in the region with cruise missiles also being used as tools to protect maritime trade routes in the region, there will be pressures built up on missile defence systems.

Arctic Countries and Missile Defense Developments

The Arctic countries include Denmark with Greenland, the United States because of Alaska, Russia, Canada, Norway, Iceland, Sweden and Finland. Countries in the region are focusing on area defence in the region for strengthened deterrence.

Owing to the Ukrainian War, Finland too focused on a strengthened 'defence by denial' capability though the desire for a credible air and missile defence capability predates the conflict.

Finland's participation in the NATO's 'Ramstein Legacy 22' highlighted its interest to integrate its own capabilities with NATO's missile defence capabilities to bolster deterrence.[22]

In 2023, Finland is reported to have made progress with long-range air defense system, the U.S.-Israeli David Sling system.[23] Israeli defense systems have Link 16 communication protocol that makes their defence system compatible with NATO defence systems.

Denmark has been focusing on an inclusive role in NATO's ballistic missile defence (BMD) framework. In fact, since 2016, Denmark sought to upgrade its frigate to BMD sensor roles in order to make NATO's BMD capability more foolproof.[24]

In 2022, there were reports that Danish Armed Forces and the

Danish Ministry of Defence Acquisition and Logistics Organisation (DALO) were focusing on integration of the SM-2 interceptors, procured through the U.S. NAVY with their Iver Huitfeldt class frigates to intercept enemy aircraft and missiles at longer distance.[25]

Not only do such frigates based BMD options provide affordable means of defensive capabilities but also survivable means as frigates are movable and hence, less difficult to track.[26]

Interoperability of its air and missile defense capabilities with NATO air and missile defense systems remains the major focus for Denmark. This would include the "ability to be part of different configurations of air capabilities within land, sea and air domains" by following NATO "standards, procedures and guidelines."[27]

In 2023, the U.S. run ballistic missile warning site in Greenland that was called the Thule Air Base was renamed as Pituffik Space Base. The region is specifically important to the United States as the Space Force guardians in the region guard the U.S. homeland against ballistic missile attacks. [28]

The upgraded Early Warning Radar weapon system is a phased array radar located in the region that could detect and "report attack assessments" of sea-launched ballistic missiles and ICBMs. Thus, Greenland forms major backbone of U.S. homeland missile defence.

Sweden's security dilemma in the recent past has worsened. This is owing to the Russia-Georgian conflict, Russia's annexation of Crimea and the recent Ukrainian War. Given this deteriorating security situation in the Baltic Region, Sweden's 'National Defence Strategy' even focuses on 'territorial defence.'

Sweden has realized these security implications and focused on its role in strengthening security in the Baltic Region. Moreover, if Sweden is to join NATO, it needs credible 'defense by denial' mechanism to support NATO air and missile defense structures. The strategic importance of Gotland, an island which is hundred kilometers off the Swedish coast provides a commanding view of the Baltic Sea.

Hence, it is necessary that Sweden possesses a credible air and missile defense capability for Sweden even more as its location lies within NATO's air defense architecture that extends from the Northern shores of Norway to Iceland and Greenland.

Even before the Ukrainian War commenced, the Swedish Armed Forces in 2021 introduced the new Patriot System which is also known as the Air Defence System 103 or LvS 103. The system reached its Initial Operational Capability (IOC) by December 2021, which means that it could now be put to service.

This would enable Swedish Armed Forces to strengthen its air defense capability. According to the Defence Minister, Peter Hultqvist, the LvS 103 would enable the Swedish Armed Forces to "counter long-range missiles and air attacks and we will also be able to fight ballistic missiles." He further explained, "[t]his is a powerful modernization and upgrade of Swedish Air Defence and Swedish defence capability as a whole."[29]

The Patriot system will be using two types of missiles: Robot 103A GeM-T and Robot 103B (PAC-3 MSE) (more optimized against ballistic missiles).[30]

Both Finland and Sweden could play a crucial role in NATO IAMD architecture in the near future. While the former has already joined NATO in early 2023, the latter is yet to join NATO officially.

Although the importance of Canada defending against strategic weapons is obvious, the government is not supportive of becoming a part of continental defence. Though there are contemplations on the benefits of focusing on continental defence which could include issues pertaining to North American Aerospace Defence (NORAD) and NATO's own IAMD archi-tecture.[31]

This is probably the reason why Canada never gave importance to construction of integrated air and missile defence architecture but instead focused on "pairing Canadian units with allied forces that have effective air and missile defence."[32]

Though the growing threats of missiles from North Korea and Iran as well as Russia continue to threaten Canada, the country is yet to be a part of the U.S. BMD program.

Nevertheless, in 2023, Canada and the United States entered into an agreement to bolster defence in Arctic with Over the Horizon

(OTH) radar installations that would operate under the NORAD Command.[33]

This could enable Canada to push their line of sight further north to be able to respond to high speed weapons effectively.

There are debates in Canada to participate in U.S. Ground Based Air Defence (GBAD) program, a step Canada refused to pursue in the past. Then Chief of the Defence Staff in 2022, Gen. Wayne Eyre declared: "in decades to come, that threat, that tenuous hold that we [Canada] have on our sovereignty, at the extremities of this nation, is going to come under increasing challenge."[34]

Norway on the other hand, operates the National Advanced Surface-to-Air Missile Systems (NASAMS) which was originally developed for providing air defense capabilities but eventually upgraded and modernized for incorporating BMD capabilities as well.[35]

Iceland possesses long range surveillance radars that are upgraded to eliminate obsolescence and increase life-span to cater to NATO's Integrated Air and Missile Defence (IAMD) architecture.[36]

For the United States, the Arctic remains strategically relevant for homeland missile defence capabilities. It hosts a greater part of the U.S. missile defence architecture meant for homeland defence.

Alaska, the region that makes the United States an Arctic country, is referred to as "the most strategic place on earth."[37]

In 2021, the United States completed construction of Long Range Discrimination Radar (LRDR) that would help track and defend against long range ICBMs and hypersonic weapons forming the backbone of U.S. layered missile defence to protect its homeland.[38]

In addition, the United States is also working on Next Generation Interceptors (NGI) to replace the existing Ground Based Interceptors (GBIs) which had myriad limitations. The interceptor would need to counter enemy missiles as well as counter measures fitted on missiles as well as counter high speed missile systems.

Hence, LRDR could complement the NGIs. There are also recommendations to retain the GBIs also in Alaska owing to the North Korean missile threats as the GBIs are undergoing Life Extension Program (LEP).[39]

In the near future, the United States could also consider deploying the Aegis Ashore system with advanced interceptors in the Arctic along with existing GBIs till the NGIs becomes a success story.

Some analysis also recommend a more holistic approach in the Arctic region with "coordinated planning" with the United Kingdom, the Baltic States, Poland and Germany to ensure that the U.S.-NATO force is able to possess an "Arctic defence coherence and enhanced deterrence posture across the Baltic-Arctic theatres."[40]

However, that would mean getting countries like Poland and the Baltic States to also stress on Arctic region militarily which could prove difficult for such states.

In addition to this, Russia has conducted missile defence tests in Arctic region which include the next generation S-500 anti-missile system that could intercept ballistic missiles, and high speed missiles.[41]

Its desire to build an Arctic 'air defence' dome called for its Northern Fleet to be armed with S-400 air and missile defence system.

In fact, in 2019, Russia deployed its S-400 missiles in Arctic Novaya Zemlya archipelago to defend against aircraft, cruise missiles and ballistic missiles.[42]

This is not the only defensive weapon deployed in Novaya Zemlya. Russia has also deployed there the S-300 surface-to-air missile (SAM) systems in 2015.[43]

The S-400s along with, S-300s and S-500 systems could form Russia's Arctic holistic 'air and missile defence' dome forming a groundwork of anti-access/area denial (A2/AD) network in the region. In its military drills in the Arctic, Russia has also fired its coastal defence missile system called the Bastion missile at sea-based targets.[44]

With Sweden and Finland in NATO alliance, Russia's security concerns in the Arctic would worsen further and hence, it could strengthen its air and missile defence capabilities. With Russian invasion of Ukraine in the recent past, Moscow is aware that Arctic region would experience credible air and missile defence developments by Arctic countries to mitigate Russian fears.

China too considers itself as a 'near Arctic" state and an "important stake holder in Arctic affairs." China wishes to become a major player in any negotiations or discussions on crucial Arctic-related decisions or policies.

China would be keen to place its submarines in the Arctic region but these submarines whether SSBNs, SSNs, or conventional submarines would need to be modified technologically in order to make them capable of operating under harsh weather and climatic conditions in the Arctic.[45]

China's increased presence in the region could mean that China could resort to air and missile defence capability independently or integrate its systems with Russia's considering that Russia and China are partners in the region or share Russian air and missile defence network. This would enable China to develop A2/AD capability in crucial choke points.

Repercussions

The Arctic region has become a hotbed for power tussle. Increased military presence of great powers further complicates the strategic stability and balance in the region.

In addition, the Ukrainian War has led Arctic states to become more apprehensive and seek for defensive means for strengthening security. This means that air and missile defense development would continue in order to assure deterrence and security to states.

Interoperability of air and missile defense components and assets would become major focus for Arctic states in order to make their defence more credible.

However, each country in the region would be focused their independent defense by denial capability too so as to operate under a sovereign defense command and mechanism.

Global powers vying for power in the region would continue to focus on sophistication of their defensive capabilities for strengthened deterrence in the region.

Great power competition in the region is leading to complex and yet most powerful chains to air and missile defence networking. As offense gets stronger in the region, defense would become more advanced and lethal against offense systems.

CRAFTING A KILL WEB FORCE: THE ROLE OF AUTONOMOUS SYSTEMS

In a visit to Quantico, I had a chance to talk with LtGen Karsten Heckl, who serves as the Commanding General, Marine Corps Combat Development Command, and the Deputy Commandant for Combat Development and Integration.

I first met him when he was Assistant Deputy Commandant for Aviation, HQMC Aviation Department. I visited him when he was Commander of 2d Marine Aircraft Wing, and I interviewed him when he commanded the First Marine Expeditionary Force.

In this visit, we had a chance to focus on the evolution of the USMC within the broader context of the joint force, and discussed in particular the coming of new generation of autonomous systems and how they fitted in or enabled the kind of force transition which the USMC is engaged in.

We started with force transition and then discussed autonomous systems and their contribution to that transition. In other words, what kind of con-ops do you want to pursue and how do the new autonomous systems support those con-ops?

It was particularly interesting to have this conversation with Heckl at this time for I had just returned from my most recent visit to MAWTS-1 where the focus is upon "the physics of combat" in force transition, to use the words of LtGen (Retired) Steve Rudder.

We started by the focus which I found at MAWTS-1 upon how to enhance the survivability and lethality of the force through signature management. This is what I wrote after my meeting in early November 2023 with Major John Edwards, the Spectrum Warfare Department Head at MAWTS-1.[46]

"In my meetings with PACFLEET this past April, a key aspect of the challenge facing the force is clearly spectrum warfare or signature management and deception.

"My takeaway from discussions at PACFLEET was very clear. Success for distributed maritime operations requires not only assured command and control but the tissue of ISR systems enabling distributed fleet operations and adding the key element of deception through various counter-ISR systems as well.

"In effect, fleet distribution built on a kill web effects infrastructure is being combined with what me be called a wake-a-mole operational capability. You can't target me, if you can't find me.

"As one key Navy leader put it to me: 'Counter-ISR is the number one priority for me, to deny the adversary with to high confidence in his targeting capabilities. I need to deceive them and to make a needle look like a needle in a haystack of needles. It is important to have the capability to look like a black hole in the middle of nothing.'

"MAWTS-1 with its work on FARPs, force distribution, new ways to do C2 such as from systems operating out of the back of Ospreys, signature management and deception is clearly working along the same lines as PACFLEET.

"I had a chance to discuss this approach with Major John Edwards, the Spectrum Warfare Department Head, when visiting MAWTS-1 in November 2023. Edwards highlighted their work in preparing the force for the spectrum management challenges they experience and will experience within a contested electronic warfare environment.

"Their focus is upon ramping up the "red" threat against blue to prepare the force for the experience they have when operating in a contested environment.

"They focus on showing the operational elements of the force the kind of spectrum signature they are creating when they operate to better understand the nature of spectrum warfare and how that affects their lethality and survivability in operations. And by knowing that one can create ways to think about signature deception as well as pointed out by PACFLEET."

It is not surprising then that LtGen Heckl emphasized the same points as the PACFLEET commander or the Spectrum Warfare Head at MAWTS-1.

LtGen Heckl argued: "It is about survivability and a key to being able to do that is signature management. We are keenly focused on reduced electronic magnetic signature management in how we think about deployment of the force and doing so with an eye to how the deployed force can integrate sensors with strike.

"It really is about a kill web in which the real value proposition is reconnaissance and counter-reconnaissance reducing your vulnerabilities and exposing those of the adversary and enabling effective strike."

It is in this context that Heckl discussed autonomous systems. "We are focusing on a broad range of autonomous systems capabilities. They aid significantly in signature management.

"If they are unmanned, you don't have the weight or equipment necessary for a man onboard whether it be a ship or an airborne system. It means as well you can get better value out of your manned aviation assets or your ships.

"With regard to our lift assets – C-130s, CH-53s, or Ospreys – they can carry the most essential elements to an EABO but can be supplemented by a variety of autonomous systems which reduces the overall signature of the force and allows for enhanced flexibility of the force."

Logistics in LtGen Heckl's view is the pacing function for a distributed force. How to sustain a distributed force?

This will be a combination of the air and sea manned assets as well various autonomous systems. He highlighted work being done for the USMC to build unmanned surface vessels to carry logistics to the point of need.

And the logistics challenge will be reduced by various ways to use autonomous systems within the kill web. He cited the opportunity to used UUVs carrying weapons able to operate virtually undetected and gain access to the sensor network to provide weapons support to deployed Marines as an example of reducing the need to deliver weapons directly to those Marines. By reducing the overall logistics burden, the Marines can focus on the use of their manned assets in a more focused manner.

In this context, it is important to realize how amphibious ships can be rethought in terms of a mothership functionality. The extant fleet of amphibious or expeditionary sea bases have flexible flight decks for mix and match rotorcraft, tiltrotor craft, decks from which to lower boats to the water, or well decks to launch from the water level, or flight decks in the case of LHAs combat aircraft.

This mix and match capability to fit the mission is a core quality of these ships. With the coming of maritime autonomous systems, USVs or UUVs can be launched with the payload appropriate to the mission, ISR surveillance, underwater detection, UAVs launched as weapons from USVs, or torpedoes or maritime strike weapons from the USVs or in the case of UUVs, torpedoes.

As such the fleet can act as picket ships preparing the way for the arrival of carrier strike fleet or surface warfare action group and participate with them in providing a combat cluster or matrix of operational depth and reach which the carrier strike fleet or surface warfare action group would not have by itself.

We closed by LtGen Heckl highlighting the importance of building out the global positioning network.

"Our GPN has been an effort now for about a year and a half. One can imagine every EABO being a potential logistics node and our ability to use a Navy 28-foot USV that draws maybe two feet of water is part of the picture. We are thinking in terms of a globally positioned network, which will include maritime pre-positioning, but the days of ships pulling pier side and depositing an iron mountain of supplies ashore are a thing of the past."

It is in this force transformation process that LtGen Heckl sees autonomous systems playing a key role. We discussed another example which resonated with the challenges facing the Australians, namely, how to provide for enhanced air-enabled striking power without having to rely on fixed bases?

Here LtGen Heckl highlighted the Marine Corps' work with the XQ-58 Valkyrie. "It is does not need a base. It can be launched from the back of the truck. It has good range and can carry a lot of payload. And its fully autonomous.

"The reason it has decent range and can carry a decent payload is that it is unmanned. Not only does human weight not come into play but also all the equipment which humans require for operating an air asset – environmental control systems for example. I think we are at the boundary or the edge of being able to incorporate autonomous systems into our force transformation."

---

1. https://www.straitstimes.com/singapore/new-multi-role-combat-vessels-to-act-as-force-multiplier-for-s-pore-navy.

2. https://3dprint.com/292662/uss-essex-first-u-s-navy-ship-to-test-3d-printing-at-sea/.

3. https://www.popsci.com/technology/navy-ship-gets-large-metal-printer/.

4. https://www.maritime-executive.com/article/uss-essex-tries-out-3d-aluminum-printing-under-way.

5. *Ibid.*

6. https://www.news.xerox.com/news/xerox-announces-sale-of-elem-additive-solutions-to-additec.

7. https://www.marinelink.com/news/d-printing-navy-builds-additive-502465.

8. https://3dprint.com/297004/us-navy-installs-meltio-hybrid-metal-3d-printer-to-reduce-repair-times/.

9. https://amfg.ai/2023/05/18/5-exciting-applications-of-3d-printing-in-the-navy/#:-:text=5%20Exciting%20Applications%20of%203D%20Printing%20in%20the,Shipyards%20...%205%205.%20Entire%203D-Printed%20Ships%20.

10. https://www.nationaldefensemagazine.org/articles/2023/3/17/navy-must-go-all-in-on-additive-manufacturing-official-says.

11. *Ibid.*

12. https://www.janes.com/defence-news/news-detail/ifc-2023-sweden-charts-next-generation-fighter-development.

13. https://breakingdefense.com/2023/11/sweden-commits-to-future-fighter-procurement-decision-in-2031/.

14. https://www.shephardmedia.com/news/air-warfare/poland-explores-loyal-wingman-options-for-f-35-fleet/.

15. https://news.usni.org/2023/11/30/the-u-s-navys-unmanned-future-remains-murky-as-china-threat-looms?utm_source=USNI+News&utm_campaign=ba6e2c844d-USNI_NEWS_DAILY&utm_medium=email&utm_term=0_odd4a1450b-ba6e2c844d-230422265&mc_cid=ba6e2c844d&mc_eid=d5b4bb05ef.

16. https://www.defense.gov/News/Speeches/Speech/Article/3507156/deputy-secretary-of-defense-kathleen-hicks-keynote-address-the-urgency-to-innov/

17. https://www.wsj.com/economy/the-u-s-can-afford-a-bigger-military-we-just-cant-build-it-7eddoe74.

18. Aaron Mehta, "STRATCOM Chief Warns of Chinese Strategic Breakout," *Breaking Defense*, Aug. 12, 2021.

19. There are exceptions to this. A recent Center for Strategic and International Studies (CSIS) war game of a Chinese attack on Taiwan allowed for prohibition of US conventional attacks on the Chinese mainland because of fears of nuclear escalation. But it did not play political decisions or nuclear threats of the kind emphasized here. See Mark F. Cancian, Matthew Cancian, and Eric Hegenbotham, "The First Battle of the Next War, Wargaming a Chinese Invasion of Taiwan," Report of the CSIS International Security Program, Jan. 2023.

20. For more on this see Paul Bracken, *The Hunt for Mobile Missiles, Nuclear Weapons, AI, and the New Arms Race* (Philadelphia, PA: Foreign Policy Research Institute, 2020).

21. Riley Mellen, "Russia May be Planning to Test a Nuclear-Powered Missile," *The New York Times,* October 2, 2023.

22. Debalina Ghoshal, "Finland's Missile Defence Choice," *European Security and Defence,* September 12, 2022.

23. Elisabeth Gosselin- Malo, "Finland is one step closer to getting David's Sling missile shield," *Defense News,* August 4, 2023.

24. "Denmark Progresses in NATO Ballistic Missile Defense Role," *Defense News,* April 22, 2016.

25. "The Armed Forces test launches SM-2 missile," *Danish Defence,* May 6, 2022.

26. "Denmark Progresses in NATO Ballistic Missile Defense Role," *Defense News,* April 22, 2016.

27. Dan Taylor, "30-year air & missile defense agreement for Danish military won by Terma," *Military Embedded Systems,* January 20, 2023.

28. Rachel S. Cohen, "Thule no more: US-run outpost in Greenland renamed Pituffik Space Base," *Air Force Times,* April 10, 2023.

29. "New era for Swedish air defence," *Swedish Armed Forces,* November 19, 2021.

30. "Air Defence System 103- Patriot," *FMV.*

31. "Canada," *Missile Defence Advocacy Alliance.*

32. Malte Humpert, "US and Canada to Step up Arctic Capabilities with Over-the-Horizon Radar and Facilities for F-35," *High North News,* March 27, 2023,

33. "Canada announces new Arctic air, missile defences with the US," *The Defense Post,* June 21, 2022.

34. Murray Brewster, "Canada's 'tenuous hold' in Arctic could be challenged by Russia, China, says top soldier," *CBC,* October 18, 2022.

35. Norway," *MDAA,* <Norway – Missile Defense Advocacy Alliance.

36. Gareth Jennings, "Iceland to upgrade long-range air surveillance radars," *JANES,* October 15, 2020.

37. Col. Michael J. Forsyth, "Why Alaska and the Arctic are Critical to the National Security of the United States," *Military Review,* January-February 2018.

38. "U.S. Military Installs Long-Range-Missile-Defence System in Alaska," *Radio Free Europe Radio Liberty,* December 7, 2021 and John Keller, "In Dyne to maintain Alaskan long-range radar to help protect from ballistic missiles in midcourse phase," *Military Aerospace,* October 5, 2022.

39. John Grady, "NORTHCOM: U.S. Needs New Ballistic Missile Interceptor by 2028 to Keep Pace with North Korea," *USNI,* March 25, 2022,

40. Heather Conley, et.al., "Defending America's Northern Border and Its Arctic Approaches Through Cooperation With Allies and Partners," *German Marshal Fund,* August 17, 2023.

41. Anwesha Majumdar, "Russia Successfully Tests S-500 Anti-missile Defence Systems Prototypes In The Arctic," *Republic World,* December 30, 2021,

42. "Russia plans to set up Arctic air defense 'dome' with S-400 missiles," *Reuters,* December 9, 2019.

43. Atle Staalesen, "Russia deploys S-300 in Novaya Zemlya," *The Barents Observer,* December 9, 2015.

44. "Russia conducts military drills in Arctic sea opposite Alaska," *Reuters,* September 16, 2022.

45. "Pentagon warns of risk of Chinese submarines in the Arctic," *The Barents Observer,* March 6, 2019.

46. https://sldinfo.com/2023/11/operating-in-contested-environments-mawts-1-works-the-spectrum-warfare-challenge/

EPILOGUE

In this final section to the book, I am including the three articles which we wrote celebrating the 30th anniversary of Ron Maxwell's epic civil war film *Gettysburg*.

Why he did the film and the relevance of going back into history rather simply reading today's values and debates into yesterday's historical eco-systems is underscored in these essays.

As was noted in an article by Janet Albrechtsen in *The Australian* published on 30 September 2023: "Seeing history as a mirror for our own concerns ... patronises the past because it turns the past into a plaything for our own prejudices and predilections," Sandbrook says....

"If society is applying modern filters of sex, gender and race to the past, that tells us something about our own time; it says nothing about that period in history....

"Speaking from his home in Chipping Norton in West Oxford-shire, Sandbrook says the worst kind of history is "the history that makes you feel smug about yourself ... It smacks of smug narcissism about our own virtue."[1]

A CONVERSATION WITH RON MAXWELL: THE 30TH ANNIVERSARY OF THE EPOCH CIVIL WAR MOVIE GETTYSBURG

September 23, 2023

By Robbin Laird and Ed Timperlake

Ron Maxwell has produced notable movies on the American Civil War. He was the film director and screenwriter for *Gettysburg* (1993), *Gods and Generals* (2003), and *Copperhead* (2013).

In its article, "A Call to Duty, The Best War Films," *The Los Angeles Times* wrote "Ron Maxwell created the most ambitious Civil War movies ever made." It is now the 30th Anniversary of the first of these civil war films and it is being celebrated appropriately enough in Gettysburg itself.

The upcoming event is described on the website *Destination Gettysburg* as follows: "Join Director Ron Maxwell and members of the Cast in Gettysburg, PA October 13-15, 2023, for a weekend long festival as the acclaimed film Gettysburg celebrates 30 years!

"In honor of the 30th Anniversary of the release of the film Gettysburg, the Virginia based Journey Through Hallowed Ground has partnered with several local organizations to create a weekend long celebration of the film.

"This festival will feature two screenings of the Directors Cut of Gettysburg, a screening of the Directors Cut of Ron Maxwell's Copperhead, cast and crew panels, signing opportunities, special tours, and lots of opportunities to experience the town and battlefield first hand."
2

Ed Timperlake, a fellow resident with Ron Maxwell of Rappahannock County, arranged an opportunity to talk with Maxwell about the anniversary and the film.

In our discussion with Maxwell, he underscored that he saw his role as a filmmaker of an historical movie to put the audience back into the period portrayed in the movie without the distortions of the present getting in the way of understanding how the people of the day lived, thought and in the case of the Civil War fought.

Filmmakers in doing an historical film can take the Maxwell

approach. This has a great advantage of allowing contemporary audiences to comprehend rather than condemn the past. It also forces the audience to think about what they themselves would have done in that historical epoch given the realities of that particular historical epoch.

Maxwell argued that the great films looking at history have this approach. We can look at the last 100 years of film and still relate to films looking at an historical period which are crafted in this manner. As examples he cites the 1957 film Paths of Glory and the 2022 film All Quiet on the Western Front, both set in the First World War.

There are alternative approaches, not practiced by Maxwell, which provide different visions of film making about history. The first is propaganda, where the past is exploited simply from the standpoint of justifying a particular currently held point of view. The second is a hybrid between accuracy and propaganda.

Here the filmmaker uses contemporary values and weaves them into the historical saga so the audience does not have to struggle with the past and can easily relate to a particular historical moment as prologue to their current prejudices or received wisdom. These films rarely stand the test of time, as subsequent generations see through their dated and over-simplified manipulations.

Looking back, we asked Maxwell the importance of the film in today's deeply divided America. He argued that it reminds us of what deep divisions can lead to, how intolerance of those who think differently and contrary to your beliefs can lead to dire consequences; in the case of mid 19th century America, a civil war.

He underscored that it was not simply regions that were killing each other in the civil war, but family members doing this.

He cautioned: "Can we learn from the past and pull back from the brink of fratricide?

We were not asking that question when the film first came out thirty years ago: We are now."

This article was first published by *Rappahannock News* on September 9, 2023.[3]

CONTINUING OUR DISCUSSION WITH RON MAXWELL

September 30, 2023

By Ed Timperlake and Robbin Laird

Our last article based on our interview with Ron Maxwell focused on the up-coming thirtieth anniversary of Gettysburg.

We were fortunate to continue our interview and to discuss his artistic approach in making movies, as both a gifted screenwriter and world-class director.

His artistic journey is amazing from NYU where as an undergraduate theater major Ron acted in plays and musicals, including the title role in Hamlet, which earned him an invitation and scholarship to attend the New York University Graduate School of the Arts, Institute of Film and Television.

After graduation he was Charlton Heston's personal assistant in Spain when Heston was directing Antony and Cleopatra. Soon afterwards Ron was a producer of the Emmy Award winning PBS series, Theater in America.

While at WNET in NYC, Ron produced and directed Sea Marks, filmed in Ireland and Verna USO Girl filmed in Germany.

Verna earned Ron an Emmy nomination as best director as well as leading to his Hollywood movies, the now cult classic *Little Darlings* for Paramount, the country-western hit movie *The Night the Lights Went Out in Georgia* for Avco-Embassy, *Parent Trap 2* for Disney, Kidco for 20th Century Fox.

Soon to follow were his Civil War epics, starting with Gettysburg, released by Warners.

As the American writer Earnest Hemingway said about his art using the written word "All you have to do is write one true sentence. Write the truest sentence that you know."

A powerful testimony empowering Ron's artistic goal of putting his audience in Civil War moments that ring true can be seen in a speech given by one of the greatest Jurists in American History, Oliver Wendell Holmes. As a Union solder three times severely wounded, Justice Holmes said poignantly that his combat generation in their youth was "touched by fire."

According to one source: "Holmes served as a lieutenant in the 20th Massachusetts Volunteer Infantry, known as the Harvard Regiment because it drew all its officers and many of its members from Harvard University. Holmes had just graduated when he departed Boston to fight for the great cause of his day – the abolition of slavery."[4]

After the war, Justice Holmes went on to commit his life to binding a wounded nation with grace dignity forgiveness and an eternal dedication to the rule of law.

With America having essentially a current cultural revolution by many who stand in certitude and judgment of the past actions of the southern solder in the Civil War it is best to embrace Justice Holmes brilliant insight about mutual respect by someone who was actually in combat:

Memorial Day

by Oliver Wendell Holmes, Jr.

An Address Delivered May 30, 1884, at Keene, N.H., before John Sedgwick Post No.4, Grand Army of the Republic

"The soldiers who were doing their best to kill one another felt less of personal hostility, I am very certain, than some who were not imperilled by their mutual endeavors.

"I have heard more than one of those who had been gallant and distinguished officers on the Confederate side say that they had had no such feeling. I know that I and those whom I knew best had not.

"We believed that it was most desirable that the North should win; we believed in the principle that the Union is indissoluble; we, or many of us at least, also believed that the conflict was inevitable, and that slavery had lasted long enough.

"But we equally believed that those who stood against us held just as sacred convictions that were the opposite of ours, and we respected them as every man with a heart must respect those who give all for their belief."

On a beautiful summer day on a mountain top in Rappahannock Country a discussion was had with Ron Maxwell about lasting art and what it means to pay homage to the past without devolving into cliché ridden shallow lecturing.

Like Hemingway and Holmes, Ron stayed true to his vision and gave all America a lasting gift in perhaps the greatest war movie ever made.

This article was first published by *Rappahannock News* on October 21, 2023.[5]

ON THE RON MAXWELL INTERVIEW: PERSONAL REFLECTIONS

October 8, 2023

By Kenneth Maxwell

Ed Timberlake and Robbin Laird's interview with Ronald "Ron" F. Maxwell on the monumental 1993 film "Gettysburg," which he directed and wrote the screenplay, provoked some interesting memories.

I was very interested to learn for instance from the Robbin Laird and Ed Timberlake interview that Ron Maxwell had performed in a school play as Hamlet. And that his success in this role had led him to the NYU Film School.

I also happened to have played Hamlet at my school, Queen's College, Taunton, Somerset in the UK in 1958. My teacher and the play's producer, Brian Watkins, very much wanted me to continue in the theatre. I did go up to London at his insistence and was auditioned by the National Youth Theatre and was invited to join the company.

I had already, however, been offered a place at St. John's College, Cambridge, by Harry Hinsley, the historian (and former Bletchley Park code breaker, although we did not know about Hinsley's war-time intelligence activity until many years later because of the strictures of the Official Secrets Act.) So in 1960 instead of going into the theatre I went up to Cambridge University much to Brian Watkin's disappointment.

I had intended to go on acting while at Cambridge and did attend the open audition for the Cambridge Dramatic Society in my first week. The auditions were being conducted by Corin Redgrave, one of the less talented members of that very talented theatre family. He was conducting the auditions seated on a very large throne in the middle of the stage I decide that this was not for me and left before my turn came.

But I do have another non-shakespearian connection to Ron Maxwell's Gettysburg.

My house "Moss Hill" in Norfolk in northwestern Connecticut, where I lived until 2004, was constructed in 1903 for Major John Barclay Fassett. Major Fassett was a hero of the battle of Gettysburg. The house was designed by the architect, Alfredo Samuel Guido Taylor, who had arrived in Norfolk in 1902. He was to play a major role in the "village beautiful" movement in New England. Norfolk's leading family's, the Battells and the Eldridges, had pioneered the movement.

Like many of New England's small towns in the 19th century, Norfolk had lost its economic base in agriculture and mill production. Yet Norfolk with its picturesque scenery, pure air, and mountain spring water, and at the time a very good railway connection, was among the towns in the Berkshires and Litchfield Hills which were reborn as summer resorts.

Alfredo Taylor was born in Florence, Italy, in 1872. He had graduated from Harvard, studied at Columbia University's School of Architecture, and in Paris at the Ecole des Beaux-Arts, returning to New York City in 1900. In the Fall of 1902 he purchased a parcel of land in Norfolk adjacent to the property recently acquired by his wife's mother and stepfather, Major John B. Fassett, who were planning to build a summer residence there.

The Fassett house, known as "Moss Hill" was Alfredo Taylor's first Norfolk project. Taylor's own house "Rubly" was built adjacent to "Moss Hill" and was ready for occupation in 1905. It was empty and in total disrepair when we checked it out in the mid-1990's but has since been refurbished.

Many of Major Fassett's books and personal belongings were in the attic, forgotten for decades, and they were still there when we moved into Moss Hill.

It took me three years to sort them all out. Major Fassett had been a member of the Harvard class of 1858. Among his fellow students was Henry Adams, later the historian and the author of "The Education of Henry Adams" an American classic.

The first edition of the book was in the attic at "Moss Hill."

Another of the students in his class was William Henry Fitzhugh Lee, the son of general Robert E Lee, later to be the commander of the confederate forces at Gettysburg.

Major Fassett had to wait for the congressional medal of honor for his heroic action at Gettysburg until December 1894. The congressional medal of honor, the highest decoration for bravery in the United States, had been conceived originally as a decoration for ordinary soldiers not for officers. It was only by the end of the decade of the 1880s that the decoration was extended to officers as well.

During the civil war, the young Fassett, born in Philadelphia, had enlisted in the 23rd Pennsylvania Infantry. On July 2, 1863, Captain Fassett was serving as the senior aide to Major-General David B. Barney, who commanded the Army of the Potomac's 1st Division of the III Corps.

When the confederates under General James Longstreet smashed the III Corps salient near the Peach Orchard, he rallied and reformed elements of General Andrew Humphry's 2nd Division on Cemetery Ridge.

Returning to the front lines he noticed the abandoned and captured artillery pieces of battery 1, 5th U.S. Regular Artillery. Realizing that the confederates could use the guns to destroy the newly reformed Union positions on Cemetery Ridge, he ordered the nearest troops, the 39th New York Volunteer Regiment of the II Corps, to charge and retake the guns. The unit commander initially refused but Fassett invoked the authority of General Winfield S. Hancock (which he did not technically have).

He then joined the vicious struggle to retake the guns. He made a conspicuous target as he was the only mounted officer.

The New York 39th succeeded in retaking the guns and Captain Fassett made a daring escape as the confederates tried to knock him off his horse and capture him. His actions secured the safely of of the Cemetery Ridge front line.

Major Fassett died in January 1905 so he did not live to enjoy his new summer residence in Norfolk. His wife, Taylor's mother-in-law, soon married again, to a Mr. Purdy, a wealthy businessman with financial interests in the railroads and engineering plants in pre-revolutionary Russia.

His papers were also in the attic at Moss Hill and I donated them to the Norfolk Historical Society.

Major Fassett was present when Abraham Lincoln gave his famous address at Gettysburg on November 19th, 1863, four and a half months after the battle. The Secretary of War's very long speech preceded the very short speech of Lincoln which is published on one page at the end of the official printing of the proceedings that day.

I have donated these proceedings, found in the attic at Moss Hill, as part of my collection at the library of St John's College, Cambridge, as well as Major Fassett's information, also retrieved from the attic, concerning the congressional medal of honor.

The permanent residents of Norfolk Connecticut today number only 1,500 people, a little less than the number of residents a hundred years ago. On the village green at Norfolk, Connecticut, there are the names of the 35 local men on the memorial to those who died during the "war of the rebellion."

Norfolk's veterans gather there in silence each Memorial Day, not only to remember those who died during the American Civil War, but of all the wars since where Americans have died.

The Union commander at Gettysburg was General George Meade. General Grant was besieging Vicksburg, Mississippi, at the time. But I have Major Fassett's lithograph of "General U.S. Grant" retrieved from the attic of his house at Moss Hill hanging on my study wall.

It is of course a pure (and happy) coincidence that I share a family name as well as the Gettysburg medal of honor winner Major Fassett's attic at Moss Hill with Ron Maxwell.

---

1. https://www.theaustralian.com.au/inquirer/the-rest-is-history-podcast-hosts-tom-holland-and-dominic-sandbrook-want-us-to-stop-moralising-about-the-past/news-story/7293639ad12c407551e27240e3e76d4f.

2. https://destinationgettysburg.com/gettysburg-the-movie-30th-anniversary-celebration/.

3. https://www.rappnews.com/opinion/comment/commentary-a-conversation-with-rappahannock-filmmaker-ron-maxwell-on-the-30th-anniversary-of-gettysburg/article_0be431f2-4f43-11ee-8e79-7bf983591397.html.

4. https://newenglandhistoricalsociety.com/touched-fire-oliver-wendell-holmes-americas-deadliest-day/#google_vignette.

5. https://www.rappnews.com/opinion/comment/commentary-ron-maxwell-staying-true-to-his-vision-for-gettysburg/article_bc0433a2-7036-11ee-ae31-2b650a651a09.html.

THE EDITOR

Dr. Robbin F. Laird is a long-time analyst of global defense issues. He has worked in the U.S. government and several think tanks, including the Center for Naval Analyses and the Institute for Defense Analyses.

He is a frequent op-ed contributor to the defense press, and he has written several books on international security issues.

He is the editor of two websites, *Second Line of Defense* and *Defense.info*.

He is a member of the Board of Contributors of *Breaking Defense* and publishes there on a regular basis.

He is a research fellow with The Sir Richard Williams Foundation.

He is also based in Paris, France, and he regularly travels throughout Europe and conducts interviews with leading policymakers in the region.

BOOKS BY ROBBIN LAIRD

Scientific-Technological Revolution and Soviet Foreign Policy. (Co-author Erik Hoffmann). 1982.

The Soviet Union and Strategic Arms. 1984 (Co-author Dale Herspring).

The Soviet Polity in the Modern Era (Co-edited with Erik Hoffmann). 1984.

Technocratic Socialism: The Soviet Union in the Advanced Industrial Era (Co-author Erik Hoffmann). 1985.

French Security Policy in Transition: Dynamics of Continuity and Change. 1985.

France, The Soviet Union, And the Nuclear Weapons Issue. 1985. Reissued by Routledge, 2020.

Perspectives on Defense futures : National Developments in Europe. (Jim Lacy co-author). 1985.

French Security Policy: From Independence to Interdependence. 1986. Reissued by Routledge in 2020.

The Soviet Union, the West, and the Nuclear Arms Race. 1986.

Soviet Foreign Policy. (Editor). 1987

Strangers & Friends, the Franco German Security Relationship. 1989

The Future of Deterrence: NATO Nuclear Forces After INF. 1990 (Co-editor Betsy Jacobs). Reissued by Routledge in 2021.

USSR and the Western Alliance (Susan Clark co-editor). 1990. Reissued by Routledge in 2022.

The Europeanization of The Alliance. 1991. Reissued by Routledge in 2021.

Soviet Foreign Policy: Classic and Contemporary Issues. 1991 (Co-editors Erik Hoffmann and Fred Fleron).

The Soviets, Germany, And the New Europe. 1992. Reissued by Routledge in 2021.

The Revolution in Military Affairs: Allied Perspectives (Co-author Holger Mey). 2004

Contemporary Issues in Soviet Foreign Policy: From Brezhnev to Gorbachev. 2008 Reissued by Routledge. (Co-editors Erik Hoffmann and Fred Fleron).

Three Dimensional Warriors: Second Edition. 2013

Rebuilding American Military Power in the Pacific: A 21st-Century Strategy. 2013. (Co-authors Ed Timperlake and Richard Weitz).

The F-35 and 21st Century Defence. 2016

Training for the High-End Fight: The Strategic Shift of the 2020s. 2021.

2020: A Pivotal Year?: Navigating Strategic Change at a Time of Covid-19 Disruption (Editor). 2021.

Joint by Design: The Evolution of Australian Defence Strategy. 2021

The Return of Direct Defense in Europe: Meeting the 21st Century Authoritarian Challenge. (Co-author Murielle Delaporte). 2020.

The U.S. Marine Corps Transformation Path: Preparing for the High-End Fight. 2022.

A Maritime Kill Web Force in the Making: Deterrence and Warfighting in the 21st Century (Co-author Ed Timperlake). 2022

Defense XXI: Shaping a Way Ahead for the United States and Its Allies. (Editor) 2022.

Defense XXII: A World in Transition (Editor). 2023.

The Role of the Osprey in the Pivot to the Pacific. 2023.

Kenneth Maxwell on Global Trends: An Historian of the 18th Century Looks at the Contemporary World (Editor). 2023

Australian Defence and Deterrence: A 2023 Update. 2023

The Coming of the CH-53K : A New Capability for the Distributed Force. 2023.

Australia and Indo-Pacific Defence: Anchoring a Way Ahead. 2023.

French Defense Policy Under Macron: 2017-2021 (Editor). 2023

The Obama Administration and Global Change (Editor). 2023

My Fifth Generation Journey: 2004-2018. 2023.

THE CONTRIBUTORS

PAUL BRACKEN

Paul Bracken is Professor of Management and Political Science at Yale University. Is he a noted expert on nuclear weapons and worked with Herman Kahn at Hudson Institute many years ago which is where the author first met him.

ROBERT CZULDA

Robert Czulda is an assistant professor at the University of Lodz, Poland. He is a former visiting professor at the Center for International and Security Studies at Maryland (CISSM) under a Fulbright Senior Award.

Dr. Czulda is an alum of the Young Leaders Dialogue of the U.S. Department of State (2010–2011) and has lectured at universities in Iran, Brazil, Indonesia, Ireland, Lithuania, Turkey, and Slovakia, as well as the National Cheng-chi University in Taipei. He is a freelance defense journalist as well and has published widely on Polish defense and related issues.

MURIELLE DELAPORTE

Murielle Delaporte is a defense analyst based in France and the United States. She has worked in the French Government and various think tanks in both France (*Institut français des relations internationales* in Paris) and the United States (East West Institute for Security Studies in New York).

She received three political science and security studies degrees from Sciences Po and Sorbonne in Paris, as well as from Georgetown University in Washington, D.C.

She has published several books and articles in both French and English on defense and strategic issues. After being a correspondent for various publications (TTU in France, Military Logistics International in the UK) and an occasional contributor to others (*FrontLine Defence* in Canada, and *Leatherneck* in the United States), she is a regular contributor to New York–based *Breaking Defense* since 2013 and a guest lecturer at Sciences Po – Bordeaux since 2017.

She is currently the editor-in-chief of a French magazine and website specialized on military and security issues – https://opera tionnels.com- which she founded in 2009. She has provided global reporting from Europe, North America, Africa, and the Middle East. She is a contributor as well to the Washington-based publication Breaking Defense.

JAMES DURSO

James Durso (@james_durso) is a regular commentator on foreign policy and national security matters. Mr. Durso served in the U.S. Navy for 20 years and has worked in Kuwait, Saudi Arabia, and Iraq.

DEBALINA GHOSHAL

Debalina Ghoshal is based in India and is a non-resident fellow, Council on International Policy, Canada, She provides regular analyses on global developments for *Defense.info*.

HARALD MALMGREN

Dr. Malmgren provided this summary of his career:

My experience with assessing forward looking costs of United States Government defense and national security programs began when I was asked by McGeorge Bundy, JFK's National Security Council Director, to leave my

Professorship at Cornell and come to work in the summer of 1962 at the Pentagon as an aide to Defense Secretary McNamara.

It was only a few weeks aer arriving in Washington that McNamara and Bundy asked me to attend the Pentagon War Room discussions of our nation's leading Generals on possible nuclear retaliation measures against the USSR in the event that talks with Soviet Union leader Khrushchev led to possible nuclear war confrontation.

The gravity of being fully involved in decisions about potential nuclear war was a shock to my orderly, analytical academic mind. How life and death calculations at the highest level of our national decision system taught me the necessity of summarizing choices of action and the respective costs in minutes and hours was a challenge of a different order of magnitude than I had ever considered.

Fortunately, the Cuban Missile Crisis was resolved peacefully. However, shortly aer, I was asked to lead an urgent analysis of the introduction by the U.S. of an An Ballistic Missile defense system. I was assigned to work with the Weapons Systems Evaluation Group which reported directly to the Joint Chief of Staff.

I was appointed as Chief of the Costing Division. This was not a lowly analysis of all the many components of such a system, but rather a concise estimate of what it would cost to develop, build and deploy such a system for top level review and a go-or-no-go decision.

Over many discussions with some of the nation's leading scientists and engineers and consolations with top logistics officers of the US military, I put forward a cost estimate of a first phase as $25 billion. I was then asked to calculate for each dollar spent by the US what it would cost the Soviet Union to penetrate such a system.

After many weeks my conclusion was that the ratio of cost of an enemy penetration of a successful deployment of a functional defense system was 7 to 1! While in 1963 and 1964 my ratio became widely used in other defense studies, it found itself in the hands of Cap Weinberger, Secretary of Defense under President Reagan.

This captured the imagination of people around Reagan and, I was told, helped Reagan's decision to announce his Strategic Defense Initiative, popularly known as "Star Wars Defense". The Soviets, I was told, were well aware of my

7 to 1 ratio rule, and it led to rapid rethinking in Moscow of how the US Star Wars" might "bankrupt the USSR".

In late 1964, I was asked by WH staff to leave the Pentagon and become Executive Assistant to Christian Herter, President Kennedy's Special Representative for Trade Negotiations. Herter had been Secretary of State near the end of the Eisenhower Administration.

As it turned out, WH staff made it clear to me that I would be a resource that NSC staff would tap into. Furthermore, the General Counsel of the Department, John McNaughton would continue to be in touch with me with regard to developments in the Vietnam War John and I had become friends at the Pentagon, and I learned he was longtime friend of McGeorge Bundy, the NSC Director.

Repeatedly I was summoned, often on Saturdays, to the Pentagon for off the record discussions on the rising costs of the Vietnam conflict and its inevitable challenges for President Johnson's domestic policy budget.

The intricacies of the guns vs. butter conflicts led me deep into budget decisions, and the politics behind budget decisions in Congress. Charlie Schultze, the OMB Director, also often dragged me informally into his internal budget disputes.

How top-level decisions on defense spending come to be made became part of my knowledge base, even though I was primarily responsible for trade negotiations with other nations until I left the Administration in 1969.

When President Nixon asked me to return to the WH to lead US trade negotiations, he did mention that he was aware I had extensive personal experience with the guns vs butter fiscal disputes that were plaguing Nixon's own priories, and asked me to remain available from me to me for in-house discussions on the continuing Vietnam War expenses and the inflation controls he had instituted.

From this personal history I retain interest in the role of defense priories and the inevitable clashes with domestic fiscal policy initiatives of any President.

KENNETH MAXWELL

Dr. Kenneth Maxwell was the founding director of the Brazil Studies Program at Harvard University's David Rockefeller Center for Latin

American Studies (DRCLAS) (2006–2008) and a visiting professor in Harvard's Department of History (2004–2008).

LT GENERAL (RETIRED) STEVE RUDDER

LtGen Steven Rudder is a retired Marine Aviator, the former Commander of Marine Forces Pacific, and aerospace advocate.

EDWARD TIMPERLAKE

The Honorable Edward Timperlake is the former Director Technology Assessment, International Technology Security, Office of the Secretary of Defense, and served on the Board of The Vietnam Children's Fund, a pro-bono project that has built 48 elementary schools in Vietnam.

Previous positions he has held include serving on the Professional Staff, House Committee on Rules focusing on illegal foreign campaign donations to the American political process. As an Assistant Secretary, Department of Veterans Affairs, he was a member of The White House Desert Shield/Desert Storm Communications Task Force.

He created the "TASCFORM" analytical methodology for measuring the modernization rate of military aircraft worldwide for both the Director Net Assessment and Central Intelligence Agency and was Principal Director Mobilization Planning and Requirements/OSD in President Reagan's first term.

His Bachelor of Science is from the US Naval Academy, and MBA from Cornell University. He is a carrier qualified U.S. Marine Corps Fighter Pilot finishing his tour as Commanding Officer VMFA-321.

PIERRE TRAN

Pierre Tran is a Paris-based journalist who focuses on French defense policies. He was a Reuters correspondent for many years and is a regular contributor to *Second Line of Defense* and *Defense.info*.

RICHARD WEITZ

Richard Weitz is Senior Fellow and Director, Center for Political-Military Analysis at the Hudson Institute.

THE SECOND LINE OF DEFENSE ANNUAL PUBLICATIONS

Beginning with the year 2020, we have published an annual publication to highlight our work during the year.

We started with 2020 and highlighted the pandemic year. After that we started the series officially with the defense series, namely Defense XXI and Defense XII.

All of these books are available in ebook and paperback versions and can be found on Amazon or other online book sellers.

DEFENSE XXII: A WORLD IN TRANSITION

The essays in this volume address the epochal change we are going through as a society.

We have highlighted some of the key developments affecting the evolution of defense and security challenges facing the United States and its key allies, as well as innovations and developments in selected military technologies and concepts of operations.

The first section brings together essays on the world in conflict in 2022, which are assessments of the challenges facing the liberal democracies as we enter a new historical epoch.

The second section focuses on lessons learned from the past being applied in the present.

The third section focuses on the allies and their reworking of their approaches to defense.

The fourth section highlights selective military innovations, including evolving concepts of operations that the U.S. and allied militaries have entertained or implemented during the year. The fifth section focuses on a specific aspect of this change, namely unmanned systems.

The final section addresses the question of future evolution of the global system.

George Galdorisi writes: *Defense XXII: A World in Transition is one of those rare books focused on political, diplomatic and military matters that will appeal to experts in the field as well as the layperson. Robbin Laird has assembled a breathtaking array of professionals and has woven together a narrative that makes this book unique. It reads like a novel, and you just have to turn to page to see what happens next.*

Professor Kenneth Maxwell underscores: "Robbin Laird has produced here a remarkably important and timely collection of essays on the most challenging moment in recent global history. And he has done so in large part by giving a voice to many of those involved in responding on a day-to-day basis to the major shifts taking place in the geo-political re-configuration of global power."

DEFENSE XXI: SHAPING A WAY AHEAD FOR THE UNITED STATES AND ITS ALLIES

This compendium of articles published in 2021 provides an overview of several key trends and themes regarding the evolution of U.S. and allied defense. We have focused on several key developments during the year in the defense domain which will have longer term impacts in the years ahead. During 2021, we visited several U.S. Naval and Marine Corps bases, as well as France and Poland as well as "virtually" Denmark and the United Kingdom.

During those visits, we interviewed many senior commanders about how they are focused on shaping a more effective military to deal with the evolving challenges from the authoritarian powers.

As former Secretary of the USAF, Michael Wynne commented: "The articles in the book, organized as they are by natural topics, will undoubtedly enhance the reader's understanding as to just how weapons and information technology and the distribution and relationship knowledge have affected and impacted the age old concept that military action is simply an extension of diplomacy by other means."

2020: A PIVOTAL YEAR?: NAVIGATING STRATEGIC CHANGE AT A TIME OF COVID-19 DISRUPTION

"2020: A Pivotal Year?" addresses the impacts of the COVID-19 disruption on global politics and provides assessments of the ripple effects felt throughout Europe and Asia. Authors based in Europe, the United States, and Australia have all contributed to this timely and unique assessment.

This is a unique book looking back at the COVID-19 impact and the dynamics of change globally. The first section of the book provides a unique look at the impact of COVID-19 on the Western societies, with Professor Kenneth Maxwell focus on the United Kingdom and Pierre Tran on France.

We continue our discussion by looking at a wide range of geopolitical dynamics, and more specifically on Europe and Australia.

We have brought together a number of our essays on historical developments of interest, spearheaded by the outstanding work of Professor Kenneth Maxwell.

We conclude by taking a look forward into 2021.

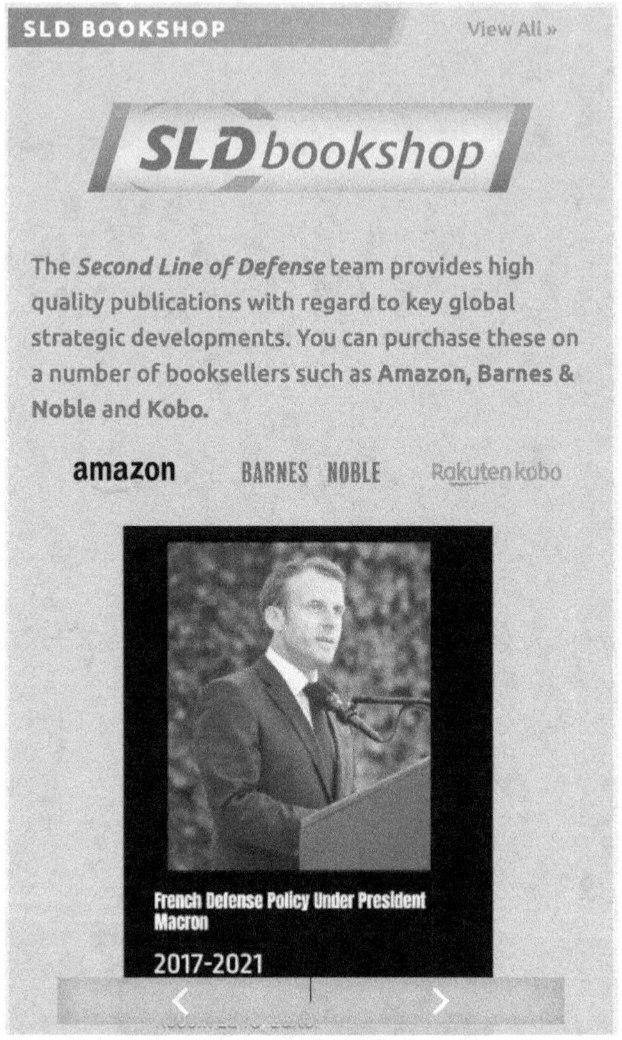

Books included in the SLD Bookshop:

An Update on MAWTS-1: 2023

French Defense Policy Under President Macron: 2017-2021

Kenneth Maxwell on Global Trends: An Historian of the 18th Century Looks at the Contemporary World

My Fifth-Generation Journey: 2004-2018

Australia and Indo-Pacific Defence: Anchoring a Way Ahead

Australian Defence and Deterrence: A 2023 Update